Praxiological Essays

The 25th volume in the series *Praxiology: The International Annual of Practical Philosophy and Methodology* brings a praxiological perspective to current issues facing our society. In sixteen brand-new essays, a team of international scholars expands praxiology beyond the borders of its historically philosophical application and uses it to address real-world problems in a variety of fields. The volume outlines new approaches and reflections on traditional praxiological method, and then applies these developments as tools in fields as diverse as ethics, psychology, sociology, economics, management, and entrepreneurship. Grounded in the tradition of the Polish praxiologist Tadeusz Kotarbiński (1886–1981), the 25th volume, entitled *Praxiological Essays: Texts and Contexts*, highlights the rich mosaic of issues perceived in the practice of human action, and carries a tradition of Praxiological inquiry forward into our contemporary philosophy, methodology, and social sciences.

Wojciech W. Gasparski is professor emeritus of the Institute of Philosophy and Sociology, Polish Academy of Sciences and Chair in Business Ethics at Koźmiński University, Warsaw, Poland.

The Learned Society of Praxiology
PRAXIOLOGY: The International Annual of Practical Philosophy and Methodology Vol. 25

Praxiology: The International Annual of Practical Philosophy and Methodology series examines fundamental issues in the theory of human action and methodological issues in such practical disciplines or sciences of the artificial, as Herbert A. Simon called them, as design and planning, technology, economics and management, as well as ethical dimension of human action. Praxiology starts from the point of view of effectiveness, and has three components: analysis of concepts involving purposive actions; critique of modes of action from the viewpoint of efficiency; and normative advisory aspects in recommendations for increasing human efficacy and ethicality.

Praxiological Essays

Texts and Contexts

Praxiology: The International Annual of Practical Philosophy and Methodology

Volume 25

Editor

Wojciech W. Gasparski

NEW YORK AND LONDON

First published 2018
by Routledge
605 Third Avenue, New York, NY 10017

and by Routledge
2 Park Square, Milton Park, Abingdon, Oxon, OX14 4RN

Routledge is an imprint of the Taylor & Francis Group, an informa business

Library of Congress Cataloging-in-Publication Data
Names: Gasparski, Wojciech, editor.
Title: Praxiological essays: texts and contexts / editor, Wojciech W. Gasparski.
Description: 1 [edition]. | New York: Routledge, 2017. | Series: Praxiology: the international annual of practical philosophy and methodology; Volume 25 | Includes bibliographical references.
Identifiers: LCCN 2017015393 |
ISBN 9781138069008 (hardback) |
ISBN 9781138102668 (pbk.)
Subjects: LCSH: Praxeology.
Classification: LCC B832.2 .P735 2017 | DDC 128/.4—dc23
LC record available at https://lccn.loc.gov/2017015393

ISBN: 978-1-138-06900-8 (hbk)
ISBN: 978-1-138-10266-8 (pbk)
ISBN: 978-1-315-10353-2 (ebk)

Typeset in Goudy
by codeMantra

In Memoriam

Brother Leo V. Ryan, C.S.V. (1927–2016)

Brother of the St. Viator Convent and professor emeritus at DePaul University in Chicago, former dean of the College of Commerce and Kellstadt Graduate School of Business at that University and President of the Society of Business Ethics. A life honorary member of the Learned Society of Praxiology.

He was a member of the International Advisory Board of *Praxiology: The International Annual of Practical Philosophy and Methodology* and co-editor of four volumes of this series.

He was not only a great man, an expert in human resource management science and business ethics, but also a lover of Poland and our true friend.

May he rest in peace and remain in our grateful memory.

Contents

Editorial

Wojciech W. Gasparski

Editor-in-chief

This is the 25th or silver volume in the series *Praxiology: The International Annual of Practical Philosophy and Methodology*. The volume is a collection of essays composed by eminent scholars who were active for the series during the last quarter of a century. They are either authors of important contributions to the discipline, editors of previous volumes, members of the International Advisory Board, or representatives of ISBEE, the organizer of the Business Ethics Olympics[1] to which a few volumes were dedicated, who accepted an invitation to contribute to this volume.

It was suggested that this silver volume of the series should be devoted to current issues and reflections approached from a *praxiological perspective*, identifying problems and arguments to open new horizons for further praxiological inquiry. The texts submitted offer a range of contexts in which a variety of new approaches, aspects, reflections, and applications are presented.

Tradition is obviously the number-one context. Therefore, it is worth noting that the volume was composed in the year of the 130th anniversary of Tadeusz Kotarbiński's (1886–1981) birth. The founder of Polish praxiology began in 1910 to work on the theory of action, which, in reference to French scholar Alfred Victor Espinas, he later called *praxiology*. From the very beginning of his philosophizing, Kotarbiński was interested directly and primarily in practicality. He was concerned with the teaching of philosophy as a basis for teachers' training accounting for the broad meaning of *teaching*—not just the work of a schoolteacher but any kind of creation and transfer of knowledge; hence, the name *teacher* also applies to a researcher, professor, journalist, writer, media practitioner, and many other people pursuing relevant professions. Therefore, it would be relevant to recall Herbert Simon's concept of *docility*:

> Because of bounded rationality, docility contributes to the fitness of human beings in evolutionary competition. By 'docility' I mean *the tendency to depend on suggestions, recommendations, persuasions, and information obtained through social channels as a major basis for choice.* Most of us who

> restrict our consumption of fats do so, not because our own experience and research has provided convincing evidence that a fatty diet is unhealthy, but because we have been told, on reliable authority, that such a diet is harmful. 'Reliable authority' is a term describing a social system and interpersonal relations within it. In large measure, we do what we do because we have learned from those who surround us, not from our own experience, what is good for us and what is not.
>
> (Simon, 1993, pp. 156–157)

Kotarbiński's *teacher* is similar to Simon's *reliable authority* concept. The reliability of such authorities is so important because they deliver content for practical behavior based on *bounded rationality*, which is the contemporary guise of ancient *practical wisdom* (*phronesis*). The notion is extremely useful now in the times of the Internet, for it has pointed out the importance of the ability to differentiate between reliable and false authorities.

The other issues among Kotarbiński's interests were: philosophical culture, particularly logical culture; therefore, he introduced reism, later replaced by concretism. Kotarbiński consolidated practical knowledge, hence he distinguished practical sciences and indicated design as their methodological differentiator. Finally, in order to avoid practical errors, he elaborated their typology. All these efforts resulted in a system worthy of the name of a *philosophy of practicality* with praxiology as a *sui generis* grammar of action.

Tadeusz Kotarbiński wrote, "The main task of praxiology is realizing, formulating, justifying and systematizing general recommendations and warnings concerning the *efficacy* of actions, in other words, their practicality" (Kotarbiński, 2002, p. 30). Efficacy—composed of *effectiveness* and *efficiency*—is the basic criterion of good work in all areas of human activity. The presence of this praxiological argument supplemented with *ethicality*, known as *the triple E* (effectiveness, efficiency, ethicality) was extensively shown in the volumes of *The International Annual of Practical Philosophy and Methodology*, published under the auspices of the Learned Society of Praxiology by Transaction Publishers at Rutgers. If you'll pardon the repetition, I would like to quote once again what I wrote in the editorial to the first volume, namely that praxiology is like the prose of Monsieur Jourdain, the protagonist of Molière's play: Everybody uses it but only a few of us know what we speak, write, or do (Gasparski, 1992, p. 3). The situation is hopefully better now, for the series has provided an opportunity to increase the number of those who are familiar with this action theory and its relevance to different types of human behavior.

Many contributions to this volume confirm the topicality of Kotarbiński's ideas. Besides explicit references to Kotarbiński's concepts, notions, and theses, it is evident that also authors of other contributions are familiar with the heritage of his or his followers' praxiological analysis of human action.

Economics—the number two context—was the first type of praxiology companion, as noted in Georges Enderle's paper. It was the proceedings of the International Conference on Praxiologies and the Philosophy of Economics organized in 1988 in Warsaw, Poland, that were published in the very first volume of the series (1992). In the Introduction to that volume, American philosopher Josiah Lee Auspitz, whose involvement in creating the series was pivotal, wrote:

> Because there was now widespread work on praxeologies, often under other names, an international conference seemed necessary to include American economists and philosophers, representatives of Scandinavian, Italian, and Eastern European work, and noted writers elsewhere in the philosophy and logic of practice action, general systems theory, theories of management, planning and design… Yet the idea of praxiology—of a discipline devoted to the relation between *praxis* and *logos*—captures central preoccupations of modern life: What is the knowledge about human action? By what 'logic' do we bring such knowledge to bear in improving action?… The Polish and Austrian foundings of praxiology/praxeology put more than the usual number of basic ideas on the table. The Polish contribution of Kotarbiński was rooted in an extreme nominalism (or a radical empiricism, as it is sometimes called) and emphasized the planned aspects of rational action; the Austrian work of von Mises presented the notion of choice as an *a priori* category and emphasized the hidden and unintended rationalities concerted by the market.
>
> (Auspitz, 1992, p. 10)

The other contexts are: different philosophical foundations; ethics and moral science companionship; psychological and/or sociological approaches;, different levels of generality; micro- and macro-praxiologies. Contexts related to spheres of praxiology applications are: administration, management, design, entrepreneurship, organization, engineering, etc. Because of so many contexts it would have been rather difficult to select one and structure the contents of this volume accordingly. Instead, the most neutral way was chosen: The essays are presented in the alphabetical order of their authors' names.

The first paper by Timo Airaksinen is devoted to an analysis of the basic praxiological concept—*effectiveness*, "which is… a complicated and demanding term to use and understand, if we do not use it in its naïve colloquial sense". He argues that "we must treat Kotarbiński's notion of action in its widest possible sense and then ask, what are those goals and how are they related to acts and action understood as work?" The contributor suggests as an issue not intentionality—"because actions and intentions go hand in hand"—but *desire* as the driving force towards the goal to be achieved as the action result.

A praxiological task, therefore, is not only instrumentality, but iterative responsiveness to the agent's needs that are induced by his or her desires.

Victor Alexandre in his paper refers to the French tradition based on the works of Abraham Moles and Elisabeth Rohmer. He notices, among other things, that we humans less frequently perform so-called *rare actions*: "the rare act is not a simple response to a rare, unforeseen, random or accidental event, but it is envisaged as an objective destined to show or demonstrate a singular praxiological or cognitive competence." Their praxiolographical analysis is presented in the paper. It is also pointed out that rare actions have specific psychological, cognitive, emotional, and socio-psychological effects.

Marek Arszułowicz in his paper presents the concept of value management from the start-up entrepreneur's point of view, especially in relation to the digital economy (*big data*) and enormous amounts of knowledge. He introduces a few implications as a suggestion for further praxiological considerations based on the Misesian 'praxeological' approach.

The next essay by Jérôme Ballet and Emmanuel Petit is also situated in the sphere of interrelations between praxiology and economics. The contributors claim that the concept of identity is important for economics. They refer to moral psychology, behavioural economics and the Nordic definition of praxiology.

The British tradition of *action learning*, originated by Reg W. Revans, is revisited in the essay by David Botham. The originator of this approach wrote that "The study of achievement, the anatomy of action, the analysis of how things are done, is, or should be, the final task of the scholar of praxiology, the theory of practice…" (Revans, 1971, p. 29).

Joanne Ciulla's essay on praxiology of collective leadership is mainly methodological, what is its context. She concludes it with question marks rather than full stops:

> So as I see it, one key moral question about the praxiology of collective leadership is: What moral pitfalls of individual leadership does collective leadership avoid and what unique moral pitfalls does it face? Are there cases where collective leadership is better (more effective and ethical) than individual leadership and vice versa?

According to her "These are not theoretical questions but ones that have taken center stage in the world today". For that reason, leadership praxiology is seen as an important part of praxiological inquiry.

A picture of the economics that is needed is sketched by Georges Enderle in his paper. He offers his most recent thoughts on economic systems hoping they help to open new horizons for praxiological enquiry. He believes that "the comprehensive conception of wealth creation and the economics of provision indicate more concretely how praxiology can be substantiated in business and the economy" and concludes with the challenge that it offers "fascinating perspectives to develop in the next 25 volumes of *Praxiology*".

The paper by Krzysztof Klincewicz refers directly to Kotarbiński's praxiology; and the argument is as follows. Western management theories are affected by some wrong concepts that hibernate in them like viruses, which results in the *sui generis* cyclical repetition of the same 'diseases'. Earlier praxiological studies—unknown in the West, for they were published mainly in Polish—combined with the existing body of knowledge, might serve as a medicine and help to cure management practice.

Olli Loukola refers to praxiological concepts via political philosophy. In particular, his paper is mainly based on the ideas of Leonidas Donskis, who died in 2016. Loukola claims, after the Lithuanian philosopher, that human identity is strongly linked with hatred. Why? The answer offered in the conclusion of his contribution reads that "Contemporary identity building takes place in the cross-tide between the disappearance of traditions, the emptiness of the liberal vision, and the struggle against alienating and coercive forces. The scare of losing your traditions, the worries of the unpredictable future, combined with the distressing idea of having to choose your identity in a social-existential void, and under the mercy of hostile powers, create together the circumstances to which hatred may seem to be the appropriate response." It seems that this context of human action is close to the issues raised by the praxiological theory of struggle (Gasparski, 2011, p. 11–16). For "the art of life is more like the art of struggle than the art of dance", as Kotarbiński wrote after Marcus Aurelius (1999, p. 198).

The article of Piotr Tomasz Makowski has two aims: (1) to explain the reason why the Kotarbiński's praxiology is a philosophy of action; (2) to answer the question 'why his action theory is hardly noticed in the mainstream of the analytic action theories despite its important philosophical content?' The essay is illustrated with cases taken from practice of human activities. Similarities and differences of Kotarbiński's and von Mises's praxiologies are also characterised.

Piotr Masiukiewicz in his contribution also refers to Kotarbiński's statements on relations between praxiology as a metatheory and organization theory. He suggests the need for the "theory and practice of praxiology in a multidimensional space of contemporary business management." He raises the following categories: the principle of purpose and proportionality, economic analysis of law, public consultations and praxiological principles related to efficiency and effectiveness of risk management in an organization as well as responsible decision-making. Masiukiewicz, who refers to von Mises's tradition as well, appeals for new praxiological tools to support effectiveness and efficiency of enterprise management. He claims that a kind of "Occam's razor" should be used to verify organizational structures, production processes, information systems of the management, and decision-making systems.

Tufan Orel draws attention to the strong relations between the varieties of design *stuffs* and the *praxiological lifeworld* which is the environment of an action. This includes some inherent elements of action (agent, activity, work) and "internal circumstances" (realization and execution, evaluation and decision making). Orel tries to show "that it is also possible to consider actions taking place in relatively autonomous and parallel environments... So, we can talk," he says, "not only about an 'intra-weaving' of the components of action, which creates *ipso facto* a special environment of an action...—a praxiological lifeworld—but also about the 'inter-weaving' of praxiological lifeworld between them".

Yet another tradition, the Nordic one of Jakob Meløe (1983)—who served as a member of the series' International Advisory Board in 1992–2000—is presented by Gunnar Skirbekk. His paper offers an excellent picture of the performance of actions by humans and observers trying to comprehend their multidimensional contexts. The issue is: "in what sense may the agents... 'know what they have to know in order to do what they do'?" Metaphorically, it is like throwing a stone in a pond and generating waves whose shapes are not necessarily regular but depend on the behavior of other agents and on the viewer's angle of seeing that complex picture. This paper is a perfect example of micro-praxiological analysis.

Mirosław Sułek in his paper suggests a top-down approach to human action theory. This approach is different from Kotarbiński's bottom-up approach to studying human actions, i.e. from one subject's actions to collective actions. Sułek assumes the existence of a 'social organism' of which human beings are a part. They "act in a competitive environment, i.e. in the world of limited resources (the so-called scarcity of goods), where they primarily struggle to *survive*, and subsequently *develop*. For this purpose, they create *social systems of action*. Scarcity of goods can only be handled in two ways: either through voluntary *cooperation*, or *struggle*", claims the contributor. The approach falls under the rubric of macro-praxiology.

In relation to the idea presented above, one may notice that the micropraxiology of Kotarbiński is the study that is relevant to explaining the essence of the atomic level (Bunge, 1979, p. 6) of human action systems, e.g. Sztylka's contribution.

Andrzej Sztylka extensively characterizes the interrelations between the praxiological and ethical dimensions of human action, summarizing Kotarbiński's analysis of action agency or authorship.

Laszlo Zsolnai, in his paper, criticizes the outcome of neo-liberalism in economics, which is a product of the Austrian approach to business activity. He criticizes fundamentalism in economics, promoting responsible decision-making instead. This is, according to the author, not a luxury but a precondition of a worthy life.

Let us stress that all of the contexts to which the contributors refer find their position under the praxiological umbrella, as is declared by them and noticeable. It is obvious that although the perspective considered as praxiological has invariant features, different authors prefer some of them more than others, or add their own. So, the final picture presented in the volume is a mosaic of issues perceived in the practice of human action and its reflection in the praxiological mirror. It proves the very fact that praxiological inquiry is present in contemporary philosophy, methodology, and social sciences, sometimes under different names, as demonstrated in the volumes published in the series so far. I am extremely grateful to the authors for their contributions. I also highly appreciate the Transaction Publishers staff for their commitment to the effective publication of the annual during the last 25 years. From this volume on, the series will be published by the renowned publisher Routledge of the Taylor & Francis group who acquired Transaction Publishers.

***

It is with great sorrow that we must inform readers that two eminent scholars, Brother and Professor Leo V. Ryan, C. S. V., and Professor George J. Klir, have passed away.

Leo V. Ryan (1927–2016), a life honorary member of the Learned Society of Praxiology, was a brother of the St. Viator Convent and management science and business ethics professor emeritus at DePaul University in Chicago. Since 1998 he was a member of the International Advisory Board of *The International Annual of Practical Philosophy and Methodology* and co-editor of four volumes of this series.

His academic functions and monastic duties were many. He was professor at Marquette and Loyola Universities (1957–1965), the Peace Corps director in Lagos, Nigeria (1966–1968), a member of the General Council of Priests of St. Viator in Rome (1968–1970), advisor and education director of schools run by the Viatorians (1980–1985). In 1972, he became the first president of the St. Viator High School in Arlington Heights, IL (1972–1974). In 1975, he was appointed dean of the College of Business Administration at the University of Notre Dame, where he worked until 1980. From 1980 to 1989, he served as dean of the College of Commerce and Kellstadt Graduate School of Business at DePaul University. In 1999, he retired from DePaul, obtaining the title of professor emeritus and holding the distinction of the Via Sapientiae Award, the highest honor for lecturers of DePaul University. He also taught at the Helsinki School of Economics and the Program on International BBA in MIkkeli Finland, as well as at Adam Mickiewicz University and the University of Economics, both in Poznan, Poland.

As the president of the Society for Business Ethics, he was instrumental to introducing business ethics in Poland. The Polish government awarded him the Medal of Merit for his contribution to the development of culture and education in the country. Leo V. Ryan is the author and co-editor of eight books and over 500 articles. He was not only a great man, an expert on human resource management and business ethics, but also an admirer of Poland and our true friend. May he rest in peace and remain, with his wise advice, for years in our grateful memory.

***

George J. Klir (1932–2016) was an eminent scholar in the field of general systems theory. He was born and graduated in Prague. After emigrating to the United States, he taught at the University of California LA and Fairleigh Dickinson University. Finally, he was a professor and department director at the State University of New York at Binghamton (1969–2007).

He was editor of the *International Journal of General Systems* and the book series *Systems Science and Systems Engineering*. He served as president of the International Federation for Systems Research and president of the Society for General Systems Research/Science. He received numerous awards and honors, including five titles of doctor honoris causa. He is the author, co-author, and editor of numerous articles and books.

In 1988, he participated in the conference *Praxiologies and the Philosophy of Economics*, organized in Warsaw, Poland, where he gave a lecture on "The Role of Methodological Principles of Uncertainty in Economics", published in the first volume of the series *Praxiology: The International Annual of Practical Philosophy and Methodology*. Prof. Klir was a member of the International Advisory Board of this series in 1992–1996.

The community of systems theoreticians owes him a great deal, as he was not only an excellent scholar devoted to the discipline, but also a person ready to help researchers in their academic development. Both his enlightened methodological advice and his concern for friendly companionship will long remain in our memories.

Note

1 This is the nickname of the International Society of Business, Economics, and Ethics world congresses, organized every four years since 1996. G. E. Four of the earlier volumes of the *Praxiology* series were dedicated to the previous ISBEE congresses: Vol. 5—Wojciech W. Gasparski & Leo V. Ryan, eds., *Human Action in Business: Praxiological and Ethical Dimensions* was dedicated to the 1st ISBEE Congress held in Tokyo, Japan in 1996; Vol. 8—Leo V. Ryan, Wojciech W. Gasparski, Georges Enderle, eds. *Business Students Focus on Ethics* was dedicated to the 2nd ISBEE World Congress held in Sao Paulo, Brazil in 2000; Vol. 19—Olli Loukola and

Wojciech W. Gasparski, eds., *Environmental Political Philosophy: Praxiological Considerations* was dedicated to the 5th ISBEE World Congress held in Warsaw, Poland in 2012; vol. 24—Timo Airaksinen and Wojciech W. Gasparski, eds. *Desire: The Concept and Its Practical Context*, was dedicated to the 6th World Congress organized in 2016 in Shanghai, China.

References

Auspitz, J. L., 1992, Introduction: An International Praxiology, in: J. L. Auspitz, W. W. Gasparski, M. K. Mlicki, K. Szaniawski, eds., *Praxiologies and the Philosophy of Economics*, Transaction Publishers, New Brunswick (USA)-London (UK), pp. 9–14.

Bunge, M., 1979, *Treatise on Basic Philosophy*, Vol. 4 *Ontology II: The World of Systems*, Reidel, Dordrecht.

Gasparski, W. W., 1992, Editorial: The Prose of Action, In: J. L. Auspitz et al., eds., *Praxiologies and the Philosophy of Economics*, Transaction Publishers, New Brunswick (USA)-London (UK), pp. 3–8.

Gasparski, W. W., 2011, Whistleblowing in the Light of the Praxiological Theory of Struggle, in: M. Arszułowicz, W. W. Gasparski, eds., *Whistleblowing: In Defense of Proper Action*, Transaction Publishers, New Brunswick (USA)-London (UK), pp. 9–20.

Kotarbiński, T., 1999, From the Issues of the General Theory of Struggle, in: T. Kotarbiński, eds., *Collected Works: Praxiology* Part One (in Polish), Ossolineum Publishers, Wrocław, pp. 66–198.

Kotarbiński, T., 2002, The ABC of Practicality, in: L. V. Ryan, F. Byron Nahser, W. Gasparski, eds., *Praxiology and Pragmatism*, Transaction Publishers, New Brunswick (USA)-London (UK), pp. 25–60.

Meløe, J., 1983, The Agent and His World, in: G. Skirbekk, ed., *Praxeology*, Norwegian University Press, Oslo, pp. 13–29.

Revans, R. W., 1971, Action, Creativity and Learning: Some Reflections upon the Nature of Achievements, *Prakseologia 39–40*, 29–50.

Simon, H. A., 1993, Altruism and Economics, *American Economic Review*, 83(2), 156–161.

Chapter 1

Trouble with Success

The Problem of Effectiveness in Praxiology

Timo Airaksinen

Introduction: The Problem of Goals

The "Three E's of Praxiology" are often said to be Efficiency, Effectiveness, and Ethics. Ethics is such a wide and complicated topic, much more so than many people tend to realize, that I do not intend to tackle it here. I try to avoid ethical and moral issues in this paper.[1] Efficiency sounds like a term in engineering science, and my suspicion is that it is a pretty well-understood concept, yet philosophers can complicate any term and topic, if they are given a chance. Anyway, I do not have anything to say about it now. We are left with effectiveness, which is, as I want to show, a complicated and demanding term to use and understand, if we do not use it in its naïve colloquial sense. Many praxiologists may want to bypass such issues and say, simply, that effective action and work reach their given goal or get the job done. In other words, effectiveness means that action reaches its goal, which is understood as an object or content of, say, the relevant intention. We can put this idea, thus effective action realizes the relevant intention of the agent. For example, I want to build a bridge and as a result of my effective action, we have a bridge, as I intended. What could be simpler? I do what I intended to do, and that is it.

It is a mistake, it seems to me, to focus solely on actions when we do praxiology.[2] This is to say that it is a mistake to focus solely on intentions, because actions and intentions go hand-in-hand. What we need are the concepts of a design, project, job, and work. We work, which entails a job that again entails a set of actions whose intentions anchor it to the real world. However, the main focus should remain at the level of work, its design and projects, which are the key concepts here.

What happens in the case of a bridge? We want a bridge; if we do not, we never start the project of building one—here, building is work, and no work may proceed effectively without a project. Now, there is a job to be done, or actually a systematically connected constellation of jobs that will result in a bridge if we succeed. If we do not succeed, we will not get a useable bridge. In this case, the failure seems quite one-dimensional: no such bridge. However, if our desires are more demanding, our failures will also be more complicated: It is possible that we get something but it is not what we wanted or aimed at. We get something but not what we wanted. We educate young men to become brave soldiers but, in the event of a failure, we do not get heroes but instead, say, violent monsters. They are still soldiers but not the kind of soldiers we wanted. The source of complication is obvious: We want a certain kind of soldier, not just a soldier as such. Actually, we rarely want a simple thing as such, in the sense that we want it without qualifications, like we wanted a bridge as a bridge. If we want a bridge *simpliciter*, the circumstances are likely to be somehow exceptional. The same can be said of the training of soldiers: We may want to train soldiers, as such, as cannon fodder, as it used to be said, but this is exceptional. We feel the need to explain it, for instance, the river is regularly flooded and we need a bridge, any bridge, in order to protect the people on the other side. Therefore, any bridge works for us; we cannot afford to be choosy. If we train cannon fodder, we are likely to be hit by moral concerns, or our reasons for such a nasty project must be exceptionally cogent. I have a hard time seeing what kinds of reasons could be mentioned, perhaps an imminent military catastrophe? Anyway, when we work for a given goal, we normally qualify this goal in various ways. We are more or less demanding. This makes the evaluation of success of the project more complicated.

Kotarbiński himself writes (1972) as follows: "In short, practical evaluation, i.e. efficacious one, comes down to the question of effectiveness and economy of action. What are effective acts? Those which lead to a chosen goal."[3] This short quotation illustrates quite well my own goals in the present paper. I want to make three comments on it. First, Kotarbiński mentions "economy action," which means, as I take it, efficiency of action, that is, the way the goal is reached with the least possible effort and, accordingly, cost. Second, in the quotation above, the term "efficacious" must mean the same as "successful," and the quotation makes perfect sense. Thirdly and most importantly, he says that effective acts are those that "lead to a chosen goal." I argue both that this crucially important statement needs to be understood correctly and that such a correction is far from easy or straightforward. To do this, we must treat Kotarbiński's notion of action in its widest possible sense and then ask, what are those goals and how are they related to acts and action understood as work?

Needs and Desires

The real problem here is this: When we start working on a project in order to realize a goal, we also want or desire this goal.[4] There are exceptions, of course: I am coerced to act in a goal-directed project that I do not like or want. I aim at the goal only because I must, in the sense that I work under a threat. This is not an uncommon situation. Also, social obligations and moral duties may result in a situation where I act and work reluctantly: It is my duty and I must do so, regardless of my negative feelings against the task as such. For instance, it is my duty to help you in distress, although you happen to be my rival in work and love. I would not want to help you except that I (morally speaking) must. I want to be a moral person and hence I do it. Here I only discuss cases where the agent is free from such constraints.

Our desires establish a goal, which we then intend to realize by means of some suitable projects. The key term here is "desire." Some people may disagree and argue that the key term is "need," and then there emerges a distinction between needs and desires; they must not be conflated.[5] This relationship is complicated, but I still want to argue that the fundamental term is "desire" and not "need." To me, there is no need without a corresponding desire. Let me explain this and then move on towards some deeper problems concerning desire and its objects in relation to the praxiological E of effectiveness.

We need a bridge over a troubled water; suppose we all agree on that, and then we start building one because we believe that our need ascription is, in a sense, valid, that is, supported by good reasons. There are no good reasons against the bridge and we believe that the bridge will bring about good results in terms of safety, economy, and welfare.

To put is simply, life is better if we have a bridge than it would be without the bridge. Also, no viable alternatives to the bridge, such as, for instance, a ferry or a tunnel under the river, seem to exist in this case. So, we design a bridge and start working on the relevant projects.

It is easy to see how the primacy of desire comes into the picture here. We desire the good effects provided by the bridge, or we say that the bridge has its good effects on our life, such that we desire them. Let us look at the case of soldiers. We need soldiers because the times are dangerous, and we train a bunch of new recruits to become heroic soldiers. We say we need more such soldiers and not mere cannon fodder. All this is based on our desire to be safe in the long run. We do not need cannon fodder because in the long run this is not a viable answer to our call for safety, and we desire safety. That is why we need more heroic soldiers. Suppose we are near-pacifists, all of us, which is to say we dislike armies and are basically afraid of soldiers. We do not like or want them as such. What we want is safety, and because we believe that the only way to be safe in the long run is to have an army and train good soldiers would we want new soldiers to be trained. We do not want them as such, but we know we need them in order to keep safe, which is what we desire. In other words, we would like to live a life of safety and without soldiers around, but we cannot if we want to get what we want. The best possible world is of course such that there are no soldiers and life is safe. The least desirable world is such that there are soldiers and life is unsafe, which is quite possible, too. In this sense, "need" is an instrumental and not a foundational concept, unlike desire and want. We want something and hence we need something that helps us realize our desire. Notice that many instruments that we need are undesirable as such. I need a root canal job, which I do not find independently desirable at all. But what else could I do if I want to live a healthy life, which is what I do? What we need is a theory of needs and desires. One way to handle this issue is by saying that need ascriptions result in conditional desires: I want the root canal job on the condition that it helps.

Why would this be difficult to accept, as it seems? The reason may well be that many desires are so basic and obvious and as if automatic that they remain in the background, unnoticed and unappreciated when we consider work and its projects. It is not worth emphasizing that we want to stay alive, lead a healthy life, have a safe environment, enjoy happiness and welfare, experience economic success, and other such good things we actually like and desire. However, simply omitting to mention those things does not imply that they would not be there as a foundation of our practical life; they are our fundamental desires. We say we want a bridge for good reasons; hence, we need a bridge because otherwise we cannot get what we want. We need a bridge because otherwise we cannot prosper, and we want to prosper. We desire prosperity, and without this common and self-explanatory desire, it makes no sense to say that we need a bridge.

Objects of Desire

Desiring something seems to entail that something exists that is the object of my desire; that is, there is a desirable thing that I actually desire, in this given case. We find this object by considering our desires. I want a bridge and hence the object of my desire is a bridge. In this way, I first desire X, where X is the object of my desire, and then I realize that I need Y in order to get X. If I do not mention X, I cannot know what I need, and in this way the concept of effectiveness loses its very meaning and content. Obviously, effectiveness and its evaluation are anchored to the idea of the object of desire via the concept of need. Effective work realizes what is needed, which satisfies the relevant desire. We work on the bridge that we need in order to live a prosperous life, which we all desire.

Here comes the bad news: Desire has no object, but without an object we cannot specify what we want; if we cannot say what we want we cannot say what we need; hence, we cannot design a project according to which we work towards its realization. Why do I then say a desire lacks an object? In everyday practical contexts, this certainly does not seem to be the case. In other words, according to a naïve approach to the interplay of need and desire, desire has its object or at least such an object can be constructed. The reason for this is obvious: In many cases, even normally, we know what we need to do to realize our goals. We work on our needs, and this (conversationally) entails that we know what we want; that is, we know the relevant object. Where do we get this object? I must now give my reasons for saying that desires have no object. Then I must explain why we still think that desires have their object. All this is necessary because the key praxiological concept of effectiveness is now under a severe threat. Finally, I will say something about how to save this essential concept. We need it, there is no question about it!

Desire has its object in a formal logical sense, namely, according to the *de re*-interpretation of desire statements. I say, "We want brave soldiers" and I mean it *de re*: We want new soldiers who are brave. I also may mean it *de dicto*: "We want that our new soldiers are brave." It is easy to see that in the *de re*-sense the objects of our present desire are brave soldiers. Here is a problem: Only if you are a stern realist in ethics can you say that such thick moral notions as "brave soldier" are referential terms or, in other words, that something like brave soldiers actually exist. The word "brave" constitutes the problem here. For an antirealist, "brave" is an idealization or a subjective construction that corresponds to no facts of the real world. One man's brave soldier looks like another man's monster. Moreover, if you look at the corresponding *de dicto*-reading of the example above, you quickly see that it allows for no object (of desire). We have soldiers whose certain attributes are what we desire, and those constitute no object. We want the braveness of soldiers. If we say we want braveness, we create a rather strange object; I do not think it is a good idea. Of course, one may say we want their braveness as a fact, and that very fact is the required object. Such an argument seems to conflate *de dicto* and *de re*-readings. Be that as it may, let us now stay at the level of *de re*-reading.

So, if this is the case, desire has no particular object. Of course, I may say, trivially, that I want a cone of ice cream, where ice cream looks like the object of my desire. I cannot discuss the problem of such trivial desires here. Here is a hint: I can ask you, what do you desire when you desire ice cream? The correct answer may well be, I take a trip back to the sunny days of my childhood. The trick is in my asking what makes ice cream desirable to you. You may well answer by saying that you got ice cream because others did, which means that you wanted to conform. In other words, you wanted ice cream because others wanted it. Actually, you needed ice cream because you wanted to conform. Simple objects may not be that simple! Moreover, I do not think we should say desire sometimes has an object, sometimes not—this sounds too ad hoc to be plausible at all. Either X is always there as a real object or it is never there. Let me explain. There is a deeper reason than those above for arguing that desire takes no real object. The new reason is this: in "I want/desire X," X ranges over such a wide field that definitely extends the realm of real things, including facts. Let me explain.

I desire so many different things. Suppose I want to desire nothing, like a good Buddhist does; I want all the good things in the world; I desire immortality, etc. In all these cases, the *de re*-object of my desire can be formulated in the formal logical sense, but such a *de re*-object may not pick out any corresponding real object, fact, or event. Its real description is empty. If I want nothing, nothingness is my *de re*-object although we have a hard time specifying what kind of a fact nothingness is, in the sense in which I desire it. But if I want not to want it, where is the requested object now? It is easy to depict a corresponding fact—I desire to desire nothing—but the success conditions of all this are quite problematic: When I successfully desire nothing, I am still desiring something. Also, when I desire immortality, I desire something that may not exist; many people know this, and yet they desire it. And no one who desires immortality may say what that really means. People desire even if the supposed object is controversial, fuzzy, or empty. This is not an exception; on the contrary, it is rather the paradigm case.

Even when I want a bridge to be constructed over the river in our little town, I need to specify what I want before you know what I want. A bridge as such is not yet the desired bridge, as every prospective bridge builder knows. We need to design a good and suitable bridge first. Now it can be asked: Once the bridge is designed and built, is it not possible to go and say that we got exactly what we wanted, which is to say that our desire had an object, the object is now realized in the real world, and the original desire is accordingly satisfied? The object of my desire is there in front of my very eyes clad in steel and concrete, ready to be used. Well, yes, the bridge is now there, and it satisfies our practical needs, but this is different from saying that we actually got what we desired: happiness and prosperity. Notice that we need the bridge in order to be happy and prosperous. It again seems that the idea that we got what we wanted results from a confusion between needs and desires. We may get what we needed (a bridge) but this does not imply that we got what we desired (happiness and prosperity).[6]

This is how the logic of desire works: I mention prosperity, happiness, and well-being (X), all of which are desires that are now internally anchored to the idea of a bridge. They cannot be achieved without the bridge. But even after the bridge, a good bridge, is there, X is still far away. Here, it is best to say that we need a bridge and forget "We want a bridge," because then we can forget the fact that what we want does not exist and never will as a realized fact in this real world. What I desire is a new possible world where we all, the future generations included, are prosperous and happy, except perhaps my enemies and rivals. I aim at such a new possible world, which world obviously cannot be a fact of this present, given, real world of ours. I want something that is out of this world. The range of my desires is always wider than this given world. In this sense, I may be able to do what I intended and realize an object I needed, but I can never get what I wanted *de re*. My desires are always larger than this given world, unlike my needs.

A Problem and Its Solutions

What does all this mean in the praxiological terms? The praxiological task is to achieve your chosen goals in a systematic, efficient, and effective manner without causing any ethical problems. The question is, accordingly, as follows: how to understand the norm "achieve your goals," if the logic of desire does not allow you to fix any definite goals? One solution is to return to the level of intentions and needs. I intend to build a bridge and by doing so I satisfy my socially understandable and morally acceptable needs. This solution certainly works in the pragmatic perspective, however dissatisfying it may be in a wider philosophical view. I do not think we can avoid the following question: "How to achieve what we desire?" I repeat the reason for this, namely, without desires, needs become impossible to satisfy. Why do I need a bridge if I want nothing? I can always ask, "Why do we need this bridge?" and the answer must be given, directly or indirectly, by referring to desires. Here is then my first simple solution: Take your desires as given and focus on your corresponding needs and formulate your intentions accordingly; in this way, you get approximately what you want. Is this enough? Why should we require more? The bridge you got may bring you one step closer to good life and prosperity. For a practically oriented person, this may indeed be enough.

Ultimately the answer rests on the question of how practical a field praxiology really is. If it is fully practical, the worries presented in this paper may well be irrational or at least they are irrelevant. We say we want all kinds of things, and then we act in the best possible practical manner. If we want a bridge, it does not really matter why exactly we wanted it; it is enough to say we agree we want it and, accordingly, we see no drastic problems with these wants and desires. If the desire is somehow outlandish or any way problematic, we need to discuss it and then reach a decision about it. If we want to build a tall fence to keep all intrepid intruders out, we also ask what we really want and whether we actually need such a fence. All this can be discussed at a fairly superficial level mentioning physical safety and protection of our lifestyle and jobs. However, there are cases where we must dig deeper, and those cases are where we need praxiology. Here is a relevant paradox: In those trivially practical cases, we do not need praxiology—Why would we? Where do we need praxiology?—in those non-trivial cases, we meet some seemingly intractable problems. However, it is exactly those problems that make praxiological concerns so important and justify our interest in it.

We also can talk about our need-claims, namely, the fact that we need someone may argue that we do not need it, and she may be right. We do not need the bridge because there is not enough traffic to justify the claim. Sometimes need claims are essentially contested, like "We need to torture our political prisoners in order to get all the information required to make us safe," where safety is what we desire. "We all hate torturing our prisoners, but we must," is a dramatic but well-known discursive move. Anyway, this shows nicely what essentially contested need-claims are like. At least we can discuss them, which may not be the case with some of our common, more fundamental desires. Some people want war and mayhem, some appreciate peace and quiet, yet these people should agree on some common goals to realize.

If praxiology is a fully practical enterprise, all that requires is that we should be able to agree on needs, which of course may not be an easy task; yet, it is a practical quest. Desires and their conflicts are, in a sense, a less practical issue. Often we just presuppose some common and fundamental desires, and hence we do not mention them at all. Sometimes what we desire are such deeply personal things that, if they are disagreeable to others, we may not know how to deal with them without power in its many disguises. Basically, any resort to power means that we do not fully respect another person's desires but we try to change them without her consent or even understanding what is going on. Power is, in its Weberian definition, a capability to change another person's actions even without her consent and against her will.[7] I do not think praxiology has much to say about these cases. Anyway, it is often advisable not to discuss desires at all.

Practical solutions are still possible, of course. We do not then worry about the objects of desire as such. We presume they exist in the sense that we construe them as real objects, or facts, in this real world and we aim at them as such. We push aside the idea that we always desire a whole new possible world, which we see as a better alternative to the present one. We also dismiss the complicated question about the role of our beliefs when we work on our needs and desires: It all depends on what we believe until we test our solutions against the always-recalcitrant real world, and even then we may refuse to believe the results. This is to say that, when he considers the E of effectiveness, a praxiologist must make a firm decision concerning the degree of required practicality of his present enterprise: Is it enough for him to consider needs and current intentions along with his satisfiability or should he go deeper into the desire that grounds those needs and intentions? My feeling is that it is a mistake to forget desires and give primacy to needs, simply because, in that case, praxiology becomes a rather trivial instrumental discipline that cannot understand human goal-directed behaviours, like design, work, and projects, in any thoroughgoing manner. It is not clear to me why we would like to restrict our research activities to such a relatively superficial level. It seems we should go deeper if we can—and we indeed can. We need to take wants and desires seriously and give them a need-independent role and status. You first ask, "What do you really want?" and you evaluate your practical success against the answer to the question. You do not think it is fundamental to ask, "Did we do what we intended to do?" or "Did we get what we need?" Both these questions are derivative and as such not deep enough.

It is of course a true dilemma that we cannot say what we want by specifying a (*de re*) object of our relevant desire. This is to say that our praxiological task is not only practical in the instrumental sense. It is practical in a much more demanding sense: We must be able to read people's desires in such a way that we know what they entail with respect to the relevant instrumental tasks. Perhaps this is enough? If we know what needs our desires presume and command, perhaps we know enough? It is then a quixotic task to require that we first fully understand our desires and only then decide what to do and what we need to do it. On the contrary, we proceed from our needs and intentions towards our desires in order to understand them, and then we can modify and correct our need ascriptions. We iterate this until we have a nice equilibrium between our needs and desires, and then we can initiate our projects and jobs hoping to do good work.

Notes

1 T. Kotarbiński says (1938) that "praxiological truths are a source of ethical uneasiness, since the mode of action most likely to succeed is frequently at odds with the immediate reaction of noble feelings," in his "On the Essence and Goals of General Methodology," in W. Gasparski and T. Pszczolowski (eds.), Praxiological Studies, Dordrecht: Reidel, 1983, p. 29.

2 Kotarbiński himself emphasizes actions; see his early 1913 article, "The Goal of an Act and the Task of the Agent," op. cit. But his concept of action is very broad; see p. 3: "Then let the entire process of the operation of all the forces taken together, which was an indispensable condition for the goal, be called the act." In other words, given a goal, all human activity that essentially contributes to its realization is what we mean by an act. Accordingly, Kotarbiński reasons from given goals to the corresponding action, so that he does not infer the goal from the description of the action. I follow in this paper the latter, causal, way of reasoning rather than his original analytical way. My problem is, anyway, how do we find the goal in question and then reach it?

3 Kotarbiński, "The ABC of Practicality" in L. V. Ryan *et al.* (eds.), Praxiology and Pragmatism, New Brunswick: Transaction Publishers, 2002, p. 31.

4 For a theory of desire, see my "An Introduction to Desire," Homo Oeconomicus 31/4 (2014), 447–461, and "Narratives of Desire," in T. Airaksinen and W. Gasparski (eds.), Desire: The Concept and Its Practical Contexts, New Brunswick: Transaction Publishers, 2016.

5 On needs and desires, see my "Desire and Happiness," Homo Oeconomicus 29/3 (2012). 393–412, pp. 397 ff.

6 On happiness and related goals, see, for example, A. C. Brooks, Gross National Happiness, New York: Basic Books, 2008.

7 See D. Wrong, Power: Its Forms, Bases and Uses, Oxford: Blackwell, 1979, p. 21.

Chapter 2

Social and Psychological Aspects of Rare Acts

Victor Alexandre

Introduction

In "The Roots of Praxiology" (*Praxiology: The International Annual of Practical Philosophy and Methodology*, vol. 7, 2000), we presented "The Structural Analysis of Actions and Its Social-Psychological Aspects". This method that we elaborated is based on the works of Moles and Rohmer (1977) and allows analyzing and representing the structure of real or fictitious acts. This method was the object of a doctoral thesis (Alexandre, 1992). Effectively, the phenomenological study of acts leads us to consider that acts form hierarchical structures (from micro-actions to macro-actions) and that these structures can be observed at each level. The acts form sequences that vary in length, and in which each unit is linked to each other at a specific distance (close ($n + 1$) or distant ($n + x$)) or a nonspecific distance by probabilities of transition whose value should decrease as the distance increases. These probabilities are reported in a double-entry table in which each entry consists of all of the units in the same order. The probabilities between each of the units are reported in the cells. These probabilities can also be expressed by dots of different sizes that are proportional to the frequency observed. We call this table a *praxiogram*, a term already used by A. Kaufmann but in a different sense. The praxiogram shows the structure of the sequence and makes it possible to clearly distinguish the frequent units of action (which precede or follow many other units) of rare units. The former generates long lines and columns which we call *units of form*. The latter generates short lines and columns that we call *units of content*. This distinction led us to reflect on dialectic frequency/rarity in the phenomenological theory of action which we only touched on in the aforementioned chapter as propositions concerning rare acts, and that we develop more here in relation to acts of both domestic and professional activity.

The Concept of the Rare Act, Nature, or Statistical Frequency

It is easy to observe that most of the acts performed each day are of the same or a very close nature, while other acts would be performed less frequently. Hence the idea that rare acts, like rare objects and rare metals and gases, exist which are distinct and have particular psychological, cognitive, emotional, and social psychological effects. This can be demonstrated by a trivial example. Driving a car implies knowledge and control over a sequence of physical movements, such as turning the steering wheel (to the right or the left), putting one's right foot on the accelerator or the brake pedal and the left foot on the clutch. The success of the action depends on the agent's judicious choice of the correct sequence at a given moment and according to the perceived and interpreted environmental constraints. The experienced driver knows these gestures. He does them often in a quasi automatic way because they are a source of comfort, security, and pleasure, even if at the end of a long journey they can become monotonous and tiresome. But suppose he has a flat tire that involves removing and replacing the tire. While the driver is an expert at driving, he is not necessarily an expert in mechanics and does not always know or no longer knows how to change a tire because such an eventuality is rare. The incident disturbs his tranquility and requires a cognitive effort: Where is the jack, the manual, the spare tire, and what is the procedure to follow while losing as little time as possible? In short, this is not a habitual act, it is *a rare act for the driver* which involves an additional overall cost and which creates a particular difficulty whose importance varies according to his schedule. However, while this act is rare for the driver, it is *frequent for the mechanic*. It is an ordinary task for him, one that he learned to do and does frequently with perfect cognitive skill, and which does not provoke any particular emotion in him apart from having accomplished his work.

This example helps to understand why it would be legitimate to conceive the rare act only in function of its statistical frequency even if the possibility of rare acts remains according to their own nature. The statistical approach stipulates that each act, whatever its nature, can be rare or frequent depending on the status and the competencies of the agent. In one case, it constitutes or is part of a "routine", but this is not so in another case. Professional training is therefore comparable to giving the operator the capacity to perform frequent acts which will be accomplished in the exercise of a profession with perfect cognitive mastery, with a minimum overcall cost and without a particular emotional content. But that does not eliminate the possibility of the existence of rare acts whose nature, content, structure, or conditions are such that they constitute exceptions and consequently require a singular expertise, a talent, or an opportunity to be accomplished. Moreover, most professional activities are not free from such acts, even if they are little likely as our example of a flat tire and, although they have little probability, they cannot be entirely excluded.

The event forced the act in the example we proposed. In other cases, the rare act is not a simple response to a rare, unforeseen, random, or accidental event, but it is envisaged as an objective destined to show or demonstrate a singular praxiological or cognitive competence. All activity of competition undoubtedly relates to this model. Human activities in general—industrial, intellectual, athletic, etc.—are not satisfied with the banality induced by repetition and the perfect knowledge that frequent acts bring, but they are guided more by a desire for innovation or progress, in other words, by a more or less chaotic tendency toward types of rare actions at a given moment. Thus, as illustrated by athletic and artistic activities, a dynamic is instituted between frequency and rarity in which the frequent act is the basis on which the perspective of the rare act is constructed. These activities are composed of numerous repetitions that the athlete or the musician does for long and tedious hours. But they are only repetitions in view of performing an exceptional act, a record (of speed or strength for example), or a public performance that will bring the artist fame and the recognition of others.

Rare Acts: The Goal of Frequent Acts

In many cases, the rare act can be considered as the goal of frequent acts, as something that gives them meaning and which, by transcending each of them, proves to be invaluable in moments of doubt, fatigue, and despondency. It originates behind the frequent act as an intention and at a psychological distance that only the operator or his mentor can determine. The rare act provides the mental support for continuing the activity, its raison d'être. Because it is mentally anticipated before it is achieved, it serves as a guide and has an energizing function. However, in order to do this, the daily activity, naturally monotonous and tedious, must be fixed on an ultimate goal, and the agent has to know how to find the future originality and singularity of the rare act in the banality of the repeated movements.

Since the question of the meaning of the act and the contribution of the rare act to the comprehension and accomplishment of frequent acts has been posed, we should refer here to acts of production such as conceived by Taylorism in which each action is broken down into simple elements called elementary movements (cf. the M. T. M. Method, Karger and Bayha, 1957). It is well-known that the aim of Taylorism was to succeed in making a complex action with a large number of operators using a small number of simple movements that are perfectly known and accomplished in the shortest amount of time. The idea of breaking down the act and the repeated performance of a fragment by the same operator is a powerful factor for increasing collective productivity. This was already observed by Smith (1776/1991) who introduced the concept of division of labor. In itself, it cannot be contested but inevitably, it leads to boredom and loss of meaning. Many years ago, a colleague stated that the civil servants' lack of motivation after ten years on the job was due to the repetition of the same daily acts and the perspective of careers that were perfectly determined and known in advance. I responded that I did not see any remedy for boredom other than the rare act. It was an attempt to be witty but not entirely, and I also recall the example of workers in a glass-blowing factory that made glasses and bottles in the west of France, who, in the old days during their lunch break, were allowed to make unique models to express their creativity and to take a break from the models imposed on them. Taylorism did seek and propose some ways to vary the content of the operator's acts (changing posts or the level of action, for example) but one can legitimately envisage that the loss of meaning is the principal reason for disinterest, and that restoring meaning always involves considering the final rare act which results from a multiplicity of frequent acts.

Rare Acts, Self-Esteem, and Self-Image

The rare act not only has a function of giving a purpose to frequent acts, it is also an indicator of the agent's self-worth, of high or low self-esteem, and as a consequence, of social recognition. The case of a magician offers a perfect example. While most agents seek the most favorable conditions, the magician is an artist who, with the full knowledge of his audience, explicitly puts himself in the most extreme situation, one that is the most opposed to successfully accomplishing his act, and he shows that he is capable of achieving what he had publicly presented as impossible. In reality, no one is convinced of the objective accomplishment of the act, because everyone knows there is a trick, but the magician is still an object of admiration. This means that for the magician as well as the spectator, the benefit as well as the purpose of the rare act are the subjects of the action.

Undoubtedly there are people who are satisfied with perfectly known frequent acts and have no desire for innovation because that would force them to make some sort of a physical or mental effort without their consent. However, other people exist with a concern for creativity and for whom the rare act is supposed to express a distinctive capacity that brings fame or a certain prestige. Each action directly or symbolically bears the mark of the person who accomplishes it. Good or heroic acts have a positive connotation and confer on their author the characters of nobility, power, and generosity. They arouse admiration. Bad acts with a negative connotation express cowardice, weakness, and violence. They lead to disapproval. These connotations of a cultural origin lead the human being to create a link between his acts that is both intimate and public, between who he is and the way that he wants to be perceived by society, or at least by his milieu. One then understands the importance of the frequency of acts in self-perception, self-image, and social judgment. The student accused of mischief will have a tendency to underestimate its frequency. He will say it does not happen often. The teacher who wants to correct him will have a tendency to overestimate the frequency and to recall all the facts of the same nature attributed to him. Thus, each one has a tendency to estimate the frequency of his good or bad acts as well as the acts of others according to the benefit or the utility he hopes to obtain. Obviously, there is nothing here related to the exact account of the acts but a general estimation which accredits or discredits the agent in his eyes or in the eyes of others.

Self-esteem (a subjective aspect) and self-image (an objective aspect) have a plausible connection with the frequency and rarity of good or bad acts. However, a more precise analysis requires moderating this statement. One will consider that a rare act with a positive connotation confers sure and sudden fame on an individual according to the importance given to the act and the subject by the social codes, in particular, intelligence and altruism (Asch, 1946). An example of this is saving someone from drowning. Other factors such as the age of the agent or circumstances can interfere. If the person is young and if he does not repeat the courageous act again, the personal attribution would tend to disappear and become a circumstantial attribution. If the act is confirmed by repetition, the personal attribution will tend to be reinforced and qualify the very nature of the person. Negatively connoted acts, such as misdemeanors and crimes, result in processes of attribution and stigmatization which probably follow the direction and the same criteria for judging the nature (essence) of the person and the circumstances. It then becomes possible to outline the principal traits of a group dynamic that is based on imitation and competition between human beings.

Rare Acts and the Group Dynamic

If the positively connoted rare act initially creates a psychological effect of admiration, it also very often creates an attempt at imitation and reproduction among subjects seeking behaviors that increase prestige.

Tarde (1898) placed imitation at the center of social behaviors and although its importance has since diminished, it remains indisputable. The frequency of the act increases when it is reproduced and little by little loses the initial quality which made its author known and admired. Inversely, the frequent acts done previously and which were replaced by it see their frequency diminish. By becoming more and more rare, acts regain some of their lost interest in the same way that ordinary objects brushed aside at a given moment for some reason (their uselessness or obsolescence) and banished to a dark attic find new consideration. The development of practices that illustrate the phenomena of the mode is subject to a double process: one solidly orientated toward innovation and the other regressive, which promotes old forms that have become more or less obsolete. Diet or fashion styles provide numerous examples. Thus over the centuries, man took the habit of eating his meals inside his house, installing better and better equipped kitchens furnished with more and more high-tech tools. However, rather early in the Middle Ages, man found the charm and practicality of eating in the countryside. This practice, which became the modern picnic, has become widespread with its own collection of recipes and accessories but it has in no way interfered with the modernization of indoor culinary spaces. The same is true for the culinary arts. A complicated and successful preparation is a rare act which brings credit to its author. Appreciated by the guests, they set about to reproduce it but when its frequency increases, the effect of the initial surprise diminishes. At a given moment, forgotten customary food dishes reappear that are simpler and whose tradition is a subjective guarantee of quality.

The rare act also has social psychological effects in the sense that it can serve as a link between those who perform the act and contribute to forming in-groups orientated toward elitism when the acts are good or gangs when the acts are harmful. There are those who climb Mount Everest, those who graduate from a prestigious university, or those who attack a bank. Even if this is illustrated by the proverb "Birds of a feather flock together", it requires a short explanation. The self-esteem that the positive rare act brings generates some isolation. When someone compares himself with others, he knows that he is not completely like them, and the others know it as well. This estrangement, which is more or less durable, interferes with the closeness usually linked to conviviality and social need. If the rare act is neglected, the benefit for self-esteem is partly or totally lost. By associating himself with others who performed the same or a similar act, the human being can satisfy both his social need and keep the benefit that comes with his act. This is a social psychological process, in other words, both psychological and social, but its expression can be observed in get-togethers with friends or public meetings, such as awards ceremonies, in the way that people speak about what they have done or describe what others have done. It is difficult for the agent to publicly discuss his positive rare act. This is considered a lack of modesty, but it is gratifying to hear others talk about it. In-depth conversational analyses would show how verbal exchanges contribute to forming self-image, not only by increasing or reducing the frequency of rare acts, but by a kind of implicit and common volition to counterbalance human relations or to restore their equilibrium by, for example, allowing an individual who has never done anything exceptional to give his ordinary acts a few particular traits to underline their worth. This is often observed at retirement parties.

The most common tendency is to hide or tone down the presentation of the negative rare act because it leads to a process of stigmatization (Goffman, 1959), which is often durable and generalized, and this explains the effect of the rare act on interpersonal communication, self-image, and the formation of a social relation. Whether the act has a positive or a negative connotation, it must be acknowledged that the act has a particular structuring power which is probably based on the laws of Gestalt field theory that integrate the different traits, even if knowledge of them remains poor or uncertain. But there are cases of rare acts that do not lead to a special emotion between two agents, as when two agents interact in the same act which is rare for one and frequent for the other. This is rather general in situations involving ticket or bank windows, interviews, or consultations, such as declaring the birth of a child at the town hall or consulting a doctor. The act of registering the birth of one's child is rare for the person doing it but the act is frequent for the town hall clerk because he repeats the same action all day long. And the act of consulting is rare for the patient while the act is identical or close to the preceding act for the doctor. In these cases, sharing the emotions which come with the rare act is difficult, even nonexistent. One knows the procedure perfectly; the other does not. Neither the empathy nor the compassion are real, but a mark of courtesy and a respect for social conventions that mask the absence of sincere feelings without altering the effectiveness of the act in any way. However, an increase in effectiveness is conceivable, as for example, in the case of the doctor whose diagnosis could be perturbed by too much compassion for his patient.

The Creation of Rare Acts

Our scientific and technological culture likes to create acts and make them known. The most perfect example of this is perhaps man's first step on the moon since millions of people saw an astronaut leave his spaceship and walk on the moon for the first time live on television. The rarity of the act was certainly due to its primacy, but also to the scientific and technological synergy which made it possible to perform a perfectly banal act (climbing down a ladder, putting one's foot on the ground, and being seen doing it by the whole world) in an exceptional context. We can draw some lessons from this symbol of modern power and engineering. It is neither the structure nor the function of the natural act of walking which rendered the act rare, but the context, the lunar space that had never been visited before by a human being. Thus rare acts can be created by applying the most natural functions of the human being to situations in perfectly unusual spatio-temporal conditions. Spatial movement, along with telecommunications, is perhaps the domain which has the greatest modern inventiveness. Man's natural resources in this area are limited. The human being with a normal constitution is capable of walking, running, jumping, climbing, swimming, and sliding. Each of these acts can find new modes, often with the help of technology. The proliferation of these modes of movement and the passion that they create increase their frequency and encourage new variations and sources of unknown sensations, which are generally developed in a context of individual or team competition.

If athletic, industrial, or another type of competition is a powerful factor in the creation of rare acts, there are easier and less expensive ways to produce them. It only requires a variation in the spatio-temporal framework or the social context in which these acts are usually found. For example, one can observe a couple making their marriage vows at the bottom of the ocean. Neither deep-sea diving nor making vows in a town hall or a religious building are rare acts in themselves. The combination of the two produces the rare act. In a more methodological way, if one cannot create a rare act, at least it is possible to create the characteristics which future acts should have in order to be qualified as rare. It suffices to construct matrices with multiple factors including the different values of the general cost factors of each action—in other words, the financial cost, the energy cost, the time cost, and the psychological cost (Mole and Rohmer, 1977)—and to note in each case the frequencies observed in a large number of acts. Empty cases appear which enable one to imagine rare acts after having defined a priori their characteristics.

Do Rare Acts Exist in Nature?

According to what we said above, it is possible to conceive only the statistical aspect of the rare act since frequency and rarity are two sides of the same process based on usage. We adopted this idea in order to express the most common rule and aimed to show that it is a key to explain the praxiological dynamic. But this does not totally dismiss the hypothesis of rare acts that are never or very rarely reproduced in nature. These acts will definitely not be found in the structure of daily life with its repetitive routines; rather, one must look for them in historical accounts, tales, fiction, and mythical or religious texts. We find facts and actions in this literature comparable to rare acts and their exceptionalness is undoubtedly the main reason which makes them vivid not only in our memory, mind, and individual affectivity but also in our collective history, even if, for some, we are free to consider them as fictitious or real. The storming of the Bastille in the history of France, the Long March in the history of China, war commemorations, ancient and modern hagiographies of imaginary heroes (Harry Potter, Superman) are examples of this type. Real or fictitious, they share a concern for small or important acts whose nature is a departure from ordinary expressions of action. They captivate the reader or the audience, they make them dream. Undoubtedly, it is not disrespectful to consider that numerous mythical and religious texts resort to the same paradigm and to see here the origin of their influence on the human mind, and consequently their real and observable influence on human behaviors.

Although acts that have a negative connotation according to the social codes (violent acts, murders, robberies, etc.) are unfortunately reproducible, strictly speaking, they may share a few common properties with rare acts. The place that they have in literature, movies, and television merits a short explanation even if it is difficult to distinguish the part that belongs to the forbidden and the part that belongs to rarity in the fascination that they arouse. They possess a certain rarity in the sense that they are only performed by a small proportion of the population and that most of the members of a given society carefully avoid them and, moreover, condemn them. If this is the case, it is undoubtedly because they hide their real nature and do not acknowledge what is forbidden. In this fictitious context where the agent does not really exist (he is an actor) and the victim does not exist either (he is also an actor), the praxiological process and the structure of the act, skillfully analyzed and presented by the novelist or the movie director, appear convincing or at least logical enough so that the reader or the audience has knowledge of the real act without feeling any kind of guilt. Moreover, we have observed that the current tendency is to add real references to fiction, as if that would increase fascination even more.

Conclusion, Rare Acts and Traces

The rare act always has a limited duration whatever its size, and nothing remains of it. Neither the agent nor the gestures, the movements, the positions, and the spectators of the rare act, like the frequent act, resist time which destroys everything inexorably. Like the frequent act, the rare act only leaves material traces such as objects, buildings, developed spaces, works of art (now with fixed or animated images), and especially linguistic traces that give an account of these rare acts. Therefore, the past rare act can be found in what serves as the memory and the real or symbolic space of conversation, in other words the world of objects and more broadly the spatio-temporal framework. The rare act marks the individual conscience, self-image and self-esteem, and it also marks the collective conscience over the long term. The spatio-temporal framework offers excellent examples of this. In general, an individual remembers where and when he was married. Disastrous events, such as a car accident or a simple fall, leave a spatial and temporal trace in the individual's memory. In a similar way, the important actions which marked the history of a group or a nation, such as a battle (particularly a victory), the signing of a treaty, or a significant group demonstration, remain in the collective memory because of the places where they occurred, although nothing remains of their materiality with the exception of some fortifications or war weapons. In order to conserve the memory of actions in a certain place, it must be made sacred so that its symbolic function prevails over its common function. The stele, the monument guards the memory of the past act, but in an incomplete way because it requires a work of interpretation which cannot be done without resorting to language, in other words, without the public discourse which is the guarantee of the authenticity of the act and the sincerity of the memory. The cyclical structure of time offers opportunities for official and public group demonstrations for commemorations and various anniversaries with a determined periodicity that can be annual or perennial. The action is not repeated during these commemorations and does not lose its status of a rare act, even if it is sometimes accompanied by recreations of its most significant aspects. It is evoked as a rare act because of the idea that the repetition of the memory is necessary to maintain group identity. This observation can also be applied to religious rites which reproduce the founding acts without altering their unique character. Putting the rare act in a spatio-temporal framework is a way to integrate it in the culture of a society, to preserve it from banality and oblivion which would make it lose its particular virtue when it has one, but also to distinguish among all of the past rare acts those which we intend to honor and those which we wish to forget.

References

Alexandre, V., 1992, L'analyse structurale des actions et ses aspects psycho-sociaux. Unpublished PhD Dissertation, Strasbourg.

Alexandre, V., Gasparski, W. W., 2000, The Roots of Praxiology, French Action Theory from Bourdeau and Espinas to Present Days, in Praxiology: The International Annual of Practical Philosophy and Methodology, Vol. 7. Transaction Publishers, New Brunswick (USA).

Asch, S. E., 1946, Forming impressions of personality; *Journal of Abnormal and Social Psychology, 41*(3), 258–290.

Goffman, E., 1959, The Presentation of Self in Everyday Life. Doubleday-Anchor. Garden City, New York.

Karger, D. W., Bayha, F. B., 1957, La mesure rationnelle du travail: M.T.M. et systèmes de temps prédéterminés, Trad. Editions Organisation, Gauthiers Villars. Paris.

Moles, A., Rohmer, E., 1977, Théorie des actes, Casterman.

Smith, A., 1776/1991, La richesse des nations. Trad. G. F. Flamarion, Paris.

Tarde, G., 1898, Etudes de psychologie sociale, Girard et Brière, Paris.

Chapter 3

Praxiological Implications for Modern Start-Ups

Marek Arszułowicz

Introduction

The modern economy offers fast computing machines that significantly cut transaction costs and promise quick communication. How would that improvement help in the value exchange between start-up entrepreneurs and customers? What aspects of human action would be affected by a sharing economy where access to knowledge is unlimited and very often free? What practical implications can be drawn from praxiological classicists in the context of the modern economy?

Every human endeavour, since the dawn of humankind until the present, regardless of its scale and scope, is a response to a stimulus that comes from reasoning based on uncertain assumptions and is aimed at satisfying that stimuli towards an uncertain future. Since the workings of a brain, be it individual or collective, naturally drive at building structures of reality, eventually this very brain can also provide conceivable justifications for each and every action despite the fact that it is unable to answer with definitive certainty ultimate life questions. For that reason, all the answers, regardless of how deeply they refer to a problem, provide but a probability of reality.

Adding to that equation the societal life of human communities, it becomes understandable that every aspect of social science is extremely difficult to predict, steer, or manage. All due to the fact that human minds and choices are unrestricted and rely utterly on a free will of choice. Consequently, the bigger the community, the greater the number of unpredicted choices and actions. No economic or political improvement or development is ever going to change it.

Praxiology provides a reasonable solution to complexity by holding the position that no human action can be falsified and that there is no possible or known way of testing probable choices providing that all other factors remain equal; therefore, an action is a legitimate justification for all choices. As the action itself provides the ultimate data for formulating laws and drawing various conclusions, then all other aspects of uncertainty that influence choice seem to be restrained by the boundaries of a specific action. Action introduces structure: It is exactly that structure that is being analysed with scientific tools and methodology. As explained by Mises (1998):

> Praxiology asks: What happens in acting? What does it mean to say that an individual then and there, today and here, at any time and at any place, acts? What results if he chooses one thing and rejects another? (p. 45)

Praxiology proposes understanding economy, the most intricate and common phenomenon in every society, by bypassing motivation which originates in deep psychological reverie and focusing instead on action that validates all choices, from the smallest to those that can be unimaginably big. As such, praxiological laws that explain economy can also serve as a tool for understanding all human actions. A person makes choices based on what he or she values most regardless of what constitutes those values.

By using praxiological methodology of deductive thinking (Rothbardian logic), we try to see how it can help to draw practical conclusions for start-up entrepreneurs in the modern economy (Rothbard, 1980). Therefore, no mathematical equations are needed, no calculations required, no numbers necessary; we purely rely on what our reasoning can develop, predict, and speculate.

Adaptability and Knowledge

Historical Perspective

Human development and progress have always been directed to achieve one particular goal: better adaptability to external circumstances. Therefore, all innovations and actions have had but one purpose: to provide better living conditions for the community. An historical perspective of humankind development can clearly prove that within a time span of hundreds and thousands of years, the lives of communities became more complex; from barter to money exchange, from rural to urban, from artistic production to international markets. All improvements followed the law of adaptability. It seems that general development rarely depended on personal choices of what is or is not valuable. All seemed to be based on the technique of trial and error that resembles Darwinian natural selection, the mechanism that allows only the best ideas to survive. But humans have had one big advantage over Darwinian methodology: They possessed consciousness, which made the whole system even more complex because there is nothing solid on which the theory of evolution of complexity can be based upon. Human choices are simply unpredictable.

What seems to be stable is the fact that human beings act to adapt. These actions follow the very same pattern of choices buried in the inner value system, which seems to change as well but with the rule of different laws. And the value system, which decides personal choices, lies at the foundation of each and every business enterprise. What else is exchanged between parties if not a set of values represented by goods (of whatever sort) or services? It seems that upon the invention of a language whose aim was to pass knowledge, and upon emergence of information technology that translates reality into a set of symbols, there seems to be a metalanguage—that of values which are constantly being exchanged. Language in business is not anymore used to target basic needs: It is used to communicate values. That seems to be a basic truth for entrepreneurs and for start-ups in particular.

Throughout the ages adaptability dictated what value would be elicited from, let's say, a piece of wood. As technology developed, so did the process of creating value from raw materials. In this sense, value remains an open question for every generation despite technological advancement. Value remains at the core of human action per se. Adaptability is a skill of generating profits and creative thoughts in any condition.

The Modern Economy

The twenty-first century economy is on the verge of a significant change; societies need to undergo a new adaptability process from an economy that has been adjusted to industrial mechanisms towards a digital or knowledge-based economy. It is impossible to speculate with ultimate certainty what the shape and functionality of the future markets will be, but even with the scarce knowledge available it is possible to deduct interdependencies between future market players. It is also possible to predict certain aspects of market behaviour based on two premises: constant adaptability as an ever-going process and value exchange. These two lie at the very centre of any exchange or trade. They constitute constant powers that seem to be unchanged in any economic system.

The fundamental question, from the perspective of a start-up entrepreneur, is as follows: With the myriad of connections, both domestic and international, would it be easier or more difficult to establish exchangeable value? The pending questions naturally follow: How can the accessibility of knowledge via the Internet help in understanding of values? What is considered to be a success or failure? How can the current action decide about future efficiency?

And the most important question still lies unanswered: What knowledge do we need to be successful in the market? In the past, knowledge was dispersed and there was no 'central planner', as Hayek put it. Hayek was defending the idea that 'a man on the spot', with his unique knowledge of the place, would know better how to distribute goods contrary to central planning, which is, by definition and technical impossibility, deprived of such a knowledge on a constant basis. Nowadays, the Internet offers plenty of information to practically everyone worldwide. In advanced societies, scanning machines in supermarkets follow two things simultaneously: They track a product as well as the shopping preferences and buying history of a customer. A similar tracking system is used by practically every online retailer. Additionally, before purchasing anything, a potential customer has the chance, means, and ability to compare a price of a commodity or service in real time worldwide. It seems that the problem of dispersed knowledge sharing has been solved. Or has it?

As Hayek explains (Hayek, 1945):

> The peculiar character of the problem of a rational economic order is determined precisely by the fact that the knowledge of the circumstances of which we must make use never exists in concentrated or integrated form but solely as the dispersed bits of incomplete and frequently contradictory knowledge which all the separate individuals possess. The economic problem of society is thus not merely a problem of how to allocate "given" resources—if "given" is taken to mean given to a single mind which deliberately solves the problem set by these "data." It is rather a problem of how to secure the best use of resources known to any of the members of society, for ends whose relative importance only these individuals know. Or, to put it briefly, it is a problem of the utilization of knowledge which is not given to anyone in its totality.

In terms of predicting human action (choices between values) all knowledge seems to be nothing but the probability of choices. Rothbard explains (Rothbard, 1980):

> For the praxiologist, forecasting is a task very similar to the work of the historian. The latter attempts to "predict" the events of the past by explaining their antecedent causes; similarly, the forecaster attempts to predict the events of the future on the basis of present and past events already known.

All knowledge is about the past. From an economic point of view, we always deal with uncertainty because we will never be sure what people *will* do.

Value

Entering the Market

The starting point of every start-up entrepreneur must necessarily begin with the action of discovering a business idea that would bring profits. From a praxiological point of view, entering the market means having goods or services that, when exchanged, would ease a certain discomfort for the customer. In other words, they must represent values that are readily exchanged for money. But how exactly can the process of discovering value be designed and executed? Is it possible to create a value adding/discovering mechanism that would be helpful for modern start-up entrepreneurs? Would access to a vast amount of knowledge be enough?

Lack of consistency between praxiologists concerning value (Eabrasu, 2011), on one hand, and its importance for entrepreneurs on the other, seems to be a strong argument for bringing it to the discussion. Even if value has been for a long time considered as less important among praxiologists, or as difficult to define, it is commonly accepted that value 'creation' or value 'discovery' or value 'adding' is a form of human action. Additionally, exchange of value and value paradox was strongly accented by Mises (1998):

> However, the classical economists failed in their endeavours to provide a satisfactory theory of value. This shortcoming forced them to abandon their ambitious plan to develop a general theory of human action. They had to satisfy themselves with a theory explaining only the activities of the businessman without going back to the choices of everybody as the ultimate determinants.
>
> (p. 63)

Establishing Sellable Values

When a customer chooses one commodity over another, or one service over another, it is done in accordance with one's value system. The system itself is not within the scope of praxiology but lies outside the discipline, namely in psychology, religion, philosophy, or maybe even ethics or other moral systems. However, from an entrepreneur's point of view, a piece of wood needs to be changed into a value-carrying item for a customer if it is to be exchanged in the market. Hence 'value problem' emerges silently, and cannot be overthrown, alongside the work of an entrepreneur. At this point, value becomes the praxiological factor because human action is required to bring the value forth. In explaining a praxiological understanding of a value system, Rothbard offers the following description (Rothbard, 1997):

> One of the great contributions of praxiology, as I have pointed out above, is that the praxiologist, the economist, doesn't know what anyone's value scales are except as those value preferences are demonstrated by a person's concrete action. In the case of my purchase of the newspaper, historians or psychologists may make more or less informed estimates of the news-dealers's or my value scales through the process of interpretive understanding, but all that the economist can know scientifically and with certainty is the preference relative to 15 cents or the newspaper as demonstrated through concrete action.
>
> (p. 91)

The point Rothbard makes is clear and understandable from the point of view of an observer (it can even be an economist) who takes note of what is happening in an existing relationship between parties in the market. But it fails to explain what actions were made by a newsagent in order to enter the market in the first place. There is no dispute as to the news dealer's oblivion to motives which drove Rothbard to buy a newspaper for 15 cents. Furthermore, it probably will never be the subject of his meditation, but for a starting entrepreneur, the idea of setting up a business would necessarily bring him to answer questions about the business's potential.

Praxiologically it should be simple: There is a goal—setting up a business, there are means by which it can be achieved—capital, product, registration, and there are actors ready to execute the plan—an entrepreneur. But what seems to be the end of the process (the achieved goal of a business) is actually the beginning of another process, namely business development. With a well-prepared business plan, short- and long-term goals are well written and designed. Yet, according to staticbrain.com, the major reasons for business failure (around fifty percent collapse after five years) are: incompetence, unbalanced experience or lack of managerial experience, lack of experience in the line of goods, or service, neglect, fraud, disaster.[1]

It is true that an entrepreneur should have certain qualities for performing entrepreneurial activities, just as a person who holds the position of a teacher or doctor should have certain qualities, but nonetheless even the best qualities and traits of character in an entrepreneur are used for better execution of value exchange. Business opportunities are, in other words, chances for value exchange between business partners. The problem lies in the ability to name those values and make them sellable in the market.

A modern entrepreneur can use an enormous amount of data to observe people's choices and their preferences. By doing so, he puts himself in a position of a 'crowd follower'. An increase in purchase of product A suggests a market demand for more varieties of product A; hence, actions are taken to produce them. However, to produce a product that is even slightly different from what competitors produce puts an entrepreneur in a position of a 'frontman' and thus increases uncertainty. Would it be worth asking, at this stage, what constitutes the customer's choice? In other words, how has his or her value system changed? According to Mises all those actions are futile (Mises, 1998):

> The basis of modern economics is the cognition that it is precisely the disparity in the value attached to the objects exchanged that results in their being exchanged. People buy and sell only because they appraise the things given up less than those received. Thus the notion of a measurement of value is vain. An act of exchange is neither preceded nor accompanied by any process which could be called a measuring of value.
>
> (p. 205)

The probable reason for clinging to human action as the ultimate tool for establishing what really is valued by customers might lie in the assumption that customers themselves do not know why they chose what they chose and it is much easier to state with certainty what they value once they have made their choice. Big companies make use of this truth and very often suggest their products as the best possible option for customers. For a long time, the name for that action was confined to the word 'advertisement' but modern technology brings so complex and intricate solutions of reaching customers that the traditional 'advertising' should be changed into 'tracing', 'spying', 'nudging', or something that would combine all these together.

Value Creating, Discovering, or Adding?

When a seller wants to raise the value of a house, he or she invests in improving its standard. From an investor's point of view, only one thing has been done at a time but the cumulative effect raises the value of the property. It can be stated that the value has been created in both eyes, that of a beholder and a creator. Would it suggest that the value system might exist independently? Taylor states clearly that such a system is impossible (Taylor, 1980):

> There is no such thing as a measuring unit of value, and this fact means that measuring the value of a thing is impossible. Value is a subjective phenomenon that eludes cardinal quantification. A thing's value is in the mind of the person who is doing the valuing, and this process of evaluating is not a matter of measurement.
>
> (p. 24)

The investor improves the standards of the property because he or she anticipates that that particular action would improve the value of the property for a potential customer not knowing who that customer might be. Should the action be taken to satisfy customer X, the investor would implore all possibilities in order to bring him satisfaction. Since in a free market the customer is anonymous, it is impossible to predict what exactly would bring that satisfaction. Yet, the investor knows that improving property standards would improve its value. Without an external system of values such actions would be futile. It is true that values cannot be measured with numbers, but somehow they are measured.

While focusing on the potential value for the market by satisfying the needs and wants of the customer, we draw our attention away from the well-established fact in economics that selfish actions miraculously bring profits for the whole society. Satisfying his own needs, an entrepreneur also satisfies the needs of others, as has been explained by Adam Smith. That is why a simple action of improving the standard of a property causes it to have a greater market value expressed in terms of monetary exchange. The value attached to a property has been noted as an 'increase' for all market players.

Mises sees value in terms of utility. Sometimes it is also expressed in terms of bringing satisfaction, happiness, lowering uneasiness, or fulfilling desires by achieving certain goals. The value system is invisible and there are no available means of measuring value; hence, the 'a posteriori' approach is reliable. What would be valuable from an entrepreneur's view are the ways of defining sellable values. Once the observations of human actions are made, there seem to be three options open for a business person: discovering a value, adding a value, or creating a value.

Discovering a value is a creative process of assessing how existing goods or services can help customers achieve their goals. Adding value is enriching existing goods or services with elements that would win the attention of customers. Creating value is introducing to the market a totally new product or service. Recalling a newsagent from whom Rothbard bought a newspaper, we might assume that he added value to an existing commodity: He created a stall for newspapers. Recalling an investor who introduced changes to his property, it can be assumed that he also added value to an existing commodity. Discovering value would entail the action of finding new ways of utilizing what already exists: Salt can be used for cooking or defrosting; music can be used for study or entertainment; a watch can be used for showing time or as a token of wealth. Creating value is apparently the most sophisticated action from the three because it aims at creating goods or services, the utility of which is highly uncertain.[2]

Geographical Location of Value. Does It Matter?

The market is a process, not a place. However, the exchange of goods takes place between people who usually come from the same background. Supermarkets, real estate agencies, car dealers, and vegetable markets operate within the boundaries of certain environment. And within that environment entrepreneurs seek their opportunities for profits. The geographical knowledge of customers helps in defining their values, as Mises explains (Mises, 1998):

> Inheritance and environment direct a man's actions. They suggest to him both the ends and the means. He lives not simply as man in abstracto; he lives as a son of his family, his race, his people, and his age; as a citizen of his country; as a member of a definite social group; as a practitioner of a certain vocation; as a follower of definite religious, metaphysical, philosophical, and political ideas; as a partisan in many feuds and controversies. He does not himself create his ideas and standards of value; he borrows them from other people. His ideology is what his environment enjoins upon him. Only very few men have the gift of thinking new and original ideas and of changing the traditional body of creeds and doctrines.
>
> (p. 46)

Similarly, Maslow's theory of human needs, though applicable on a great scale, can also contribute to the entrepreneurial search for profits. Although it is highly possible that the value system, or pyramid, can look totally different, and then the choices will follow accordingly. What conclusions can be drawn from the fact that a man acts within a geographical location and that, in general, people fulfil their needs according to Maslow's theory? Would it be enough for entrepreneurs to create a system of discovering values (and then change it into a product or service) regardless of conditions? One more element should also be considered—state intervention.

Private Value versus Law (State Intervention)

State intervention invariably compels the members of society to obey rules for social conduct by introducing laws and regulations. Additionally, apart from legal duties, citizens are also expected to observe ethical rules. The emergence of the market based on the quick exchange of knowledge necessarily brings ethical challenges for its participants. The state also brings some limitations on competition by issuing licences, permissions, and limitations. On a national level, a value seems to be going towards ethics—to the point that some activities are described as criminal or illegal. However, on a personal level, value has always had an economic meaning; they always strive at satisfying a consumer's need or desire, to ease discomfort.

Practical Implications

Role of an Entrepreneur

As Taylor clearly describes the entrepreneurial mission (Taylor, 1980): 'The whole task of having to produce to suit the wants of other persons in the face of an uncertain future is the essence of entrepreneurship', so Mises points to the source of entrepreneurial profits (Mises, 1998): 'The only source from which an entrepreneur's profits stem is his ability to anticipate better than other people the future demand of the consumers'.

Though he never explained what actions should be taken to anticipate future demands, Mises seems to complicate that matter even more: 'The ultimate source from which entrepreneurial profit and loss are derived is the uncertainty of the future constellation of demand and supply' (Mises, 1998). Not only is it uncertain what customers' demands will be, it is also uncertain in what conditions, or market environment, those demands will be manifested.

What is common in the view of these two praxiological classicists is the notion of focusing attention on the 'wants of other persons'. It can be further concluded that in order to secure a satisfactory exchange of goods in the market, prior to embarking on a desired venture, an entrepreneur should carefully examine both the environment of the business and the prevailing values of the targeted community. Regardless of how accurate those conclusions can be, they bring nothing new to the classical economy approach. What is even more, those conclusions can be derived by any entrepreneur regardless of his/her educational background. How then is the praxiological approach different?

It seems that the unique solution to the anticipated demands problem, proposed by praxiology, lies in the constant observation of human action rather than in relying on mathematical calculations to predict human action. It shifts the focus from graphs and calculations towards the choices that are actually and constantly made. Praxiology defies the notion of accurate calculation of anticipated demands, especially made on the assumption of price reduction, and instead proposes drawing conclusions from the actions performed by market actors. By doing so, it prepares an entrepreneur for sudden changes and unexpected alterations in the market. The practical application of such an approach would be the careful planning of the company's future events and targets. Those should be focused on observing value shift (actual demand) in the society. Consequently, market observations and deductive thinking seem to be more efficient tools in achieving an entrepreneurial goal of fulfilling arising demands. The only drawback derived from that approach might be discomfort and uneasiness for an entrepreneur as it sweeps away well devised graphs with anticipated future events. More uncertainty is offered instead.

The free market economy is a volatile and dynamic process with a myriad of interdependencies and constant change. The players in such a market swiftly react to each other's activities. If not a government, who or what is responsible for stimulating actions? Taylor answers (Taylor, 1980):

> The driving forces in the market process are the producer-entrepreneurs who see profit opportunities arising from potential improvements in market activities. The process of the market is ongoing because of the relentless search for profit and the resultant alterations in the market effected by competitive producer-entrepreneurs.
>
> (p. 21)

The author points towards two driving forces of the market, namely profit opportunities and competition. The former represents defining value, the latter interdependencies. Even if the environment changes these two forces remain intact; should the forces be altered that would mean a change of an economic doctrine.

Implications

The following implications have been formulated from the position of a praxiologist; conclusions are deducted from observations of customers' and entrepreneurs' actions in the market.

Implication I: Division of Labour Prompts the Creation of New Sets of Values; the Bigger the Economy the Greater Variety of Values Available

As the complexity of the market grows, so does the perception of values. Common and cheap access to knowledge allows the entrepreneur to track the value and at the same time create it. But certainty of what can be successful diminishes with the number of gigabytes of knowledge produced daily, as the value for a customer changes quickly (Mises, 1998):

> Things are valued exclusively from the point of view of the services they can render for the satisfaction of future wants. The actual sacrifices made and the time absorbed in their production are beside the point. These things belong to the dead past.
>
> (p. 491)

Consequently, the bigger the number for potential opportunities the greater the opportunity for defining and redefining values for present and potential customers. However, despite the fact that Adam Smith's theory of the division of labour has proven true in various economic systems, there is a tendency to overvalue the technological impact of machines, computing machines, and robots on human action. The threat, widely spread by traditional economy followers, predicts the elimination of jobs or job stealing in the nearest future. Nothing could be farther from the truth; hence, replacing human labour with machines caused more jobs than losses. Consequently, the introduction of new technologies inevitably, in accordance with the law of adaptability, will cause the creation of new jobs and new value exchange. Thus it would be advisable for an entrepreneur to consciously create an attitude of constant observation of value perception in the market. A fast economy causes fast changes of trends. Additionally, it might very well happen that a customer can change his/her mind over time (Mises, 1998): *Different individuals value the same things in a different way, and valuations change with the same individuals with changing conditions.*

The Internet represents reality no matter how glossy the web design is. It is true that it cuts the costs of transactions and helps to integrate dispersed knowledge, but the content needs to be created by an entrepreneur; and there is no certainty whether customers will buy goods or services, because that depends on their free will, which causes even more uncertainty. There seems to be a limit to Internet potential in the market. It stores information about the past but is unable to predict future events. That might be good news for a potential entrepreneur because his equal position in access to knowledge is secured.

Implication 2: Method of Trial and Error Imparts True Knowledge about Customers' Choices and Actually That Is the Only Method of Acquiring It

Whether the value of a product or service satisfies the needs of consumers and brings profit, this can be verified by bringing the product or service in the market. Graphic representations of expected customers' behaviour consist of no more than assumptions and speculations performed in an abstract reality. Discovery of a real value applies to the general rule of adaptability.

Once again, praxiology provides a sound explanation of loss and gain, predicting future results and technological impact with the words of Taylor (Taylor, 1980):

> There is no precision in economic calculation because of the uncertain future that pervades all activities in the market economy. An individual decision maker is unable to know precisely the future preferences of consumers, the future changes in technology, the future plans and actions of other producers, and the infinite number of other external events that will occur in the future. The gathering of empirical data as is done in establishing actuarial tables is not sufficient for the purposes of entrepreneurial activities in the market economy.
>
> (p. 30)

The loss in business is a valuable lesson; it teaches what product or service is not corresponding with the value system of the market. The wider the range of products and services available from an entrepreneur the better it would be for both: the potential customer, who has a freedom of choice, and the producer/provider, who will increase his/her chances of meeting the customer's demands. The value that the company deals with, be it discovering, adding, or creating, should be written in the company's mission statement. By focusing on the customers' values a greater manoeuvre margin is created for the company to adjust to changing demands, and this serves as a signpost for which actions should be taken to achieve its goal. That attitude was explained by Mises (1998):

> Neither the entrepreneurs nor the farmers nor the capitalists determine what has to be produced. The consumers do that. If a businessman does not strictly obey the orders of the public as they are conveyed to him by the structure of market prices, he suffers losses, he goes bankrupt, and is thus removed from his eminent position at the helm. Other men who did better in satisfying the demand of the consumers replace him.
>
> (p. 270)

Though there will not be absolute certainty regarding the choices of future customers, the storage of experience allows a focus on current trends. Companies that look for their unique system of adding/discovering value in goods and services adapt more quickly to a changing economy. It is a highly complex task, but, once discovered, it retains a company on the surface of competition despite a changing environment.

Implication 3: Fast Acquisition of New Knowledge and Switching Jobs as Needed Is Modern Economy Reality

Traditional ways of job search, job performance, and job stability are slowly becoming redundant. The current system is undergoing a global change in organizing economical life. It can be then assumed that market actors will also need to adjust to those changes and acquire adaptability skills: the ability to create in response to a constantly changing environment. Entrepreneurs will be the first who would need to learn how to adapt quickly to changing trends: *Entrepreneur means acting man in regard to the changes occurring in the data of the market* (Mises, 1998).

Implication 4: True Competition of a Free Market Is Constantly Restricted by Governments

The emergence of new businesses based on a sharing economy, such as Uber or AirBnB, is ferociously attacked by lobbies supported by governments. Free and unrestricted competition is free from any form of restrictions. At least in theory. Practically, lobbying groups put a lot of pressure on governmental institutions to block the entrance of potential entrepreneurs. Mises described the reality of his times but little has changed since (Mises, 1998):

> The entrepreneur is also jeopardized by political dangers. Government policies, revolutions, and wars can damage or annihilate his enterprise. Such events do not affect him alone; they affect the market economy as such and all individuals, although not all of them to the same extent. For the individual entrepreneur they are data which he cannot alter. If he is efficient, he will anticipate them in time. But it is not always possible for him to adjust his operations in such a way as to avoid damage.
>
> (p. 290)

Not only governments, which impose nothing but restrictions and unwanted interventions, bring about conditions unfavourable for profit maximization. Rothbard brings to the discussion a Swiss referendum in which society decided to endorse a subsidy for farmers to prevent the country from total industrialization at the expense of their own incomes. The similar voluntary deprivation of income took place in the Brexit referendum in 2016, where the majority of the society decided to cut themselves off from access to a single market. Though politically and psychologically such a decision can be understood and analysed in any possible way, from a praxiological point of view we can only state what choice has been made.

Implication 5: The Ultimate Risk Taking and Market Evaluation Lies on the Part of the Entrepreneur, No Matter How Many Technicians, Managers, and Accountants He/She Hires

It is his sole responsibility to adjust to changes. There is a controversy as to what extent a man can learn to be a successful entrepreneur by taking part in courses or studies. Business schools and university faculties worldwide offer extensive courses on entrepreneurship and the economy. If it was not believed that they would bring desired results, they would not have been offered. According to Mises, all these actions are to no avail (Mises, 1998):

> In order to succeed in business a man does not need a degree from a school of business administration. These schools train the subalterns for routine jobs. They certainly do not train entrepreneurs. An entrepreneur cannot be trained. A man becomes an entrepreneur in seizing an opportunity and filling the gap. No special education is required for such a display of keen judgment, foresight, and energy. The most successful businessmen were often uneducated when measured by the scholastic standards of the teaching profession. But they were to their social function of adjusting production to the most urgent demand. Because of these merits the consumers chose them for business Leadership.
>
> (p. 311)

Nonetheless, a praxiological rule can be applied here, namely: Take the action and see the results. There is no other way of proving who is right or wrong.

Conclusion

It was the author's intention to draw the reader's attention to problems of value management from the perspective of start-up entrepreneurs in the emerging digitalized economy in the light of adaptability and common access to an enormous amount of knowledge. Instead of providing solutions to the problems associated with value management, implications for consideration were presented. The areas for further development would include the following:

- Defining and redefining values for customers and entrepreneurs, commonly named as 'profit searching activity', should have a systemic solution.
- Safeguarding stability; a fast-changing market provides fast transactions and at the same time fast change of partnerships.
- New knowledge and skills will need to be acquired quickly and often. Since the problem of dispersed and unclassified knowledge has been significantly solved by computing machines, solution opportunities for creating new knowledge rose; consequently, the chances for creating new values (wants and needs of customers) also rose. Does the rapid increase in unclassified values frustrate entrepreneurs or make their lives easier?
- Trading worldwide means selling goods or services that represent value regardless of geographical location. Is it an advantage or burden for small entrepreneurs?
- The market has always been considered as a process, not a place. What will be the advantages of a virtual market? To what extent does it help in creating a competitive advantage and to what extent does it hinder the development of start-ups?

Notes

1 www.statisticbrain.com/startup-failure-by-industry/.
2 Creating value from an idea is a course offered by the University of Oxford.

References

Eabrasu, M., 2011, 'A Praxiological Assessment of Subjective Value'. *The Quarterly Journal of Austrian Economics* 14, No. 2 (Summer 2011): 216–241.

Hayek, F., 1945, 'The Use of Knowledge in Society', *American Economic Review*, XXXV, No. 4 (September 1945): pp. 519–30.

Mises von, L., 1998, *Human Action: A Treatise on Economics. The Scholar's Edition.* Auburn AL: Ludwig von Mises Institute.

Rothbard, M., 1980, *Praxiology as the Method of Economics, Vol. 2: Phenomenology and the Social Sciences* (June 1973): pp. 311–39. Reprinted as 'Praxiology as the Method of the Social Sciences', in *Individualism and the Philosophy of the Social Sciences.* Washington, D.C.: Cato Institute, 1980.

Rothbard, M., 1997, 'Praxiology: Value Judgments, and Public Policy By Murray N. Rothbard' *The Foundations of Modern Austrian Economics*, Edwin Dolan, ed. (Kansas City: Sheed and War, 1976), pp. 89–111; The Logic of Action One (Cheltenham, UK: Edward Elgar, 1997), pp. 78–99.

Taylor, T. C., 1990, *An Introduction to Austrian Economics.* Auburn AL: Ludwig von Mises Institute.

Chapter 4

From Behavioural Economics to Economics of Identity

Forging an Economic Praxiology

Jérôme Ballet and Emmanuel Petit

Understanding human action is a vital task in economics. Not only is it about making sense of individuals, but endeavouring at a fundamental level to understand the reactions of individuals to economic policies. From this standpoint, "it is clear that the representative agent deserves a decent burial, as an approach to economic analysis that is not only primitive, but fundamentally erroneous" (Kirman, 1992, p. 119). Behavioural economics has drawn a considerable distance between itself and the simplified homo economicus view of human action. With experimental case studies as its bedrock, it has helped paint a broader picture of human action and hence forms part of a long tradition of praxiology. According to Gunnar Skirbekk's anthology: "Praxiology in our sense is a conceptual analysis and reflective discussion of the way human activities are interwoven with their agents and with the things at which they are directed within our everyday world" (1983, p. 9). Skirbekk adds that in the Nordic tradition, praxiology is based on careful uses of examples invoking detailed descriptions and thought-experiments.

Behavioural economics is not a homogenous approach, emerging from different currents, such as experimental economics, economic psychology, and neuroeconomics (Tomer, 2007). For some authors it remains wedded to mainstream economics, having been exclusively designed to incorporate more realistic assumptions into rational decision models of action, and to describe various anomalies in rational theory (Fudenberg, 2006; List, 2008). Nevertheless, the emergence of behavioural economics suggests that another path seems to have definitively appeared on the horizon. This path carries a huge change potential for economics, but its construction requires the introduction of alternative core concepts. Indeed, although the findings of many experiments in behavioural economics suggest a different conception of an individual than homo economicus, all these findings are merely disconnected elements that should be linked to core concepts. Only then will it be possible to forge a new understanding of human action in economics. Currently, these core concepts do not exist.

We consider identity as a key core concept in improving our understanding of human action in economics. Of course, identity is not a totally new concept in economics. Recent developments have largely underlined the importance of identity for economic behaviour (Akerlof & Kranton, 2010; Davis, 2003). Nevertheless, identity has not been previously linked to findings from behavioural economics. Here we propose to build a link between these findings and the concept of identity. First, we will explore various findings in moral psychology that relate to pro-social behaviours. We will especially focus on the contribution of Blasi's model (1983). Second, we will describe the main findings from behavioural economics, concentrating on pro-social behaviours. Third, as a result of these findings, we will defend the idea that identity is a key core concept for our understanding of human action in economics. However, identity must be considered at a much deeper level than economic analysis currently provides. Blasi's model from moral psychology represents a way forward in this area.

Pro-social Behaviours and Identity in Moral Psychology

In moral psychology, after Kohlberg (1969) introduced his developmental theory of morality, cognitive approaches, such as social domain theory (Turiel, 2002), began to occupy centre stage. Cognitive theories consider that with the development of moral reasoning, the individual develops moral judgments and is then increasingly compelled to behave according to these moral judgments. Emotional theories have also entered the debate (Eisenberg, 1986; Hoffman, 2000). These underline the role emotions play in an individual's capacity to act morally, hence contrasting with cognitive theories that highlight the individual's understanding of abstract moral principles. Both approaches now acknowledge the links between cognition and emotion, but since the publication of Damasio's book in 1994, the debate hinges on the primary source of motivation: Is it cognition or emotion (Gibbs, 2003)?

Neither of these approaches is sufficient in helping us understand pro-social behaviours. As Blasi (1980) and Eisenberg and Miller (1987) outlined, cognitive-emotional motives do not guarantee moral behaviours. In each situation, an individual may experience some multiple motivational sources that push her/him towards different kinds of action. Moderators seem to interfere with cognitive-emotional motives and the identity moderator constitutes a major step. Identity influences an individual's motivation to act (Blasi, 1983; Eisenberg, 1986; Colby & Damon, 1992; Gibbs, 2003; Monroe, 2001; Nisan, 2004; among others). In all the approaches linking identity to pro-social behaviours, morality is considered motivational only if it is essential for one's sense of self, that is, if identity is related to one's sense of obligation or responsibility toward one's moral concern. Of all the models that link identity and morality, Blasi's model (Blasi, 1984, 1988, 1993, 1995) is undoubtedly the most thorough and the most persuasive. It is also unavoidable (Hardy & Carlo, 2005).

Blasi's model is based on three key features (Hardy & Carlo, 2005). First, an action is considered moral to the extent it is judged necessary for the individual. A moral action is then carried out or not carried out only if the individual feels responsible for that action. Moral judgment requires a judgment of responsibility. Moral judgment is a necessary but not insufficient condition. An individual does not only need to consider whether or not an action is right or wrong, but whether or not s/he feels a responsibility to be consistent in terms of that action. Second, the individual develops a moral identity. For each individual, being moral is more or less a central feature of her/his sense of self. And third, the individual is inclined to behave consistently with her/his sense of self. Self-consistency is a main feature of human development. Based on these three key assumptions, the individual acts in a pro-social manner because s/he establishes a moral judgment about an action to be taken, s/he feels responsible for that action, and the action is important if it is to remain consistent with her/his moral identity.

Of course, there are potentially as many variations in the assessment of the action-context as there are individuals. Blasi (1993, 2004) sees the variations between individuals as being explained by the structure of their identities. He distinguishes the contents of one's sense of self and the maturity of one's identity, which is subjectively rooted in one's personal experience. When identity matures, the sense of self becomes more internal and personal: it is less shaped by relationships and other external factors. To summarize, the structure of one's identity lies at the junction between moral motivation, either cognitive or emotional, and action. And, as the structure of identity is dependent on subjective experience, the link between motivation and action is controlled by the individual's identity. However, Blasi's model does not only highlight the central role of identity as a moderator. Through the third assumption, it also stipulates self-consistency. The individual behaves in accordance with his/her identity. Identity is then not only a moderator between motivation and action; it is the node that connects motivation and action.

One of the main findings from Blasi's model is that differences in individual behaviours must be understood not through differences in moral capacities (such as moral reasoning and moral emotion) but through differences in moral desires (Blasi, 2004). For this reason, Nucci (2004) describes Blasi's model as an 'ethical egoism' model of morality. Nevertheless, we disagree with Nucci because it is not the desire to behave consistently in terms of one's sense of self that constitutes moral motivation. On the contrary, it is because an individual has a moral motivation that s/he acts according to her/his identity. The self-consistency assumption does not operate at the motivational level. It operates at an intermediate level between motivation and action. The desire to be self-consistent does not preclude moral motivation. Instead, it stipulates that moral motivation is transformed into moral action according to the maturity of the individual's identity. In this model, the key to our understanding is how a mature identity develops.

Of course, Blasi's model is not free from criticism. Hardy and Carlo (2005) emphasize five elements for discussion. First, some moral behaviours are automatic and not deliberate. How should this kind of moral behaviour be integrated within the self-consistency assumption? Second, identity maturity is generally constructed before adulthood. So, how can moral actions be related to identity before this period? Third, the process of identity development is not discussed in Blasi's model, whereas it is an important issue in understanding why some individuals make a strong connection between their identity and moral concerns and why others do not. Fourth, emotion is an important factor in identity development, so emotions may reside at the motivational level as well as at the identity level. Considerably more research should be conducted in this area.

If we move beyond these criticisms, it is clear that the importance of Blasi's model is the inclusion of individual identity in the analysis of pro-social and moral behaviours. Since the advent of Blasi's model, understanding the relationship between moral motivation and moral action has undoubtedly required us to take individual identity into account. Although a much larger body of empirical research on moral identity is needed (Hardy & Carlo, 2005) to confirm Blasi's thinking, several empirical studies already support the idea that the more individuals see moral motivations and values as important for their sense of self, the more they are likely to act morally (Aquino & Reed, 2002; Pratt, Hunsberger, Pancer, & Alisat, 2003; among others).

Pro-social Behaviours in Behavioural Economics

Usually, economists assume that people are rational *and* selfish. Rational individuals maximize their own utility or satisfaction without paying attention to the utility of others. However, Gintis (2000) reminds us that "in neither the everyday nor the narrower economic sense does rationality imply *self-interest*. It is just as 'rational' for me to prefer to have to enjoy a fine meal as for me to enjoy the meal myself". Behavioural economists probably think that the theory of choice decision is wrong, but rather than abandon the theory altogether, they want to revise it. Consequently, they propose new models of human action which acknowledge that individuals have a richer set of preferences than is traditionally considered. They recognize, specifically, that people might be able to exhibit social or 'other-regarding' preferences in an economic context (Camerer, 2003; Camerer, Loewenstein & Rabin, 2004).

Numerous economic experimental studies have shown that people can be cooperative, confident, reciprocatory, fair, and even altruistic when they play games in a laboratory context or in the field. For instance, Ketelaar and Au (2003) show that people holding a natural tendency to act selfishly are more cooperative when they experience guilt. Bosman, Sutter and van Winden (2005) point out that anger, irritation and contempt trigger the loss of income in a negotiation game, restoring a sense of fairness. In a recent meta-analysis, Johnson and Mislin (2011) highlight the robustness of experimental evidence about trust and reciprocity; they also reveal that relatively minor variations in protocol can produce substantial shifts in measured trust behaviour.

Behavioural economists use traditional experimental games, such as the Prisoner's Dilemma and the Public Goods Game, and new specific experimental frameworks such as the Ultimatum Game (Güth, Schmittberger, & Schwarze, 1982), the Dictator Game (Forsythe, Horowitz, Savin & Sefton, 1994), the Investment Game (Berg, Dickhaut, & McCabe, 1995), and so on. Initially, when experimentalists found that some experimental findings were not consistent with the predictions of the standard economic model, they discussed the presence of behavioural 'anomalies' (Camerer & Thaler, 1995) and suggested that participants might be confused and make errors. With the accumulation of experimental evidence, economists have gradually abandoned the idea that the pursuit of self-interest is the only motivation for individual decision-making. They have therefore attempted to understand how and why pro-social types of behaviour emerge in an experimental setting. In particular, they have tried to understand how social norms or 'social preferences' are constructed by (1) stressing the important role of emotions and affect, (2) revealing the crucial impact of the context in which decisions are made, and finally (3) highlighting specific determinant aspects of personality.

One simple way to illustrate the huge contribution of this rich and abundant literature is to focus on a specific pro-social behaviour such as altruism. In economics, the Dictator Game (DG) is considered as providing a widely used and simple minimalist environment for investigating altruism (Forsythe *et al.*, 1994).[1] According to the game theory approach, the DG offers a very simple theoretical solution: a rational dictator who cares only about maximizing selfish payoffs should give nothing to the receiver. However, a lot of experimental evidence shows that dictators usually give an average amount of between 20% and 30% of the endowment to the receiver (Camerer, 2003). Often, a majority of dictators give a positive amount to recipients. Because strategy is not an issue in the DG, economists usually conclude that giving is the consequence of pro-social types of behaviour, which include pure altruistic preferences, the 'warm glow' of decision making (Andreoni, 1990), or a concern for the equality of the resulting allocation (Fehr & Schmidt, 1999; Bolton & Ockenfels). Bolton and Ockenfels (2000) assume that individuals have a symmetrical dislike for inequality. Fehr and Schmidt (1999) introduce the notion of self-centred inequality aversion, in which the agent dislikes all inequality but cares more about this when at a relative payoff disadvantage.

However, recent experimental studies have revealed the importance of affect, context and personality, making the picture more complex.

For instance, it has been argued that giving in the DG might arise from a desire by participants to appear to be acting in a socially appropriate way because their individual behaviour is being observed by others (Koch & Normann, 2008). As the equal sharing norm is extensive, fairness might be driven by a desire for social esteem in relation to this norm. It is thus possible that many dictators are motivated to give what they think receivers expect them to give. In particular, Haley and Fessler (2005), and Rigdon, Ishii, Watabe, and Kitayama (2009) demonstrate the power of expectations by means of a small trick: the presence of a stylized eyespot on the screen or three dots in a 'watching-eyes' configuration (signifying presumably the idea that 'you are being watched') is sufficient to significantly increase the level of donations. These findings imply that donations in the standard DG do not necessarily reflect a real taste for fairness or altruism, but rather a real concern for appearance. Several other studies sustain the idea that feelings of shame are capable of promoting altruistic behaviour in the DG. Brañas-Garza (2007) provides an extra piece of information to the dictator ('Note that the recipient relies on you."), reminding participants that their position in the game is advantageous but unfair. The purpose of the sentence is to call the participant's attention to a particular moral rule, thereby creating a shameful context which successfully and intensively motivates altruistic behaviour. In their experiment, Dana, Cain, and Dawes (2006) also show that dictators are more selfish in a situation where the information is withheld from the receiver, who no longer has any information about how her/his payoff is determined, than in a situation where the receiver obtains this information. Neilson (2009) formally demonstrates that a context-dependent model, in which any utility function depends not only on the final allocation but also on the characteristics of the problem choice faced, usefully indicates reluctance i.e. the distributors of the money would prefer to avoid the opportunity to give, and shame, i.e. the distributors of the money would prefer to hide the fact that a choice has been made.

To sum up, as highlighted by Guala and Mittone (2011), these findings suggest that the Dictator Game is a useful experimental design to identify the way moral or social norms shape individuals' altruistic behaviour. They show in particular that individuals have a plurality of motivations (selfishness, altruism, equity, reciprocity) which arise in relation to the situations where decision-making takes place, and depend on individuals' personalities.

Preferences, Identity, and Human Action in Economics

The findings from moral psychology, similar to those from behavioural economics, suggest that homo economicus is a morally immature individual who is probably lacking in an identity. In fact, homo economicus is the archetype of the impartial, independent, clear-sighted, emotionless 'hero' that the contemporary psychologists refer to ironically when evoking the Vulcan, Mr. Spock, from the popular sixties television series 'Star Trek' (Charland, 1998). Davis (2003) offers a sound critique of the concept of the individual in mainstream economics: Mainstream economics has rejected a conception of the individual based on her/his private psychology because private psychology is by nature inaccessible to the observer. And as clearly pointed out by Marshall (1890), motives are always an inner dimension of decision-making that economists cannot observe, whereas behaviours are observable. In the same vein,

Hick (1956, p. 6) confirms that economic theory "makes no claim, no pretence, to be able to see inside their (individuals') heads". With the revealed preference axiom (Samuelson, 1938), mainstream economics has developed a tautological theory in which behaviours are explained by behaviours (Sen, 1973). This is all the more problematic as very different motives could lead to the same kind of behaviour (Ballet & Barillot, 2006). In fact, for mainstream economics, the very issue of motives is rejected. More recent attempts to bring psychology back into economic theory, notably via game theory, have concentrated on rationality rather than human psychology (Davis, 2003). The large amount of effort invested in taking moral motives into account in economics is a kind of cost-benefit analysis neutralization of moral motivations, as can be seen in Becker's theory of culpability (1996) (see Ballet & Barillot, 2006). In such a theoretical context, it seems difficult to enhance the conception of the individual in economics.

Recently, identity has been incorporated into economics. This new insight remains mostly based on external factors that shape identity. Akerlof and Kranton's (2010) work is a good example of this kind of development in economics. Unlike Blasi's model from psychology that emphasizes internal factors e.g. maturity, economics treats identity as a constraint on choices. Individuals have only an alternative choice between conformity to social roles (what others expect in terms of individual behaviour), and nonconformity (what costs individuals have to take into account). This reasoning is in perfect harmony with the homo economicus concept. Identity is not an entrenched personal feature of the individual: it is only a cost-benefit choice. Such reasoning has no advantage over the heterodox approach of the embedded individual (Davis, 2003). Paradoxically, the socially embedded individual in heterodox economics is more fruitful for our understanding of the individual identity because there is less of a focus on the individual than in mainstream economics. However, because the focus is on the embedding context, heterodox economics sets aside individual choice. More specifically, it reduces the choice to an alternative of accepting or rejecting the role and identity characteristics expected by others (Luchini & Teschl, 2005).

One of the main features of Blasi's model must be taken into account if economics is to construct a more convincing individual identity model: the desire to be self-consistent.

Blasi (2004) underlines that individual differences in moral desires explain differences in moral behaviours. Moral desires in his model are linked to the desire to be self-consistent i.e. to be consistent with one's sense of self. In economics, the distinction between first order and second order preferences refers to the same issue. Jeffrey (1974) highlights this when he states that an individual may prefer to smoke rather than not to smoke, but s/he may also prefer to prefer not to smoke rather than preferring to smoke. S/he has second order preferences that contradict the first order preferences, for instance, because s/he knows smoking is bad for her/his health. After this first order/second order distinction was put forward, a large number of attempts have been made in economics to integrate second order preferences (see Arnsperger, 1998; Bolle, 1983; George, 1998; Hirschman, 1985; Nehring, 2006; Sen, 1977; Stanovich, 2008; among others). Sen (1977) was undoubtedly the first in economics to endeavour to tackle the issue of multiple motivations with preferences over preferences, or meta-ranking. The technique of preferences over preferences (the ranking of ranking) is a way of integrating different types of individual motivations into the analysis. Each motivation carries with it a ranking of feasible actions. An action, which is ultimately chosen by the agent, depends first of all on the rankings made on the basis of each of her/his preferences, but also on the actual ranking of motivations. This may illustrate the individual's moral behaviour. With Sen's proposal we can integrate moral motivation, a primary element in Blasi's model, but we have to set aside the link to the desire for self-consistency.

Nozick (1993) points out the potential conflict that can result between first order and second order preferences. For example, when an individual prefers to smoke but prefers to prefer not to smoke, it is because the individual lacks rational integration in her/his preferences structure. The mismatch between first order and second order preferences may be attributed to fast and slow thinking (system 1 and system 2) (Kahneman, 2011). However, Velleman (1992) suggests that a motive for rational integration itself solves the issue. This motive is the motive to behave 'in your name', as it adds a motivational force to other motives. For Velleman (1992), this motive corresponds to the function of agency. Velleman's point of view is similar to Blasi's when Blasi (2004) states that identity maturity reflects an increasing sense of agency, leading individuals to appropriate certain aspects of themselves and to reject others. The desire to be self-consistent is increasingly developed alongside identity maturity, forging the individual agency.

Understanding human action in economics supposes that we seriously tackle the issue of identity, not only through conformity to social roles, but at the other end of the spectrum, through agency, which is regarded as maturity in one's sense of self.

Conclusion

Human action is vaguely linked to identity in economics. Certainly, economics has now taken moral motives on board, in particular as part of the debate on second order preferences. However, much work is needed to extend the debate and solve the issue of rational integration. Moral psychology, and notably Blasi's model, could aid progress in economic analysis. To be self-consistent is a motive for action that adds motivational force to other kinds of motives. Identity should not be conceived merely as conformity to a social role; it should be conceived as the essential feature of individuals, one that leads to human action.

Note

1 In this game, one participant, who is called the "dictator", is given an amount of real money (for instance, ten dollars) that he has to distribute however he likes to an anonymous participant who is called the "receiver" or the "recipient". The receiver, who hence knows the dictator's instructions, must accept whatever distribution the dictator makes, even if the dictator gives her/him nothing.

References

Akerlof, G. A. & Kranton, R. E., 2010, *Identity Economics: How Identities Shape Our Work, Wages, and Well-Being.* Princeton, Princeton University Press.

Andreoni, J., 1990, Impure Altruism and Donations to Public Goods: A Theory of Warm-Glow Giving. *The Economic Journal*, 100(401): 464–477.

Arnsperger, C., 1998, Engagement Moral et Optimisation Individuelle, in F. R. Mahieu & H. Rapoport (Eds.), *Altruisme, Analyses Économiques*, pp. 191–214, Paris, Economica.

Aquino, K. & Reed, A., 2002, The Self-importance of Moral Identity. *Journal of Personality and Social Psychology*, 83: 1423–1440.

Ballet, J. & Barillot, S., 2006, Methodological Aspects of Altruism in Economics, in J. Ballet & D. Bazin (Eds.), *Positive Ethics in Economics*, pp. 41–62, New Brunswick and London, Transaction Publishers.

Becker, G. S., 1996, *Accounting for Tastes*. Cambridge, MA, Harvard University Press.

Berg, J., Dickhaut, J., & McCabe, K. (1995). Trust, reciprocity, and social history. *Games and economic behavior*, 10(1): 122-142.

Blasi, A., 1980, Bridging Moral Cognition and Moral Action: A Critical Review of the Literature. *Psychological Bulletin*, 88: 104–124.

Blasi, A., 1983, Moral Cognition and Moral Action: A Theoretical Perspective. *Development Review*, 3: 178–210.

Blasi, A., 1984, Moral Identity: Its Role in Moral Functioning, in W. M. Kurtines & J. L. Gewirtz (Eds.), *Morality, Moral Behavior, and Moral Development*, pp. 129–139. New York, Wiley.

Blasi, A., 1988, Identity and the Development of the Self, in D. K. Lapsley & F. C. Power (Eds.), *Self, Ego, and Identity: Integrative Approaches*, pp. 226–242. New York, Springer.

Blasi, A., 1993, The Development of Identity: Some Implications for Moral Functioning, in G. G. Noam & T. E. Wren (Eds.), *The Moral Self*, pp. 99–122. Cambridge, MA, MIT Press.

Blasi, A., 1995, Moral Understanding and Moral Personality: The Process of Moral Integration, in W. M. Kurtiness & J. L. Gewirtz (Eds.), *Moral Development: An Introduction*, pp. 229–253. Needham Heights, MA, Allyn & Bacon.

Blasi, A., 2004, Neither Personality nor Cognition: An Alternative Approach to the Nature of the Self, in C. Lightfoot, C. Lalonde, & M. Chandler (Eds.), *Changing Conceptions of Psychological Life*, pp. 3–25. Mahwah, NJ, Erlbaum.

Bolle, F., 1983, On Sen's Second-order Preferences, Morals, and Decision Theory. *Erkenntnis*, 20(2): 195–205.

Bolton, G. E. & Ockenfels, A., 2000, ERC: A Theory of Equity, Reciprocity, and Competition. *American Economic Review*, 90(1): 166–193.

Bosman, R., Sutter, M., & van Winden, F. (2005). The impact of real effort and emotions in the power-to-take game. *Journal of Economic Psychology*, 26(3): 407–429.
Brañas-Garza, P., 2007, Promoting Helping Behavior with Framing in Dictator Games. *Journal of Economic Psychology*, 28(4): 477–486.
Camerer, C., 2003, *Behavioral Game Theory. Experiments on Strategic Interaction*. Princeton, Princeton University Press.
Camerer C., Loewenstein G. & Rabin M., 2004, *Advances in Behavioral Economics*. Princeton, Princeton University Press.
Camerer, C. & Thaler, R. H., 1995, Anomalies: Ultimatums, Dictators and Manners. *The Journal of Economic Perspectives*, 9(2): 209–219.
Charland, L. C., 1998, Is Mr. Spock Mentally Competent? Competence to Consent and Emotion. *Philosophy, Psychiatry & Psychology*, 5(1): 67–81.
Colby, A. & Damon, W., 1992, *Some Do Care: Contemporary Lives of Moral Commitment*. New York, Free Press.
Damasio, A., 1994, *Descartes' Error: Emotion, Reason, and the Human Brain*. New York, Putnam.
Dana, J., Cain, D. M., & Dawes, R. M., 2006, What You Don't Know Won't Hurt Me: Costly (but quiet) Exit in Dictator Games. *Organizational Behavior and Human Decision Processes*, 100(2), 193–201.
Davis, J. B., 2003, *The Theory of the Individual in Economics: Identity and Value*. London, Routledge.
Eisenberg, N., 1986, *Altruistic Emotion, Cognition, and Behavior*. Hillsdale, NJ, Erlbaum.
Eisenberg, N. & Miller, P. A., 1987, The Relation of Empathy to Prosocial and Related Behaviors. *Psychological Bulletin*, 101: 91–119.
Fehr, E. & Schmidt, K. M., 1999, A Theory of Fairness, Competition, and Cooperation. *Quarterly Journal of Economics*, 817–868.
Forsythe, R., Horowitz, J. L., Savin, N. E. & Sefton, M., 1994, Fairness in Simple Bargaining Experiments. *Games and Economic Behavior*, 6(3): 347–369.
Fudenberg, D., 2006, Advances Beyond Advances in Behavioral Economics. *Journal of Economic Literature*, 44: 694–711.
George, D., 1998, Coping Rationally with Unpreferred Preferences. *Eastern Economic Journal*, 24(2): 181–194.
Gibbs, J. C., 2003, *Moral Development and Reality: Beyond the Theories of Kohlberg and Hoffman*. Thousand Oaks, CA, Sage Publications.
Gintis, H., 2000, Strong Reciprocity and Human Sociality. *Journal of Theoretical Biology*, 206: 169–179.
Guala, F. & Mittone, L., 2010, Paradigmatic Experiments: The Dictator Game. *The Journal of Socio-Economics*, 39(5): 578–584.
Güth, W., Schmittberger, R. & Schwarze, B., 1982, An Experimental Analysis of Ultimatum Bargaining. *Journal of Economic Behavior & Organization*, 3(4): 367–388.
Haley, K. J. & Fessler, D. M., 2005, Nobody's Watching? Subtle Cues Affect Generosity in an Anonymous Economic Game. *Evolution and Human Behavior*, 26(3): 245–256.
Hardy, S. A. & Carlo, G., 2005, Identity as a Source of Moral Motivation. *Human Development*, 48: 232–256.
Hicks, J. R., 1956, *A Revision of Demand Theory*. Oxford, Oxford University Press.
Hirschman, A. O., 1985, Against Parsimony: Three Easy Ways of Complicating Some Categories of Economic Discourse. *Economics and Philosophy*, 1(01): 7–21.
Hoffman, M. L., 2000, *Empathy and Moral Development: Implications for Caring and Justice*. New York, Cambridge University Press.

Jeffrey, R. C., 1974, Preference among Preferences. *The Journal of Philosophy*, 71(13): 377–391.
Johnson, N. D. & Mislin, A. A., 2011, Trust Games: A Meta-Analysis. *Journal of Economic Psychology*, 32(5): 865–889.
Kahneman, D., 2011, *Thinking, Fast and Slow*. New York, Allen Lane.
Ketelaar, T., & Tung Au, W. (2003). The effects of feelings of guilt on the behaviour of uncooperative individuals in repeated social bargaining games: An affect-as-information interpretation of the role of emotion in social interaction. *Cognition & Emotion*, 17(3): 429-453.
Kirman, A., 1922, Whom or What Does the Representative Individual Represent? *Journal of Economic Perspectives*, 6(2): 117–136.
Koch, A. K. & Normann, H. T., 2008, Giving in Dictator Games: Regard for Others or Regard by Others? *Southern Economic Journal*, 75: 223–231.
Kohlberg, L., 1969, Stage and Sequence: The Cognitive Developmental Approach to Socialization, in D. A. Goslin (Ed.), *Handbook of Socialization Theory and Research*, pp. 347–480. Chicago, IL, Rand MacNally.
List, J., 2008, Homo Experimentalis Evolves. *Science*, 321(5886): 207–208.
Luchini, S. & Teschl, M., 2005, Is There Personal Identity in Economics? A Discussion of J. B. Davis 'The Theory of the Individual in Economics: Identity and Values', *Ethics and Economics*, 3(1), https://papyrus.bib.umontreal.ca/xmlui/handle/1866/3328.
Marshall, A., 1890, *Principles of Economics*. New York, MacMillan.
Monroe, K. R., 2001, Morality and Sense of Self: The Importance of Identity and Categorization for Moral Action. *American Journal of Political Science*, 45: 491–507.
Nehring, K., 2006, *Self-Control Through Second-Order Preferences*. Unpublished paper, Department of Economics, University of California.
Neilson, W. S., 2009, A Theory of Kindness, Reluctance, and Shame for Social Preferences. *Games and Economic Behavior*, 66(1): 394–403.
Nisan, M., 2004, Judgment and Choice in Moral Functioning, in D. K. Lapsley & D. Narvaez (Eds.), *Moral Development, Self, and Identity*, pp. 133–160. Mahwah, NJ, Erlbaum.
Nozick, R., 1993, *The Nature of Rationality*. Princeton, NJ, Princeton University Press.
Nucci, L., 2004, Reflections on the Moral Self Construct, in D. K. Lapsley & D. Narvaez (Eds.), *Moral Development, Self, and Identity*, pp. 111–132. Mahwah, NJ, Erlbaum.
Pratt, M. W., Hunsberger, B., Pancer, S. M. & Alisat, S., 2003, A Longitudinal Analysis of Personal Value Socialization: Correlates of Moral Self-ideal in Adolescence. *Social Development*, 12: 563–585.
Rigdon, M., Ishii, K., Watabe, M. & Kitayama, S., 2009, Minimal Social Cues in the Dictator Game. *Journal of Economic Psychology*, 30(3): 358–367.
Samuelson, P. A., 1938, A Note on the Pure Theory of Consumer's Behaviour. *Economica*, 5(17): 61–71.
Sen, A. K., 1973, Behaviour and the Concept of Preference. *Economica*, 40: 241–259.
Sen, A. K., 1977, Rational Fools: A Critique of the Behavioural Foundations of Economic Theory. *Philosophy and Public Affairs*, 6: 317–344.
Skirbekk, G. (ed.), 1983, *Praxiology: An Anthology*, Bergen, Universitetsforlaget.
Stanovich, K. E., 2008, Higher-order Preferences and the Master Rationality Motive. *Thinking & Reasoning*, 14(1): 111–127.
Tomer, J. F., 2007, What Is Behavioral Economics? *Journal of Socio-Economics*, 36(3): 463–479.
Turiel, E., 2002, *The Culture of Morality*. Cambridge, UK, Cambridge University Press.
Velleman, J. D., 1992, What Happens When Somebody Acts? *Mind*, 101: 461–481.

Chapter 5

Aspects of Human Action

David Botham

I have chosen to present my paper in two parts. The first part, "In Search of an Ontology", investigates the importance of relationships in the world of research and identifies a small number of individuals from very different backgrounds who in their different ways have had a major influence on my own thinking. The second part, "Contributions of R. W. Revans", expands a former paper written for *Praxiology: The International Annual of Practical Philosophy and Methodology*, Volume 6, published in 1998.

In Search of an Ontology

I began preparing my thinking for this paper by considering the areas and subjects that have had the greatest impact over the last sixty years of my life. If I were to list them as a broad nomenclature they would be in the following intellectual disciplines.

Material and Behavioural Science and Modern Jazz

Unlike many subject areas that appear separated for the convenience of the layout of the printed page, they have a high level of integration, with each shaping and influencing the other in a kind of cerebral triangulation that I believe powers my dialectical reasoning. Movingly, Gregory Bateson in his introduction to his challenging book, *Mind and Nature: A Necessary Unity* (1980), listed all the individuals who in one way or another had contributed to his literary work. It was a long and impressive list that honoured a very wide variety of contributors. Moreover, it had a humbling effect on those that studied the book later, including myself.

I have similarly reflected on those individuals that I've had the good fortune to work alongside and learn from, including those I've failed to understand from the above mentioned disciplines. I am clear, however, that it would be impossible to write this or any other paper without the influence of such people. Therefore, it is my sincere hope that this contribution will influence and encourage all those who read this 25th edition of the series "Praxiology" to actively engage in the understanding of human action.

An Interpretation of Human Thinking

"... to learn to think, you must have a teacher who can think;... the essence of all our problems is bad thinking, and the only medicine is better thinking" (Engel, 1972). It would appear necessary in the human psyche to ascertain and elaborate on definitions created from different disciplines in order to create order, especially when a new genre is being sought after for the first time. Free thinkers, such as impressive extemporising jazz musicians Kessel (1923–2004), Ellis (1921–2010), and Peterson (1925–2007), seemingly create highly complex thought processes that rapidly flow through their minds. Such effects are staggeringly beautiful but at times, for the less confident, are creatively scary and unnerving. But even more importantly, music as a process, it is argued, is 'self-ontological', especially jazz (Davies 2004, p. 3; Kania, 2008). Authentic performances of musical works are the bases of this judgement.

Kessel and Ellis were two of the greatest jazz guitarists of this era. Although differing in technique they had an impressionable respect for each other's virtuosity; often demonstrated as they accompanied each other. Moreover, they each played alongside the great pianist Oscar Peterson as separate accompanists, easily reaching the self-ontological authenticity demanded.

The second group are by contrast to the first very different. They were not great improvising musicians as such, but great philosophical virtuosos representing different genres.

But, like jazz, they too influenced each other. For example, Revans (1907–2003) was influenced by Macmurray (1891–1976) and Bateson (1904–1980); whereas they all were influenced by Hegel (1770–1831) and Feuerbach (1804–1872). So it is relatively safe to say that they have all indirectly played the 'music' of continuing influence. However, it has been most regrettable that some radical thinkers (musicians) are partially or totally ignored when they are at their finest, resulting in isolated exclusion. It is true that the individuals acknowledged here were in their own ways very successful in establishing new levels of performance and positional thinking, but they were only recognised years later. But, as one notable thinker put it in a private conversation, as he reflected on his long career which bore all the scars of academic segregation and isolation: *"It is only when an idea has been thoroughly ridiculed for at least fifty years will it ever become acceptable."*

Some defenders of this confrontational behaviour argue that it stems from the conviction that most if not all scientists feel duty bound to prove that their contemporaries could be wrong, both in their conclusions and theories, thus justifying academic attack as a necessary and responsible act. One thing has to be said: Not all levels of human attack, especially in the academic and music world, are a negative and overall disadvantage. Some attacks, although initially painful, have undoubtedly produced more mavericks in both the academic world and music world, the above-mentioned being outstanding examples.

Some would argue that Bateson's maverick attitude to conventional research culminated in huge breakthroughs in both 'hard' and 'soft' methods and methodologies. It is claimed that Bateson once asserted that he was not interested in scientific research that relied on billiard balls and sticks to justify its existence. He was more interested in living species such as crabs and orchids and the relationships that existed between them; and even more importantly, the relationship he had himself to such species. I would argue that the relationship between research and the self is not only at the heart of ontological thought but is "praxiological thinking".

Distinguishable Differences between Method and Methodology

As these form the most important part of any research inquiry, this paper includes them as an integral of everything else discussed so far. This is to say that any notion of the described praxiological experience would indeed be valueless without the insightful rigour of a methodologist interpreting human action. Otherwise we would attempting to make sense of data rather than information which in the end would make very little difference to the way we think. For the sake of clarification, there are critical yet often overlooked differences between method and methodology.

The term *method* connotes planned procedures which allow research to be strictly managed in order to gather all data. Lewin's action research model is a sensitive procedural method occasionally used to introduce, monitor, and record human action and reaction. Methodology, on the other hand, is interested in processes. Instead of loyally following the rules governing the procedural method, methodology often critically evaluates method, often resulting in modification and change.

Similarly, some classically trained musicians eagerly gravitate towards reading and playing music within the rules and boundaries previously set by composers and arrangers. From experience there are very few classically trained players who feel comfortable without this procedural notation; as such, their behaviour is close to those operating and loyally following a research method. That said, there are very necessary reasons for both 'reading the music' and loyally following a tried and well tested research method. Stewart (1998, p. vii), for example, puts an obvious but well-considered view, based on his own practical experiences as a working musician and composer:

> Far from stemming the flow… of ideas (following the notes) is more likely to encourage them. As far as spontaneity goes, if you are the sort of person who likes to just grab an instrument and play, or make up songs in your head, being able to notate music won't change that, but will enable you to jot ideas down before you forget them. In my own case, I can barely remember what I played yesterday.

'Jazz Methodology'

This metaphor is drawn largely from the field of modern jazz and will be used throughout this next section. Like modern jazz musicians (Kessel; Ellis; Peterson, for example, to name but a few), methodology seems understandable only to those who have a clear and deep understanding of method and its logical structure. They themselves create the necessary strain, energy, and tension between each other so that varying degrees of theoretical difference are presented as intellectual challenges.

It might be argued that quantitative research of the traditional kind has a natural gravitas towards method rather than methodology, believing that it has a more superior basis upon which to establish a more rigorous argument stemming back to the rules upheld by the crown princes of positivism. By contrast, qualitative approaches tend to draw upon the methodological processes themselves as their principal research instruments accompanied by considerable explanations that argue for selectivity and reasoning as a direct attack on so-called traditional procedural methods.

Jazz methodology is a processual phenomenon, which, like melodic jazz, enjoys and celebrates its own methods of spontaneous composition as it draws upon many complex influences, all of which become at some stage part of the performers' individual repertoire. Like well-presented research, jazz of this genre has a deep fundamental grounding, and jazz methodology, despite its highly creative process which leads into more processes, hence its processual characteristics, has a significant intentional connection from beginning to end.

Research powered by this approach will discover the rigour that exists between method and methodology and the relationship between the research itself and indeed the researcher. Sufficient practice in jazz methodology leads to fundamental forms of action learning, which is itself an established form of creative or musical ontology that is aware of and critical of its own processes.

The relationship between praxiological thinking and action learning has already been justified (Gasparski and Botham, 1988, pp. 147–148). Part Two of this paper is an extension of the previous argument. By deliberate design it stays close to Revans's own accounts of three distinct educational experiments (1980, p. 46) that took place in India, Australia, and Belgium.

Contributions of R. W. Revans

Action Learning: Learning to Learn Through Doing. (Revans, 1980: 214, 296–297)

It should be clearly stated at the beginning of this section that there is officially no reliable definition for action learning. Revans, the originator of the process, vehemently refused to state any consistent definition and instead went to great pains to say: "what action learning was not" (Revans, 1980, pp. 305–315), eventually publishing a short book bearing this title. This does not mean that others have ignored the need for definition as the expanding literature suggests; it would not be an over-exaggeration to assert that hundreds of individuals have treated action learning like fool's gold only to discover, as many trainers, lecturers, management consultants, and postgraduate students have, that the processual dynamics surrounding action learning deny a clear single definition. This stated, there have always been those since the early inception of the process that have constantly asked for a single definition.

Revans (1979), having been pressed yet again by what he called 'half scientists' acting as purveyors of the process and wanting to market action learning to create expansion in management education, wrote:

> Action Learning has spread across the world; its programmes are to be found as far away as India and Australia; there has been more than one of interest in from America, and one recent report on the future of management education in Europe, issued by the Commission of the European Communities in Brussels, comes out strongly in favour of action learning as compared with methods of academic tradition (a classic example of saying what it isn't without defining what action learning really is).
>
> There is, on this account, some curiosity as to the nature of action learning, since little was known of it in Britain. The literature was scattered through a wide range or journals, and there was little that could be read as a concise summary of its theory or as brief record of its practice. Nor did it help to observe, however accurate the observation, that the only way to find out what action learning may be was to become actively in it. If the idea was to be given a trial, those prepared to give it must have some notion about its nature.
>
> argued Revans (1979)

This short note therefore tried to claim how action learning had been borne out of the speed with which the world was changing; to discriminate between action learning and traditional instruction; to offer a condensed guide to its logistics; and to suggest a few propositions in its methodology that our experience of it had revealed.

The inclusion of this note was to illustrate some of the tensions and challenges surrounding Revans himself as he faced serious opposition from university colleagues concerning the evolution of action learning in the UK in and around 1979. The following is a summary of the salient points raised in Revans's paper:

1 The first paragraph illustrates the optimism Revans had in 1979 despite the fierce objections of so-called fellow academics. Those that did support his concepts always anticipated his continuous optimism, which never relented throughout his long life. Unlike some of his contemporaries, he

was extremely fit both physically and psychologically. His sheer athleticism always served him well during his moments of adversity (consider his remarkable athletic achievements coupled with his disciplined scientific mind). To say Revans was a man of substance would be an understatement. Although he had moderate physical stature, he was (1980) once described as true 'giant' amongst those who, for one reason or another, came to work alongside him, some of whom considered him a polymath and bestowed him with the complimentary title 'the professors' professor'.

2 Paradoxically, the fierce attacks Revans encountered made him attractive to others, including leading statesmen and stateswomen, in particular, the former president of India, Mrs Indira Gandhi. The following is a direct and unmodified extract from *Action Learning: New Techniques for Management* (1980, p. 69), used to demonstrate part of the contextual relationships Revans had with others less hostile to his ideas.

"In 1973 Dr John Marsh, former Director-General of the British Institute of Management, gave to Mr Praxy Fernandes, Government of India, a copy of the Nile Project. Mr Fernandes at once saw the significance of action learning and, with the official help of the Council for Technical Education and Development in Overseas Countries, I was asked to discuss with the Indians the possibilities of action learning as a medium for them to make more effective use of their immense talents."

According to Revans, "Mr Fernandes was not only a shrewd administrator… but also a considerable philosopher". Revans found his views upon the nature of knowledge "as welcome as an oasis in my academic Sahara," for Revans had been raised in the "austere school of experimental physics which taught one could never know what the atom actually was; all we could hope for was to observe how it apparently behaved. Action learning descends from this ethic; something exists not for what it is, but by what it can do". He also argued that "It is idle, indeed fraudulent, to take students through certain text books except as the overture to application that can test the rigour of the argument".

Revans's fundamental ideas here illustrated, taken from a publication in 1980, never changed throughout his long life. As such, they became fixed points in the action learning process whereby future programmes could be and were often judged.

They also show his great appreciation for those who took his concepts seriously enough to apply them themselves. Rarely if ever did he turn down the opportunity to meet with those working with action learning, once remarking: "I will meet with any group at any venue as long as I can learn something from them myself."

One of the most powerful insights concerning the nature of action learning is that pertaining to its application. Like other maverick thinkers such as Bateson, Lewin, and Macmurray, Revans firmly believed in practical application as the only reliable test for theory.

Take for example the ontological statement by Macmurray proffered in his book, *The Self as Agent* (1953, p. 15), an explanation greatly favoured by Revans: "All meaningful knowledge is for the sake of action; all meaningful action is for the sake of friendship." From this it might be argued that praxiology and the learning of anything has an ultimate sociological purpose and, as such, failing to do so is indeed an endeavour failed.

Revans's Impact on Australia

It is clear that Revans had planned to have a marked impact on India and those charged with the task of developing the economy, such as the government civil service (1980: 82, p. 83): "In May 1978 I had the privilege of talking with about a hundred senior officers of the Department of Personnel and Administrative Reform of the Government of India". That said, according to his own report, Revans appeared to be disappointed with the general response from India.

Approximately six months later, Revans visited Australia where he spent three weeks discussing his ideas with various public service boards and other government bureaucracies. The poor state of the Australian economy seemed to be the principal stimulus behind the acceptance of action learning. Dr Roy Gilbert of the Public Service Board of Victoria produced a paper 5 May 1978. In his paper he asserted the following:

> I heard Prof Revans talk at Deakin University in February 1977; I supported his philosophy and so decided to experiment. A small group of Public and Private sector managers met after the Deakin University seminar with a view to running an action learning programme. Five organisations… agreed to participate in the programme (but) unfortunately some withdrew at the last moment.

It would appear that this difficult start placed considerable pressure on Gilbert and his colleagues attempting to recruit acceptable programme replacements. It has to be said that other action learning programmes have struggled with recruitment and retention problems despite impressive levels of initial interest from various organisations in the public and private sectors alike. (See "Action Learning at GEC" in *More than Management Development*, Casey and Pearce, eds., 1977, pp. 48–57.)

Gilbert and his colleagues adapted their approach and introduced what they called an 'Internal Action Learning Programme'. This programme consisted of four participants who agreed to exchange their jobs for four weeks and meet as a small group called a set with a set adviser. The overall purpose of each individual project was to improve the efficiency and effectiveness of their organisational departments.

During a four-week secondment, each set was charged with a responsibility of meeting with fellow set members twice weekly for two hours per meeting.

A programme evaluation suggested that this particular action learning programme was a clear success with plans to introduce several more in:

Conservation
Public works
Premiers education
Law and
Local government

Part of the marketing literature designed to encourage participatory enthusiasm includes statements like:

> Any recommendations are automatically implemented because the head of the work unit in the project is a member of the set. There is no imposition of ideas from the outside. People participate because they seek the opportunity to step out of their jobs for a month.

The robust structure of the design of this particular programme suggests unique durability seldom achieved with some action learning programmes. Repeated evaluations of any action learning programme indicate that losing sight of the clear objectives of the programme drastically affected participant attendance. This is a common problem, which eventually weakens the whole structural strength of any action learning programme, despite 'rescue and re-booting interventions' by programme enthusiasts.

One strategy designed to encourage participant continuity was to offer academic recognition leading to post-experience/graduate qualifications. However this could and often did create different tensions between the key parties involved. For example, the fundamental nature of action learning is based on the concept of social learning, which places the responsibility for learning on the shoulders of every participant set member as against a traditional reliance on tutors or professional consultants, no matter how gifted they might be.

As can be anticipated, neither tutors nor professional consultants were included in this programme except for some operating as set advisors. This suggests that Revans himself played a major part in the design and implementation of this Internal Action Learning Programme despite the prominence of Gilbert.

Revans, throughout his long career, was consistently opposed to individuals acting as tutors, consultants, and especially facilitators. He was the strongest and the most demanding, insisting that learning in action learning had to be left to true participants. These powerful restrictions have always placed huge strains on more recent action learning programmes, especially those which were college- or university-based. The acceptance of qualified academics by Revans was never reconciled. To others, however, the realisation that a reasonable level of inclusiveness was a sensible way forward for development of action learning programmes to survive and eventually flourish in college and university settings, was to find legitimate roles for academic staff; otherwise, the initiative would be under severe attack and destroyed, no matter how noble the philosophical concept.

Therefore, few action learning programmes have been entirely successful for academic institutions where severe power struggles between programme participants have been at their strongest with participants seizing both power and control and ignoring those attempting to help. As one distraught set advisor put it: "I don't know what to do; my set have thrown me out!"

This was a sad statement from a very sensitive member of a fine academic support team obviously trying to assist in a set advisor role. This incident of 'set rejection' was never resolved to the satisfaction of this particular set advisor and as such it proved to be fatal for future action learning; his early enthusiasm was lost, and he became one of the fiercest opponents of further programmes offered in his university department; the entire action learning endeavour closed within one-and-a-half years, regrettably fulfilling some of Revans's prophecies concerning the behaviours of some academic staff in UK universities.

Gilbert and his colleagues addressed some of these tensions by compromising and collaborating with pre-existing development programmes:

"Action learning principles have been introduced into (the traditional Management Development Programme). It is now designed as follows:

> A group of 20 relatively senior managers are nominated by their Departments, and first meet for half a day. At this seminar they must spell out the aims, functions and criteria for performance evaluation of their own respective work units. They initially work in five groups of four, and then report to the total group. One week later they meet as a group of 20, for a period of three days, to discuss general strategies for improving efficiency and effectiveness. This three day programme is opened by a Minister of the Government or by a shadow minister of the opposition. On the last day they break up into the five sets of four to develop specific strategies for their own work units. After a further six weeks the five sets gather again to discuss progress and difficulties and after twelve more weeks the total group of 20 meet for a day to discuss progress with an invited Permanent Head. Unlike those within the internal action learning programme, the 20 managers must carry on with their day to day work during the twelve weeks; All Departments are now (1980, p. 89) participating in this programme, whereas before the action learning elements were introduced only a minority of Departments did so. It is learning by doing. It gets results".

This description of a modified action learning programme or more correctly a modified existing management development programme suggests a highly task-focussed non-academic approach that yielded an impressive success rate.

It should be noted that both of Gilbert's programmes were operated without the cooperation (or interference) of any academic institution. As such, no academic qualifications and, hence, no syllabuses were created.

From experience of working closely with Revans (nineteen years) there were very few individuals he had confidence enough in to allow them near one of his own action learning programmes, either in the design or management of, save a few exceptions. Roy Gilbert was such an exception, manifesting in the design of the program previously alluded to.

That stated, it should be noted that despite Revans's endless energy and enthusiasm it was a physical impossibility for him to work with every action learning programme he had introduced especially as his central ideas began to expand. Such a realisation forced him to invite some he knew from small organisations like the Action Learning Trust.

Selection, it has to be said, was complex and severely scrutinised by Revans, especially if they were employed as management lecturers or consultants, which he chose to call 'half scientists'.

Revans's Impact on Belgium

"*What is an honest man, and what need I do to become one?*" (1980, p. 297) Until a few years ago, this statement was presented by Revans and others as the most important question ever raised in the evaluation of any action learning programme.

The statement was derived from a group of epigrams which illustrated what participants had to say about their own subjective experiences of action learning housed within the Inter-University Programme, Belgium 1968. Revans (1980, pp. 41–42) wrote the following:

> I… offered my services to the Belgians, and spent the next 10 years in exile. I worked for a single institution (having left the University of Manchester discontentedly) founded and run by a remarkable man; the Institution was the Fondation Industrie-Universitie' and its managing director was Gaston Deurinck. Although the developments of action learning were, during those ten years, confined almost entirely to Belgium, it is also clear that a slow cultural preparation was maturing all over the world; business was awakening to the fact that management cannot be taught by professors of management.

It is important at this point to consider some of the issues of this new and novel action learning programme and compare it with the former mentioned Indian and Australian programmes:

First, twenty chief executives representing twenty different organisations were required to submit real pre-existing organisational problems to the programme. The nature of each problem was such that it had to be inter-departmental.

Revans's guidance concerning the choice of suitable problems included: "(Problems with) some embarrassment to the top of management to different reasonable, honest and experienced men would suggest different approaches, according to their personal value systems and individual achievements".

Second, participant selection was equally stringent. Each applicant had to convince a jury of chief executives concerning suitability: "The senior managers (participants) were expected to reveal... that they were not investing up to nine months of their lives... in order to become merely expert in more management techniques, computer programming financial analysis or sophisticated mathematical methods (1980, p. 44) The encouragement to be given to these senior men, to be known as fellows, was that they might be able, in conditions where nobody around them could see what to do because they had not before encountered such conditions, to suggest what might be the more useful questions to pose."

Third, having nominated both a problem and a fellow, the participating enterprise had to prepare itself to receive into itself a visiting fellow from another enterprise in the programme. The first step in preparing for this was the appointment of a client, a member of the senior staff, perhaps even the president of the enterprise, "who could be said, more than any other person, to own the problem nominated for attack".

It might also be necessary for the enterprise to identify a "counterpart to the visiting fellow," and it would be essential for the client to make it thoroughly known throughout the enterprise that its top management was serious about the project and expected the support of all concerned with it. The fellows were brought together, with some of the chief executives of the participating enterprise, to decide upon the programme of exchanges; there are certain simple rules to govern these, if the learning of the visitors and of the visited is to be worthwhile.

Fourth, twenty fellows were then allocated to the five universities and built into sets; "the only rule found to be important about the constitution of sets was that they respected the language, French or Dutch, which the participant/fellows regarded as their mother tongue, however well they spoke the other".

The fellows were given a short induction course to prepare them to enter their receiving enterprises with an opening balance of self-confidence; this, of course, has been progressively shortened as the programme has matured, and "*is now no more than three weeks, one third of its original length*". For the next three months they were four days a week in their receiving enterprises and came together on the fifth in their sets to discuss their problems and progress with the other three or four members. This first spell of three months is called the 'diagnostic phase' of the programme; during it, the fellows were expected to identify the nature of the problem they have been posed and to outline an action plan that might be implemented with the support of their clients—and of any other resources available within the programme as a whole.

Fifth, at the end of the diagnostic phase, the fellows were taken to America, where they were able to present their accounts and proposals to business school experts in order to receive different interpretations. At the end of the American visit, they returned to the 'therapeutic' phase of the programme, spending a further three months persuading their receiving enterprises to put their plans into effect.

The unique term: structure d' acceuil (1980: 45, p. 294) was borne near this phase of the programme; Revans later described the term as a 'framework of welcome'. This term became one of the most important philosophical labels for both the Belgium Inter-University Programme and subsequent action learning programmes, especially those established in the Revans Institute, University of Salford, 1995–2005. But the Inter-University Programme stands out as the most advanced action learning programme of all time. The central theme of tackling unfamiliar problems in totally unfamiliar settings has been rarely attempted by anyone ever since this particular programme.

The Inter University Programme was designed and implemented by two of the most ethical men of their generation, namely R. W. Revans and G. Deurinck. Not many action learning programmes, if any, have concluded with an evaluation that exposed a participant's perception of his own degree of honesty.

"What is an honest man and what need I do to become one?"

Afterword

I have attempted in this to draw upon thinkers who in their lifetimes implemented their thoughts into action.

It is true that most of the individuals were categorised as mavericks who followed their own beliefs especially when such beliefs challenged traditional ideas. It is also true that that the maverick mind attracts other maverick minds, similar to molecules that have the same or similar chemical structures.

One final thought: If we are moving towards a place wherein we naturally offer each other Revans's 'structure d'acceuil', then it is my view that a practical philosophy of human action, or at least an interpretation of it, will always play a vital part in a world of change.

Acknowledgements

I was delighted to be reunited with my dear friend and colleague, Professor Wojciech W Gasparski and indeed pleased when he invited me to make a contribution to the series of 'Praxiology'.

References

Bateson, G., 1980, *Mind and Nature, A Necessary Unity*, New York: HarperCollins.

Casey, D. and Pearce, D., 1977, *More than Management Development: Action Learning at GEC*. Farnham: Gower Press.

Davies, D., 2004, *Art as Performance*, Malden: Blackwell.

Engel, M., 1972, *Steps To An Ecology Of Mind* by Gregory Bateson, San Fransisco: Chandler Publications.

Gasparski, W. W. and Botham, D. 1988. *Praxiology: The International Annual of Practical Philosophy and Methodology*, Volume 6.

Kania, A., 2008, *New Waves in Aesthetics* edited by Stock, K. and Thomson-Jones, K., New York: Palgrave Macmillan.

Macmurray, J., 1953, *The Self as Agent*, London: Faber and Faber.

Revans, R. W., 1979, *Action Learning, Its Terms and Character*, Unpublished Paper, May.

Revans, R. W., 1980, *Action Learning: New Techniques for Management*, London: Blond and Briggs.

Stewart, D., 1998, *Reading and Writing Music*, San Francisco: Miller and Freeman Books.

Chapter 6

The Praxiology of Collective Leadership

Joanne B. Ciulla

Leadership is a delicate dance between people who play various formal and informal parts that are determined by fluctuating types and degrees of power and influence. The choreography for this dance depends on the interplay between the context and the dancers—sometimes the chorus is more important than the lead dancer. Over the years, leadership scholars have been engaged in trying to understand this dance. Most of the research has tended to focus on *the* leader and how the leader influences followers. However, recently scholars have shifted their focus away from individual leadership to collective leadership. Leadership is a psychologically, morally, and emotionally complex relationship that results in people working together towards particular goals. As such, the praxiology of collective leadership is far more difficult to study than individual leaders and it raises some challenging ethical questions.

In this essay, I will begin by examining some of the methodological and epistemological issues in leadership studies research. From there I will explore a few of the moral questions related to doing research on collective leadership, and then reflect on whether collective leadership is superior to leadership by an individual.

Research in Leadership Studies

Over the past few years, some leadership scholars have become concerned about the fact that research in leadership studies has been dominated by positivist research. Much of the empirical research in leadership studies tends to conform to the latest fashion. If you look at publications over the past twenty years or so, you will see that they have been dominated by studies of charismatic, transformational, authentic, and ethical leadership. Most of these theories focus on the individual leader. They became popular, in part, because they have a questionnaire that allows researchers to collect data. Researchers tend to believe that data gives their findings more stature than other forms of qualitative research. While this research is useful it gives a somewhat fragmented picture of leadership. For example, in studies using a construct called 'ethical leadership' (Brown *et al.*, 2005), the questionnaire does not measure the ethics of leaders but rather the perception that subjects have about what ethics is and whether they think their leader is ethical. One of the questions is "Conducts his/her personal life in an ethical manner" (Brown *et al.*, 2005, p. 125). This study is useful in showing the relationship between perceptions of ethics and leader effectiveness but it does not tell us much about the actual ethics of leadership, nor was this the researchers' intent.

When I started working in leadership studies in 1991, I read through the literature, and rather than take in certain findings from various studies, my first instinct was to figure out what was going on in the research. In one of my early papers on leadership studies, "Leadership Ethics: Mapping the Territory" (1995), I was struck by the fact that researchers frequently confused prescriptive and descriptive statements about leadership. They would describe what leaders *are* when what they meant is what leaders *ought to be*. The *ought/is* distinction plays a fundamental role in metaethics, which is the study of the logical, metaphysical, epistemological, and linguistic presuppositions of moral language and practice. The most famous discussion of this comes from David Hume (1888/1968) who said that you cannot logically derive an *ought* from an *is*. In other words, just because something is a certain way does not mean that it logically follows that it ought to be or should be that way. In the twentieth century, Moore (1993) called this distinction the 'naturalistic fallacy'. Philosophers have debated this idea over the years, but the distinction is a useful one for leadership researchers, who are aware of the adage 'there is no such thing as a value-free social science,' but still fall into talking about what leaders 'are' when they are really describing an ideal type. So, does the description of authentic leadership (Walumbwa *et al.*, 2008) come from how leaders really are (a set of empirical statements) or is the description a set of ideas about how they should be? It would seem to be the later since researchers then set out to find people who lead this way. When these ideal types are applied to real leaders, the description of a leader's behaviour is often theory-laden. One is struck by the fact that when researchers talk about theories such as transformational (Bass, 1985) and authentic leadership, they tend to claim the most admired leaders in history as falling into their camp. Yet in some cases, the reality of these leaders' intentions, agency, and actual behaviour, rather than fitting the mould of the theories, is instead moulded to fit the theories (Ciulla, 2013).

Normative Assumptions in Research

The unacknowledged underlying normative assumptions behind research in leadership studies are striking but not surprising. There are many discussions in the literature about finding the definition of leadership, which on closer examination, are really about what constitutes a *good* leader. I remember a very spirited debate between the prominent leadership scholars Joseph Rost, Bernard Bass, and Ronald Heifetz over whose definition of leadership should be used in leadership studies research. It took place during session at the Kellogg

Leadership Studies Project in 1996. The idea that agreeing on a definition of leadership would somehow propel the field forward seemed as far-fetched then as it does now. As I argued back then, the meaning of the word *leadership* is a social and historical construction (Ciulla, 1995). Hence, the definition debates were not about what leadership is, but what it should be. In other words, people weren't debating about the meaning of leadership, they were debating about the meaning of good leadership, which means leadership that was both effective and ethical (Ciulla, 2011).

It was also clear that some of the mainstream ideas about leadership are constrained, because most of the research was on business leaders, and some of it is almost indistinguishable from management literature. Hence, there was a tension between ideas of leadership in business, which is more like a dictatorship or oligarchy, and more democratic leadership in government, social movements, or communities. Moreover, the literature has not only been distorted by the dominant context of the research, it is limited because it lacked meaningful contributions from the humanities, which are about what humans are like, how they feel, their moral aspirations, and the way they see the world, and their relationships to each other.

One reason why James MacGregor Burns's book *Leadership* and his theory of transforming leadership was so influential is because he derived his theory from real leaders in history and used some of the research in social psychology to understand them. Burns's book inspired Bernard Bass (1985) to develop his theory of transformational leadership. Early on, Bass stripped the normative and relational elements from Burns's theory in favour of the individual charismatic model of leadership that was popular in leadership studies in the late 1980s and early 1990s. Leadership scholars sometimes lump Burns and Bass together and view them as having a leader-centric or heroic-leader focus. On the surface, it looks like this is what Burns is doing, because his book only discusses influential political leaders in history. However, Burns's theory rests on the values of democracy and the dialogue that leaders and followers have with each other about values. The influence in his theory is reciprocal. The theory itself is very much about the relationship between leaders and followers and how they influence each other in very fundamental ways. More recently, scholars now call what Burns described as 'relational leadership'.

When I look at the literature on relational, collective, and post-heroic leadership, I ask: Why are researchers writing about this? I see new language, but I do not really find anything that cannot be found in literature from the humanities. Literature across cultures and time tells us quite a bit about how people see and understand leaders, group actions, and the relationship between leaders and followers. Books ranging from *The Bible*, Greek comedies and tragedies, Shakespearean plays, fairy tales, and novels from *Don Quixote* to *Moby-Dick* do this. Yes, there are heroes in literature, but there is also quite a bit of shared, collective, and post-heroic leadership going on, too. As many authors note, literature on relational and collective leadership serves as a kind of corrective to a literature that has become dominated by the heroic or individualistic approach to leadership. Articles and research on post-heroic, relational, and collective leadership are not about leaders changing; they are partly a reaction to the way that leadership research has regarded leaders because of disciplinary restrictions and the dominant context in which researchers study it.

Attributions of Agency

Perhaps the fact that so many researchers focus on individual leaders instead of relational and collective leaders tells us something important about the way that researchers and most people think about leadership itself. Meindl *et al.* (1985) argue researchers, like other people, fall prey to the 'Romance of Leadership'. The romance comes from the conscious or unconscious belief that leaders have more control over outcomes than they actually do. It is a heroic or wishful thinking view of the leader as a kind of Wonder Woman or Superman. I suspect that the tendency in the literature to focus on the individual leader may extend to a deeper set of beliefs that most people hold about psychology, agency, and responsibility. We believe in personality; we believe in free will and autonomy; but we also tend to believe that most forms of group action can be traced through a causal chain to one person who is the prime mover or, in a complex system, 'the butterfly'. In one of the last conversations I had with Burns about leadership, he told me that he thought that leaders were really just initiators who set things in motion. Moreover, the ability to identify agency is fundamental to how we think of responsibility. Attributions of agency become more complicated once you move from studying individual to collective leadership. So, rather than simply writing off the leader-centric bias of researchers as the 'Romance of Leadership', I think that individual notion of a leader is still a key consideration in regard to questions of moral accountability, even in the case of groups.

Taking Responsibility

The most ethically distinctive aspect of being a leader is that leaders receive praise or blame for the good and bad things that happen under their watch—even when they know nothing about them or have nothing to do with them. In these cases, normal notions of agency that include the intent, capacity, and causal connection to an action do not always apply. We basically think of leaders as people whose role is to take responsibility for a group, organization, or country. To *take* responsibility means to accept the role of someone who gets praised, blamed, and has a duty to clean up problems. *Taking* responsibility is different from *being* responsible in the sense that a leader may not be personally responsible for doing something or even ordering that something be done. This does not mean that leaders always take responsibility, but followers usually hold them responsible. The expectation to take responsibility is clear to anyone who has noticed how bad leaders look when they fail to do so.

Of course, we may attribute responsibility to a group; however, collective responsibility is more complicated and controversial than individual responsibility. The first obvious consideration is whether we should regard a collective as the same as or something different from its parts?

If it is the same as its parts and the parts have different intentions or do different things, then can the individuals be held equally accountable because they are part of the group (Downie, 1969; Narveson, 2002; Weber, 1978)? Even in the case of collectives, one may want to make distinctions between individuals in the collective who are more or less responsible for something. Furthermore, collective leadership raises the question of whether it is fair to make a group responsible for the behaviour of one or a few members. This becomes especially important when a group does something harmful. Should we consider members who agree to something on par with those who came up with the idea and/or convinced the group to do it? Are group members like individual leaders who, because of their membership, are held responsible for things that they do individually and collectively?

Intentions

In business ethics, corporate responsibility also raises problems about collective responsibility. Blaming and punishing a corporation for doing wrong is not enough for most stakeholders. Both the legal system and the public want to see the causal chain unraveled. They want to know who did what and who knew about it. Some have argued that corporations are not persons because they do not have moral agency or intentions (Goodpaster and Matthews, 1982). Yet, when a corporation does wrong, it is not because it has no conscience, it is because the people in it have no conscience. When we say that an individual leader is responsible for something, we mean that she was free to do something and that she intended to do it. Understanding what free will and intention mean in the context of groups is more difficult to sort out, especially in regard to intent. If an intention is a mental state, then can we attribute a mental state to a group?

Some philosophers believe that collective responsibility and the collective intentions needed for it are possible. For example, Peter French (1984) says that corporations and other collectives can be responsible if they have a structure that allows people to rationally choose a concerted action, enforces group standards that allow the group to talk about their conduct, and group discipline. They also have to have defined individual roles that allow people in the group to exercise certain powers. On this account it is the member's consent to the structure, norms, and of roles of the group members that makes it responsible for its actions. This approach to collective responsibility works better in explaining the moral agency of corporations or formal organizations than it does for social movements that do not usually have these structures.

Larry May offers a somewhat metaphysical account of intention. He believes that groups have what he calls a 'pre-reflective intention' (1987, p. 64), which is an intention that group members have not yet had. This sort of intention stems from the structure of a group and the relationships between people in it. The intention is neither a collective nor an individual intention. It stands above individuals in a group as if it were a collective intention. We see collective intention in mobs where a catalyst ignites a group emotion, but in the somewhat calmer setting of a corporation, group intentions may be more defused. Other philosophers attempt to derive something analogous to group intentions from their shared 'interest in each other's interests' (Feinberg, 1968) and group solidarity (McGary, 1986). This description seems better suited to social movements where individuals are fighting for or against the same things that affect their lives.

Responsibility, agency, and intentionality are not only part of the praxiology of leadership but they are fundamental aspects of the very idea of leadership. They are especially important in understanding collective leadership because they not only relate to ethics, they are central to how one identifies a group as having collective leadership. In other words, one cannot identify if collective leadership is taking place without implicitly or explicitly giving an account of a collective's agency, intention, and how individuals in the group and the group itself are accountable for what it does. In short, I would argue that accountability is part of what identifies something as collective leadership. Responsibility is built in to the very concept of leadership whether it is collective or individual. Also, if context determines what leadership looks like, then leadership is a social construction and as such it inevitably is about individuals, groups, and moral values. Thus, like individual leadership, collective leadership is also an inherently normative concept.

Is Collective Leadership Better?

While on the one hand, collective leadership offers a more comprehensive and realistic way to think about leadership in democracies, social movements, and other contexts. On the other hand, there appears to be an underlying assumption—as is the case with other leadership theories such as transformational and authentic leadership theories—that there is something *good* about collective leadership or that it is better than individual leadership. As Fairhurst (2007) notes, some researchers and strict constructionists even think that individual leadership itself is bad. As I have argued (1995), this is because the very ideas of 'leader' and 'leadership' include moral suppositions about responsibility, accountability, care, etc. When individuals become leaders they face potential ethical problems that stem from power, ego, self-interest, etc. It is not clear that collective leadership would avoid such problems. Groupthink and other aspects of group dynamics may also limit a collective's ability to behave ethically and rationally. One might argue that collective leadership is superior to individual leadership because there are more checks against unethical behaviour in a group than there may be with individual leaders. Another argument for the moral superiority of collective leadership might be based on the dangers of giving any individual too much power over others. This kind of individuality is not only bad for other people but it can evolve into institutionalized power. As Michael Foucault argues, "we have to promote new forms of subjectivity through the refusal of this kind of individuality that has been imposed on us for several centuries" (Foucault, 1994, p. 336). We see individual leaders face these moral pitfalls, but why wouldn't collective leadership cause some of the same problems?

In leadership research and in the world today and in the past, we see less of Foucault's problem and more of a growing willingness for people to relinquish their responsibility and inadvertently hand over their freedom to leaders in exchange for what are often false promises by so called 'strong' leaders. These 'strong' leaders are often populists who convince followers that they can make better decisions and take better care of them than other groups or democracies. The idea of a wise and benevolent despot can start to look better than a mercurial body of legislators in a Parliament or Congress. This view is not unwarranted because we also see democracies can make bad decisions about policy or their choice of elected leaders. Sometimes this is because citizens fail to obtain the knowledge they need to make informed decisions and fail to take their collective leadership responsibilities seriously. In the end, it comes down to whether democratic and other forms of collective leadership exemplify 'the wisdom of crowds' (Surowiecki, 2005) or the 'extraordinary popular delusions and the madness of crowds' (Mackay, (1841) 2012).

So as I see it, one key moral question about the praxiology of collective leadership is: What moral pitfalls of individual leadership does collective leadership avoid and what unique moral pitfalls does it face? Are there cases where collective leadership is better (more effective and ethical) than individual leadership and vice versa? These are not theoretical questions but ones that have taken centre stage in the world today. Ever since WWII, Westerners have hailed the establishment of democracy in other countries as a measure of progress in freedom and the quality of the human condition. Yet, according to data from Freedom House index on democracy, freedom has been declining annually since 2005 (Taub, 2016).

The values of collective leadership in representative democracies such as liberty, justice, and equality are so powerful that it is difficult to imagine that anyone living in a democracy would ever want to give it up for an all-powerful leader. Nonetheless, a recent study based on the European World Values Survey found that the number of people who thought that living in a democracy was essential has plummeted and is very low among young people (Foa and Mounk, 2016). This is only one study that may or may not be alarming. However, it illustrates the fact that even if collective leadership, especially democracy, is better than individual leadership or dictatorship, when it fails and the right sort of individual comes long, people are willing to cast their lot with individual leaders who all rarely turn out to be wise and benevolent despots. This is probably what Winston Churchill meant when he said that democracy was the worst form of government except for all the others.

References

Bass, B. M., 1985, Leadership and Performance Beyond Expectations, New York: Free Press.

Brown, M. E., Treviño, L. K., and Harrison D. A. 2005, 'Ethical leadership: A social learning perspective for construct development and testing', Organizational Behavior and Human Decision Processes, 97: 117–134.

Ciulla, J. B., 1995, Leadership Ethics; Mapping the Territory, The Business Ethics Quarterly 5.1: 5–24.

Ciulla, J. B., 2011, Ethics and effectiveness: The nature of good leadership, in D. V. Day and J. Antonakis (Eds.), The Nature of Leadership 2nd edn, Thousand Oaks CA: Sage, pp. 508–540.

Ciulla, J. B., 2013, "Searching for Mandela: The Saint as a Sinner Who Keeps on Trying." In D. Ladkin and C. Spiller (Eds.), Authentic Leadership: Clashes, Convergences and Coalescences, Northampton, CT: Edward Elgar, pp. 152–175.

Downie, R. S., 1969, "Collective Responsibility" Philosophy 44: 66–69.

Fairhurst, G., 2007, Discursive Leadership, Thousand Oaks, CA: Sage.

Feinberg, J., 1968, Collective Responsibility, Journal of Philosophy, 65: 674–688.

Foa, R. S., and Mounk, Y., 2016, The Danger of Deconsololidation: The Democratic Disconnect, The Journal of Democracy, 27.3: 5–17.

Foucault M., 1994, The Subject and Power, Michel Foucault: Power, James D. Faubion (Ed.), New York: The New Press, pp. 326–348.

French, P., 1984, Collective and Corporate Responsibility, New York: Columbia University Press.

Goodpaster, K. E. and Matthews, J. Jr., 1982, Can a Corporation Have a Conscience? Harvard Business Review 60(1): 132–141.

Hume, D., 1968, A Treatise on Human Nature, Oxford: Clarendon Press.

Mackay, Ch., 2012, Extraordinary Popular Delusions and the Madness of Crowds, New York: Simon & Schuster.

May, L., 1987, The Morality of Groups, Notre Dame: University of Notre Dame Press.

McGary, H., 1986 Morality and Collective Liability, Journal of Value Inquiry 20: 157–165.

Meindl, J. R.,. Ehrlich, S. B., and Dukerich J. M., 1985, The Romance of Leadership, Administrative Science Quarterly 30(1): 78–102.

Moore, G. E., 1993, Principia Ethica, Cambridge: Cambridge University Press.

Narveson, J., 2002, Collective Responsibility, Journal of Ethics, 6: 179–198.

Surowiecki, J., 2005, The Wisdom of Crowds, New York: Anchor Books.

Taub, A., 2016, How Stable Are Democracies? Warning Signs Are Flashing Red, The New York Times, p. A7.

Walumbwa, F. O., Avolio, B. J., Gardner, W. L., Wernsing T. S. and Peterson S. J., 2008, Authentic Leadership: Development and Validation of a Theory Based Measure, Journal of Management, 34(1), pp. 89–126.

Weber, M., 1978, Economy and Society, Vol. 1, Berkeley: University of California Press.

Chapter 7

Old and New Perspectives on Economic Systems

Georges Enderle

In Appreciation for the Studies in Praxiology

From its beginning in 1992, *Praxiology: The International Annual of Practical Philosophy and Methodology* has been concerned with human action in business and the economy, discussed especially in volumes 1, 5, 8, 9, 14, 16, and 17. While I did not know about this important initiative in the early years, I was very pleased to discover that the view of action-oriented business ethics I had tried to develop in Western Europe (Enderle, 1993a, 1993b) actually had its counterpart in Eastern Europe. Since then, I think, both sides have understood and pursued "the final purpose of business ethics [as] a 'new practice' consisting of improving the ethical quality of decision making and acting at all levels of business ... at the micro (individual), meso (organizational) and macro (systemic) levels" (Enderle, 1993b, p. 138). Interestingly, the 'triple E' of effectiveness, efficiency, and ethicality (curiously, reminding me of my family name) constitutes both approaches, although effectiveness and efficiency are less articulated in my approach that expects them to be part of good (positive) economics.

With the fall of the Berlin Wall in 1989 and the collapse of the Soviet Union in 1991, many voices in the West proclaimed victory of capitalism. Frankly speaking, I was not of that opinion because the dissolution of one economic system does not justify the legitimacy of another system. My mentor and friend Arthur Rich had just published *Business and Economic Ethics: The Ethics of Economic Systems* (Rich, 2006; in German 1990). He asked in his self-critical and self-effacing way if this volume hadn't appeared too late. Seemingly, the triumph of capitalism answered the question of the ethics of economic systems once and for all. The answer I gave him at that time, that it wasn't too late indeed, has been confirmed and even more validated today as when I wrote my preface in 2006. Ten years later, in 2016, the question of the ethics of economic systems has become even more urgent after the global financial crisis and the drastic increases of economic inequality in most countries. Therefore, I offer my most recent thoughts on economic systems to this silver volume of *Praxiology*, hoping to help open new horizons for praxiological enquiry.[1]

Characterization of Economic Systems with One Dominant System Criterion

The *Oxford Dictionary of Economics* defines an economic system as "the part of the social system composed of institutions and customs related to production, distribution and consumption of goods and services. Important characteristics of an economic system are property rules and the degree of economic planning: examples are traditional, capitalist, socialist, and mixed systems" (Black *et al.*, 2009, p. 132). As part of the social system, it is related to the political, legal, cultural, and other systems and embedded in nature. Given the far-reaching impact of economic systems, whether addressed explicitly or not, it is imperative to clarify the essential components of an economic system, its implied economic paradigm, its ethical criteria and its purpose in substantive terms.

There are many different ways of characterizing and evaluating economic systems, explicated in an immense body of literature (see, among others, Hall and Soskice, 2001; Heilbroner, 1987; Kromphardt, 1991; Nove, 1987; Rich, 2006). While numerous authors discuss the concepts of capitalism and socialism, only few systematically reflect on the criteria for comparing different economic systems.

In his pertinent analysis of economic systems, Jürgen Kromphardt (1991) notes critically that economic systems have been characterized with one dominant system criterion, deducting—as a theoretical construct—'pure' economic systems. At the same time, it has been conceded that the realized economic systems are mixed forms which need additional characteristics for their description and analysis. The main proponents of one dominant system criterion are Karl Marx and Walter Eucken.

For Marx the dominant system criterion is the ownership of the means of production as the legal expression of relations of production which characterize an economic system. The distribution of ownership of the means of production determines who can make decisions about production, whether these decisions are made in a decentralized manner by many people or in a centralized fashion by few, and how exchange and distribution of goods are regulated. The owners of the means of production would determine also the forms of division of labour and cooperation. And the division of society in classes would be determined by ownership relations: When, for instance, a part of society controls the ownership of the means of production, then this part constitutes the ruling class while the non-owners form the ruled class. For Marx two basic economic systems result from the application of this dominant system criterion: Capitalism, in which the means of production are owned by a few people while the majority is formed by the non-owners, and socialism, in which the means of production are owned by society.

For Walter Eucken (1950) a different dominant criterion characterizes an economic system, namely the making of plans in an economy. He argues that economic activity always happens only through economic planning and would be impossible without setting and executing plans. If all economic activities in an economy happen on the basis of a single central planning, we speak of a 'centrally planned economy'. On the other hand, if economic activities occur based on more than one plan, we have a 'market economy' in which the various decentralized plans need to be coordinated.

A first choice of the dominant system criterion is the ownership order ('Eigentumsordnung'). It originated from Karl Marx and his materialistic conception of history. The ownership of the means of production and—more broadly speaking—the relations of production determine the form of the division of labour and cooperation, the rules of exchange and distribution of goods, and the relations between the ruling and the ruled class. However, the relations of production and the legal ownership relations go hand in hand only if all rights of disposal on the means of production result from ownership and all rights of disposal are in the hands of the owners. This, though, is not the case when in an economic system of private property parts of the rights of disposal are regulated by the state. Then, with the change of the rights of disposal, the relations of production change while the legal ownership relations remain the same. Moreover, the extent of the rights of disposal by the state also depends on how the decisions taken by individual owners of means of production are coordinated with decisions among themselves and with suppliers. Therefore, it is not possible to analyse the relations of ownership without the processes of coordination.

This impossibility is confirmed by developments in the private sector—observed already by Berle and Means (1932)—in which legal ownership (e.g. of shareholders) and the rights of disposal (e.g. of management) can be, and often are, separated. In line with this separation, the modern school of property rights (see Alchian and Demsetz, 1973, and others) places its main focus on the distribution of the rights of disposal (which reach beyond the means of production).

A second choice of the dominant system criterion is the way of coordination: How decisions about production, distribution, and consumption in an economy are coordinated with each other and, if necessary, revised. This coordination decisively determines what is produced and how and for whom it is produced. At the same time, it influences the distribution or allocation of the factors of production in the different locations and procedures of production. Advocates of this second view are Walter Eucken (1950) and Paul Hensel (1970), who see in the planning of economic activity—either central or decentralized—the dominant criterion of an economic system. However, it is questionable that all economic activities are based on planning and that only two forms of planning (i.e. central and decentralized) actually exist.

The System-Theoretical Approach by Neuberger and Duffy

Against the approaches of one dominant system criterion, Egon Neuberger and William Duffy (1976) propose a system-theoretical approach that differentiates the economic system into three subsystems of the decision-, information-, and motivation-structures, called the '*Decision-Information-Motivation-Approach*'. It focuses on the basic analytical category of decisions (akin to neoclassical economics), accounts for the role of economic and social power (in response to Marxist critique), considers not only the decision makers but also the executors of their decisions, and assumes that all members of an economic system have to make decisions.

The decision-making structure is defined by the authority of making decisions in the economic realm and by their distribution among the economic subjects (individuals, groups, organizations). Because these subjects have different objectives, the developments and outcomes of the economic system vary as well, depending on the type and sources of the distribution of decision-making power among the members of society, which can be direct (when the subjects make their own decisions) or indirect (when the subjects influence other decision-makers in order to favour their own objectives). In sum, the decision-making structure is characterized by the sources of decision-making power (such as traditions, force, legal titles, and, above all, property), the subjects (individuals, households, enterprises, other organizations, and governmental agencies), their fields (e.g. production, distribution or consumption) and the distribution (or concentration) of the decision-making power as well.

The information-structure consists of the ways decision-relevant information is collected, passed on, processed, stored, reprocessed, and utilized. As such, information about the environment in general and the decisions of other decision-makers in particular is received and utilized by the decision-makers, it is a key component of the coordination-process that is essential for assuring consistency among interrelated decisions of various decision-makers and hence for the efficiency of the economic system. The two most important coordination-arrangements are the macro-economic binding planning and the market.

The motivation-structure relates to the ways decision-making power in an economic system is directed by objectives, executed and enforced. Because Neuberger and Duffy assume that the objectives of the subjects of decision-making are exogenously given (i.e. not part of the economic system), they only consider how decision-makers with their power can influence the decision-making of others (i.e. by influencing others' possibilities or consequences of actions or their evaluation of alternative actions). Therefore, the decision-makers need to know four types of relevant motivation to act in an economic system in order to choose the most effective method of influencing others: (a) Reliance on tradition or common obligations. (b) Appeal to egoism in order to increase prosperity or respect among people. (c) Appeal to solidarity or voluntary subordination of individual objectives under the objectives of the group. (d) Coercion. Accordingly, the decision-maker will choose the most appropriate system of incentives and coercion. It goes without saying that by assuming the objectives of economic subjects as exogenously given, decision-making within the economic system is understood in a merely instrumental sense. The questions of moral and immoral objectives cannot be raised and addressed within the economic system.

Kromphardt's Three-Pronged Conception of the Economic System

After discussing the approaches mentioned above, Kromphardt proposes his own conception of the economic system and applies it to a variety of capitalistic economic systems. It draws on various approaches (some mentioned above) and proposes three sets of criteria:

a Criteria of ownership and rights of disposal: Who participates in the economic processes of planning, decision-making and controlling with regard to production, distribution, and consumption?
b Criteria of information and coordination: With the help of what information systems are individual decisions coordinated?
c Criteria of motivation: What objectives do various decision-makers pursue and how do they behave in carrying out their decisions?

The characteristics of a capitalistic economic system are summarized by Kromphardt as follows (1991, pp. 41–42):

Decisions: This set of criteria highlights the *capitalistic* nature of the system. Private owners of the means of production or their authorized representatives make decisions on the production of goods and services in a mostly decentralized manner (though arrangements may occur) for an anonymous market. These decision-makers form a minority of the economic subjects. The majority, namely the labour forces *without* owning the means of production, can decide—free of feudal attachments—to which owner of the means of production they offer their labour for pay.

Coordination: This set of criteria emphasizes the system as a *market economy*. In markets where suppliers and demanders compete with each other, the prices are set by the suppliers, agreed to by suppliers and demanders or determined by exchange-like institutions. From these processes result the market signals (indicators of prices and quantities such as prices of goods, delivery times, inventories and wages on the labour market). They *inform* the suppliers about sales and profit possibilities and *coordinate* the suppliers' decisions among themselves and with the decisions of the demanders (processors, traders, consumers).

Motivation: This set of criteria characterizes the driving forces of the system. Rational and individualistic motivation determines the profit-oriented action of capitalists and—less exclusively—the behaviour of non-owners. For this view, Kromphardt draws on Karl Marx, Werner Sombart, and Max Weber. All three authors assume that the objectives of economic activity are defined, first of all, within the economic system (not exogenously as Neuberger/Duffy claim). Marx sees the novelty of capitalism in the reversal of the relation 'commodity—money—commodity' into the relation 'money—commodity—money*' and defines the objective of the capitalistic entrepreneur as profit (i.e. the net revenue of [money* − money]). Similarly, Sombart understands the immediate objective of the decision-makers of production not as the satisfaction of the needs of real people, but as the accumulation of money (i.e. 'Erwerbsprinzip'), which, though, allows for different subjective goals.

According to both Sombart and Weber, the predominant motivation in capitalism is 'rational' and 'individualistic'. Rationality means systematic planning and scheduling, regular execution, meticulous calculation, etc. Individualistic motivation characterizes the owners of the means of production who strive for achieving their objectives individually and in competition with others. But also the non-owners tend to behave individualistically, particularly when they are incentivized by material advantages.

While Kromphardt's three-pronged conception is very helpful to compare economic systems, it leaves many important questions unanswered. First, what paradigm of economics is the appropriate foundation of such comparisons? Second, what ethical criteria are basic for evaluating economic systems? Third, how may the purpose of an economic system be defined in substantive terms? The following explorations—further developed in Enderle (2013)—draw particularly on publications by Amartya Sen, Arthur Rich, Georges Enderle, and Marvin Brown.

Questions of the Economic Paradigm, Ethical Criteria, and Substantive Purposes of Economic Systems

In his book *On Ethics and Economics* (1987) Amartya Sen distinguishes two approaches to economics in the history of economic doctrines: the engineering approach and the ethics-related approach. The first primarily focuses on logistical issues: what means should one choose in order to achieve as efficiently as possible, under very simple behavioural assumptions, goals that are given from elsewhere? The second, going back to Aristotle, involves a broader understanding of economics. It also comprehends problems of human motivation and the judgment of social achievements that cannot be disconnected from the ethical questions of the good: How should one live and how should we foster a good society?

These two approaches involve very different understandings of goodness in business and economics. In the engineering approach, goodness qualifies the logistics and efficiency of the system, which are often conceived as 'mechanisms' or, more recently, as evolutionary principles. No free space is left for decision-making outside the demands of the tightly determined system. Often rationality is equated with internal consistency of choice and maximization of self-interest. With this limited understanding of freedom and rationality, human action understood in a broader sense cannot be accounted for. By the same token, there is no ethical responsibility beyond the so defined role responsibilities in the system. With regard to the judgment of social achievements (economic performance of society, social well-being, redistribution policies, etc.), the engineering approach claims that interpersonal comparisons of utility are impossible. This means that, from an 'economic' point of view, one cannot evaluate the state of an economy and judge whether it is 'good' or 'bad'. Economic science supposedly can provide only the means; the ends—at best—have to be studied independently and systematically by political philosophy.

In contrast, the ethics-related approach involves a broader understanding of rationality that includes also other-regarding motivations and legitimate reasoning about ends. It provides free space for decision making and, therefore, ethical responsibility at all levels: the individual (micro-), the organizational (meso-) and the systemic (macro-) levels. Human action has an indispensable place in this approach. Moreover, although difficult to achieve, interpersonal comparison as a necessary condition for judging social achievements is not declared impossible. As Sen argues, it can be achieved in terms of 'human capabilities', avoiding the aggregation problems with utilities.

To sum up, the ethics-related approach defines goodness in business and economics by an 'internal' and an 'external' dimension as the term 'ethics-related' indicates. The internal dimension includes a broader conception of rationality and accounts for human motivations and social and individual ends. The external dimension relates to the indispensable role of moral and political philosophy. In other words, business and economics is not a hermetically sealed, value-free realm, but suffused with ethical values and norms incorporated in motivations and ends. At the same time, it needs philosophical reasoning to obtain goodness in a full sense.

Arthur Rich, the late dean of Protestant social ethics in German-speaking countries, clearly adopts the ethics-related approach in his book *Business and Economic Ethics: The Ethics of Economic Systems* (2006) and provides an extensive discussion on the question of meaning and purpose in the economy (pp. 269–298). In order to examine the ethical quality of an economic system, he develops an ethical foundation and explicates seven criteria (creatureliness, critical distance, relative reception, relationality, fellow-humanness, fellow-creatureliness, and participation). Throughout his work, he applies his guiding principle for business and economic ethics: "That which is not economically rational cannot really be humanly just; and that which contradicts human justice cannot really be economically rational" (pp. 74–75). In other words, goodness in business and economics needs both economic rationality and human justice. It can be achieved neither by disregarding in an utopian manner the economically correct in economic questions nor by eliminating human justice as a social-ethical postulate from the economic sphere, in the name of the frequently invoked 'autonomy' of the economy.

Inspired by Sen's ethics-related approach and Rich's ethics of economic systems, Georges Enderle (2009) proposes 'a rich concept of wealth creation' as the purpose of business and economics in contrast to the maximization of share values and profits and the vague notion of 'value creation'. Wealth consists of four types of capital: natural, economic, human, and social capital, similar to the definition of well-being by the OECD (2013). It is a combination of private *and* public wealth and includes a productive *and* a distributive dimension and material *and* spiritual aspects. The activity of creating (i.e. making something new *and* better) is distinct from possessing and acquiring wealth and is situated in the time horizon of sustainability in terms of 'expanding real freedoms that people have reason to value' (Sen). Because the wealth of an economy is a combination of private and public wealth, far-reaching implications result for the roles of market institutions and self-regarding motivations. Forming only one part of the economy, markets are basically limited in creating wealth because they fail in creating public wealth; in other words, collective actors (governments, communities, etc.) are necessary as well. Moreover, self-interest, a strong driver to create private wealth, lacks the motivational force for creating public wealth; for creating public wealth, other-regarding motivations such as solidarity, compassion and justice are indispensable.

A fourth, alternative approach of conceptualizing economic systems is advanced in Marvin Brown's book *Civilizing the Economy. A New Economics of Provision* (2010). The author advocates moving from the current economics of property to a 'new economics of provisions'. Making provisions occurs through many systems: food, clothing, housing, health care, education, credit, security, transportation, entertainment, politics, and others. In contrast to capitalism and socialism, these systems of provisions are organized through civic conversations. Basically, citizens without exclusion are the subjects of these conversations. They are guided by the ethics of reciprocity—epitomized in the Golden Rule 'Do unto others what you want them to do unto you'—which includes the reciprocity of exchange, participation and civic deliberation. The civic view is explained with a new understanding of labour, land, and money, aiming at building up civic systems of provision—the purpose in substantive terms proposed by this alternative approach.

Conclusion

To compare and evaluate economic systems, Kromphart's three-pronged approach including decision, coordination and motivation helps better than the approach of one dominant system criterion to characterize the crucial differences of systems. However, these three components are of a formal nature and need to be substantiated. Praxiology and the action-oriented approach provide free space for human action with regard to decision, coordination and motivation. Sen's ethics-related approach offers a paradigm of economics that emphasizes ethicality within and beyond the economic systems while integrating the engineering approach that accounts for effectiveness and efficiency. The seven ethical criteria developed by Rich define 'human justice' and its relation to 'economic rationality'. Finally, the comprehensive conception of wealth creation and the economics of provision indicate more concretely how praxiology can be substantiated in business and the economy. In brief and without doubt, there are fascinating perspectives to develop in the next twenty-five volumes of praxiology.

Note

1 I thank Sage Publications for the permission to reprint (to a large extent) my entry on "Economic Systems" in the Second Edition of the *Encyclopedia of Business Ethics and Society*, edited by R. Kolb.

References

Alchian, A., Demsetz, H., 1973, The Property Rights Paradigm. *Journal of Economic History*, 33:1, 16–27.

Berle, A. A., Means, G. C., 1932/1999, *The Modern Corporation and Private Property*. New Brunswick, NJ: Transaction Publishers.

Black, J., Hashimzade, N., and Miles, G., 2009, *Oxford Dictionary of Economics*. Oxford: Oxford University Press.

Brown, M. T., 2010, *Civilizing the Economy. A New Economics of Provision*. Cambridge, UK: Cambridge University Press.

Enderle, G., 1993a, *Handlungsorientierte Wirtschaftsethik. Grundlagen und Anwen—dungen*. Bern/Stuttgart: Haupt. [Action-oriented Business Ethics. Foundations and Applications].

Enderle, G., 1993b, What Is Business Ethics? In: Dunfee, T. W. and Nagayasu, Y. (eds.). *Business Ethics: Japan and the Global Economy*. Dordrecht/Boston/London: Kluwer Academic Publishers, pp. 133–150.

Enderle, G., 2009, A Rich Concept of Wealth Creation beyond Profit Maximization and Adding Value. *Journal of Business Ethics*, 84, Supplement 3, 281–295.

Enderle, G., 2013, Defining Goodness in Business and Economics. In: Hösle, V. (ed.). *Dimensions of Goodness*. Newcastle upon Tyne, UK: Cambridge Scholars Publishing, pp. 281–302.

Eucken, W., 1950, *Die Grundlagen der Nationalökonomie* [The Foundations of the Political Economy]. Vol. 6. Auflage. Berlin: Springer.

Hall, P. A., Soskice, D., 2001, *Varieties of Capitalism: The Institutional Foundations of Comparative Advantage*. Oxford: Oxford University Press.

Heilbroner, R., 1987, Capitalism. In: Eatwell, J., Milgate, M., and P. Newman (eds.). *The New Palgrave. A Dictionary of Economics*. Vol. 1. New York: Stockton Press, pp. 347–353.

Hensel, P., 1970, *Das Verhältnis von Allokations und Wirtschaftssystemen* [The Relationship between Allocation Systems and Economic Systems]. In: Boettcher, D. (Hg.). Beiträge zum Vergleich der Wirtschaftssysteme. Berlin: Duncker & Humblot.

Kromphardt, J., 1991, *Konzeptionen und Analysen des Kapitalismus. Von seiner Entstehung bis zur Gegenwart*. Dritte Auflage. Tübingen: UTB Vandenhoeck.

Neuberger, E., Duffy, W. J., 1976, *Comparative Economic Systems: A Decision-Making Approach*. Boston: Allyn and Bacon.

Nove, A., 1987, Socialism. In: Eatwell, J., Milgate, M., and P. Newman (eds.). *The New Palgrave. A Dictionary of Economics*. Vol. 1. New York: Stockton Press, pp. 398–407.

OECD, 2013, *How Is Life 2013? Measuring Well-Being*. Paris: OEDC Publishing.

Rich, A., 2006, *Business and Economic Ethics. The Ethics of Economics Systems*. With an Introduction by G. Enderle. Leuven: Peeters. P. 694. English translation of *Wirtschaftsethik* by Arthur Rich (Volume I 1984, Volume II 1990), supervised by G. Enderle.

Sen, A., 1987, *On Ethics and Economics*. Oxford, New York: Blackwell.

Chapter 8

Tadeusz Kotarbiński's Typology of Economisation Measures and Its Relevance for Modern Management Science

Krzysztof Klincewicz

Introduction

The paper discusses an approach to improving the efficiency of organisational activities and processes, originally proposed by the Polish philosopher and praxiologist Tadeusz Kotarbiński in the 1950s. The approach remains relatively unknown to international readers, but offers useful insights to theorists and practitioners of the process management. It will be contrasted with the developments of the management science in the twentieth century to demonstrate the separation between the Western management discourse and the Polish praxiological tradition. The present body of knowledge in the field of management science could benefit from the conceptual cross-fertilization with Kotarbiński's contributions. The typology of economisation measures discussed in the paper remains relevant for modern organisational practices and offers a set of measures that could be applied to address practical problems which were overlooked by management theorists. The paper demonstrates the timeless benefits of this selected praxiological framework and will hopefully encourage further re-discoveries of models, concepts and tools that were developed by the Polish praxiologists in the twentieth century.

Kotarbiński's Typology of Economisation Measures

Polish organisational researchers in the mid-twentieth century were avid followers of praxiology, interpreted in line with Bourdeau's original concept of the science of functions (Bourdeau, 1882/2000, p. 28) or Espinas's quest for practical rules and techniques (Espinas, 1897/2000, p. 47). They were looking for universal principles of human action, applicable in different organisational contexts. The political and economic conditions of the non-market, socialist economy limited the reception of certain US-originated management concepts and encouraged the development of their own frameworks that would also be applicable to not-for-profit organisations and state-owned companies. In modern times, these strives for generalisability could be turned into an important asset that facilitates the application of the frameworks to various types of organisations, regardless of their business models and governance structures.

Tadeusz Kotarbiński's typology of economisation measures was presented by its author as 'postulates for economic modes of action' (Kotarbiński, 1961/1999). These postulates were not considered a full-encompassing classification but merely a set of directives (Kotarbiński, 1958, p. 147). Kotarbiński offered his own interpretation of the term 'economic' by positing that an economic action will deliver more outputs with comparable inputs, or the same outputs with significantly less inputs required (Kotarbiński, 1961/1999, pp. 340–341). This could translate into a more efficient use of resources (inputs), increased rate of outputs (e.g. products manufactured), reduction of time and money, or of human efforts (energy). Aligned with the praxiological tradition, Kotarbiński emphasized the subjective character of economisation, which should not only be associated with timeand finance-related savings. For one person, 'more economic' travel would mean saving transportation time (e.g. to allow more opportunities for sightseeing), while another social actor would link the economic aspect to the reduction of travel-related fatigue (through more comfortable transportation, the relaxed passenger would better perform activities following the trip) (Kotarbiński, 1961/1999, p. 341). When printing a document, some people would consider the use of a smaller font (in order to present more text on the same page), while others decide to use the increased font size (facilitating reading and reaching out to more potential readers) (Kotarbiński, 1961/1999, p. 341). As demonstrated by these examples, economic does not necessarily mean 'performed at a lower cost', but rather takes into account individual preferences of the person performing the action. Kotarbiński presented several variations of his typology of economisation measures, combining some measures into one type or separating them, and the list below describes fifteen measures based on two representative literature sources (Kotarbiński, 1958, pp. 147–177; Kotarbiński, 1961/1999, pp. 340–351).

1 **Minimizing interventions**—Trying to do as little as possible, reducing the necessary efforts, so that ideally no intervention is required at all. This could be achieved by: a decision to maintain the inertia and the status quo (e.g. *laissez-faire* type of management) as long as it is beneficial for the person concerned; refraining from actions until the right moment; replacement of materials by less work-intensive alternatives (e.g. purchase of a ready-to-eat meal instead of cooking); selection of better inputs (e.g. exploiting minerals that are closer to the surface or locating a warehouse closer to the factory in order to reduce the need for transportation); repairing tools or machines instead of replacing them. It is important to remember the subjective character of economisation; people valuing their time are likely to prefer ready-to-use meals, while persons interested in saving money might rather prefer to cook by themselves. As described by Kotarbiński (1961/1999, p. 343), the purchase of a seasonal ticket might

not be more economic than buying tickets for each individual ride—it depends on the individual preferences related to the time spent buying and validating these tickets, as well as travelling frequency.

2 **Pure invigilation**—Observing instead of intervening, but at the same time remaining alert and ready to intervene whenever needed. This measure can be combined with the delegation of tasks to other employees or the use of technologies to replace human efforts—in both cases, performers of the desired actions need to be supervised. It could be implemented in a broader socio-political context, e.g. when governments refrain from market interventions (comp. the notion of invisible hand and beliefs in efficient, free markets) or when they support the capacity building instead of direct social transfers ("*Give a man a fish and you feed him for a day; teach a man to fish and you feed him for a lifetime*").
3 **Anticipation**—Involving: earlier actions preparing ground for the expected outcomes (e.g. planting seeds to grow plants or vegetables, buying inputs in advance, especially when their prices are lower; prophylactics of diseases; designing products to make them easier to recycle); resorting to already accomplished and irreversible deeds (fr. *faits accomplis*) that might privilege one actor; or formulating request in such a way that a person's failure to act or respond by a given date will be interpreted as a certain course of actions (Kotarbiński, 1958, p. 161).
4 **Potentialisation**—Demonstrating the ability to act without any actual action, e.g. by showing a gun or military potential, installing security cameras or scarecrows, or conditionally suspending penalty. It might also lead to the elimination of (potentially) unnecessary efforts, e.g. a host refrains from sweetening coffee or tea served for guests, but offers them the possibility to add sugar to their drinks by themselves (Kotarbiński, 1958, p. 164).
5 **Automation**—Making actions easier to perform, with less efforts owing to training, repetition and standardisation (comp. efficiencies achieved through mass production) or imitation (copying others whenever useful instead of striving for originality). Kotarbiński's use of the term 'automation' did not refer to tools, machines or technologies that nowadays are commonly associated with the term (comp. measure no. 9—instrumentalisation).
6 **Cumulation**—Performing two or more activities at once. This could result e.g. from the previously described automation, which reduces the physical or emotional involvement, allowing people to repeat certain actions and at the same time, think about other matters or work on other problems.
7 **Simplification**—Reorganising work to make activities less complex and easier to perform, e.g. by dividing them into a smaller number of elements or reducing the number of activities.
8 **Immanentisation or internalisation of actions**—Using reflection instead of physical efforts, analysis and conceptualisation instead of trial-and-error.

The measure resembles the concept of double-loop learning (Argyris, 1977), popular in management literature, where organisational participants draw lessons learned from their earlier, unsuccessful activities and modify the course of actions rethinking the sources of earlier failures.

9 **Instrumentalisation or externalisation of actions** (also referred to as: **mechanisation)**—Means using instruments, tools, and technologies to facilitate actions. The notion of instruments might be relatively broad, encompassing e.g. written documents (to replace human memory). Whenever economic, externalisation might also lead to the reduction of cogitation and promote actions (i.e. directly contradicting the previously-described immanentisation).
10 **Coordination**—Taking measures to ensure that individual actions are not contradictory or conflicting.
11 **Ordering in time**—Setting up the optimal sequence of actions, which might include the following examples: reversing the order of actions if needed; pacing the actions at specific intervals; combining the sequence of actions to gradually increase effort and subsequently allow the acting person to rest.
12 **Ordering in space**—Deciding about the most economic location of actions, e.g. to reduce the time or costs needed to transport, commute, move, or reach out for materials.
13 **Planning**—Gathering knowledge about the future and selecting desirable courses of actions (related to measures no. 3—anticipation and no. 8—immanentisation).
14 **Organising**—Combining elements in a structure that offers opportunities to better meet the objective shared by these elements (Kotarbiński, 1961/1999, p. 348).

Kotarbiński suggested that this set of directives was not exhaustive nor did it include mutually exclusive measures (Kotarbiński, 1958, p. 147). Several other measures could be identified in Kotarbiński's writings, including: inventing/innovating (to introduce radical changes and surpass the results achievable merely by imitation, see: Kotarbiński, 1961/1999, p. 347) and reusing the by-products of other actions or waste (Kotarbiński, 1958, p. 173).

The typology was relatively simple and applicable to multiple social contexts, both in formal organisations and in daily life. Whenever a gap arises between the observed organisational situation and expectations or objectives formulated by managers, 'gap-reducing' actions are desirable (Ansoff, 1965, pp. 25–26), and Kotarbiński's framework offers practical recommendations. The following sections of the paper will attempt to contrast Kotarbiński's contribution with the broader international discourse of the management theory, demonstrating that the Polish philosopher offered a solution to organisational problems that were diagnosed but not adequately addressed by Western researchers, particularly in the field of process management.

Western Management Theory Departing from Simple, Universal Principles

Even though Kotarbiński's model is not widely-known to scholars, it might offer useful insights both to theorists and practitioners. The following section will position it within the broad discipline of management science, explaining how it emerged from the early twentieth century tradition of 'scientific management' that subsequently evolved in Western countries. As it will be demonstrated, the Polish praxiological tradition remained faithful to the origins of operations management, and if re-discovered, it could enrich the present business practices. Regrettably, the theoretical propositions by Kotarbiński and his followers felt into oblivion in Poland in the 1980s and 1990s, when strives for economic modernisation led to the accelerated adoption of Western management concepts and intentional rejection of the local heritage of organisational theory, erroneously considered by many as linked to a fundamentally different economic system (see also: Kostera, 1995).

The Polish praxiology was successful in paralleling the Western management discourse that started with the works of Frederick W. Taylor, Frank and Lillian Moller Gilbreths and Henry Gantt, as well as a Polish researcher Karol Adamiecki, and was focused on improving work processes and organisational operations. As Peter Drucker suggested, the heritage of the so-called scientific management consisted in 'making work productive' by means of analysis of operations and use of specific tools that help combine these operations into production processes, quantity and quality, so that their directions could subsequently be controlled (Drucker, 1985, p. 199). This approach is associated with the names of Taylorism (as a tribute to Taylor) and Fordism (thanks to Henry Ford's introduction of mass production as a novel way of optimising repetitive manufacturing tasks). The famous assumption, attributed to Taylor, was the existence of 'one best way' of executing each activity or process, with management researchers charged with using scientific methods to identify these optimal means. Even though management scientists, inspired by Bertalanffy's general systems theory, accepted later the principle of equifinality (stating that any desired end state of a system can be attained by multiple alternative means), Polish praxiologists stayed within the confines of the analytical tradition of scientific management, centred around individual activities, processes, and operations that could benefit from efficiency improvements.

In the Anglo-Saxon literature, strives for improvement of individual processes or activities became associated with the quantitatively-oriented Operations Research, suitable for well-defined, structured problems that could be represented through mathematical models (Herrmann and Magee, 1953; Thomas, 2012), or with the game theory, focused on finding optimal solutions to interactions between two or more players (Dixit and Nalebuff, 1993). The heritage of scientific management was associated with a 'mechanistic organisation' (Morgan, 1986, p. 22), resembling a machine, with both Taylorism and

Fordism attracting significant criticism. Morgan drew a parallel between the mechanisation of manufacturing companies and the wide-spread occurrence of bureaucratic organisations, with both tendencies expected to ensure the speed, clarity, regularity, reliability, precision, and efficiency (Morgan, 1986, p. 24–25). Since empirical experiences with such organisations yielded disappointing results, the tradition faced fierce criticism in Western countries, even though it had been actively pursued both in Eastern Europe and Japan. Critics pointed among others to the importance of people and informal structures in organisations (Scott1986, p. 53–54), as well as to the complexity of organisational goals, making the optimisation of operations particularly difficult (Scott, 1986, p. 52).

In reaction to this criticism, management scholars started differentiating types of production processes (Drucker, 1985, p. 213) and looking on an organisation as a whole rather than through the lens of individual activities, borrowing from sociological perspectives including the followers of Max Weber (see e.g. sociological contributions presented in the initial issue of the first scientific journal dedicated to management science: *Administrative Science Quarterly*—Parsons, 1956), inspired also by more practice-oriented propositions of Peter Drucker from his books published in the late 1940s and 1950s. Researchers considered hierarchically decomposed objectives of companies (Drucker, 1985), interpreting them as outcomes of negotiations between organisational participants and decisions based on limited information (Ansoff, 1965, p. 35), or explored the relations between structures, operations and strategies (Chandler, 1972, p. 13).

Edith Penrose's theory of the firm contributed to further shifts in the focus of management scholars by highlighting the importance of the firm 'as a collection of productive resources' (Penrose, 1959/1995, p. 24) instead of individual, optimizing decisions (Penrose, 1959/1995, p. 13–14). Joan Woodward (1965) set new theoretical directions by focusing on organisational variables such as structure, type of technology or production system, and looking for cross-organisational regularities. This approach contributed to the development of the so-called contingency theory in management science, which was looking for the optimal designs and courses of actions depending (contingent) on specific external and internal conditions to ensure the best fit between an organisation and its environment (Morgan, 1986, p. 60). It further shifted the research interests away from the search for optimising principles, refuting Taylor's strives for 'one best way'. The ontological foundations of the contingency theory might thus be interpreted as an underlying, implicit assumption that no universal rules could be identified with respect to organisations and the process of organising. This methodological approach yielded numerous middle-range principles, constructed in the following way: "If a condition A in the organisation or its environment occurs, then B is likely to maximize the organisational effectiveness or efficiency". With the passage of time and the accumulation of the body of research, the description of the condition B became increasingly complex and less typical for an actual organisation, with subsequent researchers identifying further limitations of the previously formulated principles.

The contributions of the contingency theory were criticised for failed attempts to describe the social realm by means of a vast collection of scientific principles, which turned out to be excessively complicated in their applications, not always empirically verified (Scott, 1986, p. 61), often very distant from the actual organisational practices and thus not applicable in a given case. Some critics were even resorting to a derogatory term 'cow sociology', suggesting that management scholars following the contingency approach emulate agricultural researchers. They strive for increases in the milk production outputs, while supporters of the contingency theory apply similar principles to organisations and their participants (Scott, 1986, pp. 60–61). Nevertheless, the approach inspired numerous practitioners, such as, for example, the bestselling book *The Mind of the Strategic* by McKinsey's Japanese partner Kennichi Ohmae (1982) proposed to transform strategic thinking into a series of questions, with specific courses of actions recommended after a long list of yes-no questions has been answered and the organisational problems have been narrowed down so that the application of abstract principles is possible (Ohmae, 1982, pp. 18–25).

Breaking away with the contingency theory paradigm, Tom Peters and Robert Waterman (1984) offered an alternative approach to management research by focusing on a subset of successful companies (purposefully selected sample of individual companies-case studies) and looking for their 'best practices' that could offer useful lessons learned for other organisations. They once again tried to identify relatively simple but universal rules, albeit on a corporate-wide, strategic level, such as e.g. closeness to customers, importance of autonomy and entrepreneurship, productivity through people or need to focus on an organisation's most successful activities while disregarding others ('stick to the knitting'). This tendency to simplify the complex, strategic matters and offer straightforward recommendations for managers was adopted by numerous other management scholars. For example, Michael E. Porter's book, discussing techniques for achieving and maintaining competitive advantages (Porter, 1985) introduced a set of analytical tools and highly abstract propositions, which interestingly were not supported by any empirical evidence provided or cited in the book. In a similar manner, Oliver E. Williamson formulated his version of transaction cost economics as a new research paradigm, focused on a transaction as the unit of analysis (Williamson, 1998, p. 41) and resorting to abstract concepts such as asset specificity (Williamson, 1998, p. 95) or governance structures linked to 'the efficient boundaries problem' (Williamson, 1998, p. 97).

The enthusiasm for universal and simple rules that could be applied to organisational strategies and operations was finally curbed by scholars adopting the ontological and epistemological assumptions of the so-called interpretative paradigm (also referred to as: interpretativism, organisational symbolism, or organisational ethnography), who highlighted the diversity of organisational forms, the importance of personal experiences, emotions, attitudes and values, as well as the inability to formulate physics-like laws or principles in the highly unforeseeable social world (Burrell and Morgan, 1979, pp. 260–275; Gabriel, Fineman, and Sims, 2000, pp. 5–6).

The above-described evolution of management theory in the twentieth century directed the Western scholars towards research avenues that were divergent from Kotarbiński's interests, and undermined the attempts to identify relatively simple and universally valid optimisation principles. Interestingly, the discipline of management encompassed also contributions of practitioners, whose propositions remained closer to the praxiologist's contribution, as it will be described in the following section of the paper.

Western Management Practice Looking for Process Improvement Techniques

Even though the dominant discourse in management science diverged from the initial research foci, methods and propositions formulated by the precursors of scientific management, after several decades, approaches similar to Kotarbiński's model started attracting attention of business practitioners. The scientific management was abandoned by theorists in the US and Europe, but it remained relevant and popular in Japan. The Japanese approaches to operations management supplemented Taylor's perspective by the need to ensure flexibility in manufacturing systems (Schonberger, 1982, p. 133), appreciating the importance of the 'human factor' (with employees perceived rather as a community than independent individuals), relying on team work and continuous improvement, and thus going beyond simple process optimisation (Womack, Jones, and Roos, 1991). This transformed, re-born and improved version of Taylorism returned to Western countries as part of the 'work simplification' tradition, incorporating the elements of Taylorism, Fordism and the Japanese quality control movement. It nowadays remains an important perspective in operations management, accompanied by the previously-described business management and the approaches relying on the use of IT systems to support processes (Harmon, 2010, p. 38). The contribution of Japanese process improvement practitioners revealed an important trade-off between cost and quality (Li and Rajagopalan, 1998), with the traditional Taylorism focused on optimising costs (alongside time and work efforts), and its Japanese derivative putting more value in predictability, compliance, and meeting customer expectations.

In their strides for improvements, organisations could benefit from process discontinuities, induced by breakthrough technologies that could radically increase the organisational efficiency (Utterback, 1994, p. 201). In the 1990s, such a disruptive role was associated in particular with the diffusion of

Information Technology (Hammer and Champy, 1993, p. 83), including centralised databases, client-server environments and workflow systems allocating tasks to individual workers based on predefined process templates. Instead of simple adjustments of existing processes, Michael Hammer and James Champy promised 'a business revolution', as stated by the subtitle of their bestselling book (Hammer and Champy, 1993). They advocated 'starting over' (Hammer and Champy, 1993, p. 31) or 'fundamental rethinking and radical redesign of business processes' (Hammer and Champy, 1993, p. 32), dubbed 'business process re-engineering' (BPR). Consequences of the 'BPR revolutions' turned out detrimental for many implementing organisations (see e.g. Rigby, 2001, pp. 156–157), and the management discourse leaned towards less radical, more evolutionary approaches to process management. Advocates of the evolutionary 'business process improvement' (BPI) were criticising the radicalness of BPR. Thomas H. Davenport offered an alternative view on organisational changes that could be understood as process innovations (Davenport, 1993, p. 171), suggesting that business improvement could involve both radical innovations and incremental improvements, implemented either as one-time modifications or as continuous cycles of changes (Davenport, 1993, p. 24). Despite the popularity of process management methodologies, most of them are focused on analysis and monitoring of processes but do not offer ready-to-use tools or principles that would be directly applicable to close the identified performance gap (Siha and Saad, 2008). The business process improvement supporters proposed a framework called ESIA, an acronym of the terms: *eliminate, simplify, integrate and automate* (Peppard and Rowland, 1995, p. 181–193). ESIA allows one to analyse individual business processes and interactions between them, identifying the potential for specific improvements. Interestingly, this approach is similar to Kotarbiński's economisation measures, described in this paper, but more simplistic, disregarding some of the potentially useful improvement techniques that had been identified by Kotarbiński.

Another parallel could be drawn between Kotarbiński's model and an analytical framework of cost drivers, proposed by Michael E. Porter. While presenting the model of value chain, Porter suggested that the value chain-based analysis of costs of corporate operations could take into account cost drivers that 'determine the cost behaviour of value activities' (Porter, 1985, p. 70). In order to optimize the operations and related costs, managers should better understand the underlying logic of their operational model, captured by the list of specific cost drivers identified by Porter (1985, pp. 70–83), including: economies of scale, learning, patterns of capacity utilisation, linkages, interrelationships, integration, timing, discretionary policies, location and institutional factors. The presence and extent of applicability of a given cost driver will directly influence the operations and their costs, thus offering improvement opportunities. Some cost drivers might contradict others or reduce their beneficial impacts, so the awareness and exploitation of cost drivers helps establish cost advantages and optimize corporate operations. As in Kotarbiński's typology, Porter recommends specific courses of actions to help organisations derive economic benefits from individual, identified cost drivers. In its quest for improving organisational operations, Peter Senge's management bestseller *The Fifth Discipline* (Senge, 1990) resurrected and repurposed systems dynamics, an approach previously used as a quantitative way of modelling comprehensive, physical or social systems. Senge's book offered a new life to systems dynamics turning it into a way of understanding the complexity of organisations and abandoning the quantitative modelling used by his predecessors. According to Senge, by following traditional improvement pathways, we are prone to becoming 'prisoners of our own *thinking*' (Senge, 1990, p. 27). Insights into organisational problems should be of a more systemic nature, taking into account the intricate and not easy-to-see-through networks of relations affecting organisations. Senge proposed 'system archetypes' (Senge, 1990, p. 378–390), recurring patterns of dependencies and feedback loops present in multiple spheres of life, including in organisations. These generic patterns are usually overlooked as organisational participants do not know how to identify and analyse them. Senge's use of system archetypes is relatively close to the previously described approach of Kotarbiński, even though both have different points of departure. Senge posits that by carefully analysing organisational interdependencies, business practitioners could uncover hidden relationship patterns, consisting of multiple positive or negative feedback loops, which—once identified and named—might be addressed by specific managerial activities, as specific recommendations are formulated for each identifiable system archetype. At the same time, Senge's perspective paved way for researchers by emphasizing the need to identify complex and sometimes counter-intuitive interdependencies in management science.

Another perspective complementary to Kotarbiński's model has also been developed in the fields of product design and technology management. Beliefs in the optimisation potential of product development projects contributed to the creation of value engineering, an approach introduced by the US company General Electric in the 1940s. Value engineering was used to improve end product performance through better understanding of relationships between components and their redesign (Peppard and Rowland, 1995, p. 18). In the same historical period, but separated from the achievements of American business enterprises, the Soviet researcher Genrich Altshuller started his quest for a set of rules that would optimise the development of new technical products and generate inventions in response to identified technical problems. The quest yielded positive outcomes in the following years, resulting in the establishment of the inventive algorithm ARIZ and the theory of inventions called TRIZ. Altshuller's approach relied on a systematic search for new solutions to a given technical contradiction, that was considered superior to the traditional use of trial-and-error (Altszuller, 1972, pp. 17–19). Some of the 'inventive principles' identified by Altshuller rules and algorithms stimulating the emergence of inventions—resembled Kotarbiński's proposals (e.g. separation, unification, counter-balancing or pre-arranging), but they were primarily applicable to technical problems not business processes (Altszuller, 1972; Mann, 2007, pp. 215–230). Nevertheless, after the recent re-discovery of TRIZ in Western countries, its principles have also been successfully used to support the re-design of business operations (Harmon, 2010, pp. 70–71).

Discussion

Kotarbiński's list of economisation measures answers to the demands of management practitioners, who have been looking for practical process improvement techniques. The framework is significantly more sophisticated than the ESIA model of business process improvement, and offers more comprehensive insights into the available optimisation potential. It parallels the other above-described tools and techniques, including Porter's cost drivers, Senge's system archetypes and TRIZ' inventive principles, and deserves a place among popular and practically useful organisational frameworks.

The use of Kotarbiński's typology might encounter limitations, related to the highly abstract nature of the principles. A trade-off exists between the specificity (or situational embeddedness) and the generalisation potential, with uncertain applicability of the principles in some practical situations. Kotarbiński himself declared that he was looking for "as broad as possible technical generalisations" (Kotarbiński, 1958, p. 7) intended to improve human actions, in line with the praxiological interests in universal regularities that impact various spheres of human lives as well as organisational operations. The present paper could open up new avenues for research, as the typology of economisation measures might be combined with contributions of other, above-listed models, and subjected to comprehensive empirical verification in order to increase the specificity of findings, which seem particularly relevant for business organisations and corporate processes.

The paper offered an overview of a contribution of the Polish praxiologist, which was relatively little known at the international level but could easily be applied in the field of business process management. It demonstrated the usefulness of the Polish praxiological research from the mid-20th century and might encourage further literature studies to assess the originality and relevance of other frameworks and principles described by Tadeusz Kotarbiński. The diffusion of management ideas and concepts could be compared to the spread of viruses, including the phenomenon of cycling, when certain virus strains (ideas) remain hibernated for a number of years but resurface again to inspire the practitioners (Klincewicz, 2006, p. 189). At the same time, these ideas might be subjected to 'antigenic drifts', with small but continuous changes in the 'genetic material', which reinforce even minor misrepresentations in the diffusion process (Klincewicz, 2006, p. 191) so that new applications could be developed and research findings could be combined with the existing body of knowledge.

References

Altszuller, H., 1969/1972, *Algorytm wynalazku* [*Algorithm of Invention*], Wiedza Powszechna, Warszawa.

Ansoff, I. H., 1965, *Corporate Strategy: Business Policy for Growth and eEpansion*, McGraw Hill Book Company, New York.

Argyris, Ch., 1977, 'Double Loop Learning in Organizations', *Harvard Business Review*, 55(5), pp. 115–125.

Bourdeau, L., 1882/2000, 'Praxiology as the Science of Functions', in: Alexandre, Victor and Gasparski, Wojciech W. (eds.) *The Roots of Praxiology: French Action Theory from Bourdeau and Espinas to Present Days, Praxiology: The International Annual of Practical Philosophy and Methodology*, Volume 7. New Brunswick, NJ—London, Transaction Publishers, pp. 21–43.

Burrell, G. and Morgan, G., 1979, *Sociological Paradigms and Organizational Analysis: Elements of the Sociology of Corporate Life*, London, Heinemann Educational Books.

Chandler, A. D., Jr. 1972, *Strategy and Structure: Chapters in the History of the American Industrial Enterprise*, Cambridge, MA—London, The MIT Press.

Davenport, T. H., 1993, *Process Innovation: Reengineering Work through Information Technology*, Boston, MA, Harvard Business School Press.

Dixit, A. K. and Nalebuff, B. J., 1993, *Thinking Strategically: The Competitive Edge in Business, Politics, and Everyday Life*, New York—London, W. W. Norton & Company.

Drucker, P., 1985, *Management: Tasks, Responsibilities, Practices*. New York—Cambridge, Harper Colophon Books.

Espinas, V. A., 1897/2000, *The Origins of Technology* (excerpts), in: Alexandre, Victor and Gasparski, Wojciech W. (eds.) *The Roots of Praxiology: French Action Theory from Bourdeau and Espinas to Present Days, Praxiology: The International Annual of Practical Philosophy and Methodology*, Volume 7. New Brunswick, NJ—London, Transaction Publishers, p. 45–91.

Gabriel, Y., Fineman, S. and Sims, D., 2000, *Organizing & Organizations: An Introduction*, 2nd ed., London—Thousand Oaks—New Delhi, Sage Publications

Hammer, M. and Champy, J., 1993, *Reengineering Corporation: A Manifesto for Business Revolution*, New York, Harper Business.

Harmon, P., 2010, 'The Scope and Evolution of Business Process Management', In: vom Brocke, Jam and Rosemann, Michael (eds.), *Handbook on Business Process Management*. Springer Verlag, Berlin Heidelberg, p. 37–81.

Herrmann, C. C. and Magee, J. F., 1953, '"Operations Research" for Management', *Harvard Business Review*, 31(4), pp. 100–112.

Klincewicz, K., 2006, *Management Fashions: Turning Best-Selling Ideas into Objects and Institutions*. New Brunswick, NJ—London: Transaction Publishers.

Kostera, M., 1995, 'The Modern Crusade: Missionaries of Management Come to Eastern Europe'. *Management Learning*, 26(3), pp. 331–352.

Kotarbiński, T., 1958, *Traktat o dobrej robocie* [*Treatise on Good Work*], Wrocław-Warszawa, Zakład Narodowy im. Ossolińskich.

Kotarbiński, T., 1961/1999, *Postulates for Economic Modes of Action*, Estratto Rivista Methodos, Milan, 13(51–52), pp. 175–187—translated into Polish as: *Zalecenia ekonomicznych sposobów działania*, [in:] Kotarbiński, Tadeusz. *Dzieła wszystkie. Prakseologia, część I*. Wrocław-Warszawa-Kraków, Zakład Narodowy im. Ossolińskich, Wydawnictwo Polskiej Akademii Nauk, pp. 340–351.

Li, G. and Rajagopalan, S., 1998, 'Process Improvement, Quality, and Learning Effects', *Management Science*, 44(11), pp. 1517–1532.

Mann, D., 2007, *Hands on Systematic Innovation*, 2nd ed., Clevedon, IFR Press.

Morgan, G., 1986, *Images of Organization*, Newbury Park-London-New Delhi, Sage Publications.

Ohmae, K., 1982, *The Mind of the Strategist: Business Planning for Competitive Advantage*, New York, Penguin Group.

Parsons, T., 1956, 'Suggestions for a Sociological Approach to the Theory of Organizations—I'. *Administrative Science Quarterly*, 1(1), pp. 63–85.

Penrose, E., 1959/1995, *The Theory of the Growth of the Firm*, Oxford-New York, Oxford University Press.

Peppard, J. and Rowland, P., 1995, *The Essence of Business Process Re-Engineering*, New York-London, Prentice Hall.

Peters, T. J., Waterman, R. H., 1984, *In Search of Excellence: Lessons from America's Best-Run Companies*, New York, Warner Books.

Porter, M. E., 1985, *Competitive Advantage: Creating and Sustaining Superior Performance*, New York, The Free Press.

Rigby, D., 2001, 'Management Tools and Techniques: A Survey', *California Management Review*, 43(2), pp. 139–160.

Schonberger, R. J., 1982, *Japanese Manufacturing Techniques: Nine Hidden Lessons in Simplicity*, New York, The Free Press.

Scott, W. R., 1986, *Organizations and Organizing: Rational, Natural, and Open Systems Perspectives*, 2nd ed., Englewood Cliffs, NJ: Prentice-Hall.

Senge, P. M., 1990, *The Fifth Discipline: The Art & Practice of the Learning Organisation*, New York-London, Currency Doubleday.

Siha, S. M. and Saad, G. H., 2008, 'Business Process Improvement: Empirical Assessment and Extensions', *Business Process Management Journal*, 14(6), pp. 778–802.

Thomas, W., 2012, Operations research vis-a-vis management at Arthur D. Little and the Massachusetts Institute of Technology in the 1950s, Business History Review, 86, pp. 99–122.

Utterback, J. M., 1994, *Mastering the Dynamics of Innovation: How Companies Can Seize Opportunities in the Face of Technological Change*. Boston, MA: Harvard Business School Press.

Williamson, O. E., 1998, *The Economic Institutions of Capitalism*, New York, The Free Press.

Womack, J. P., Jones, D. T., Roos, D., 1991, *The Machine that Changed the World. The Story of Lean Production*, New York, Harper Perennial.

Woodward, J., 1965, *Industrial Organization*: Theory and Practice, London, Oxford University Press.

Chapter 9

Hatred—A Challenge to Contemporary Collective Identity

Olli Loukola

> God, grant me the serenity to accept the things I cannot change, the courage to change the things I can, and the wisdom to know the difference.
>
> —Serenity Prayer, Reinhold Niebuhr (1892–1971)

Human identity is the kind of notion which contains both a promise and a menace. When an identity is found, discovered, or created (depending on how one conceptualizes 'identity'), it gives a person or a group of persons self-confidence about who or what they really are, where their defining roots lie, what sorts of ties and commitments this entails, and in what aspects is one different or similar to others. These are surely some of the central and most important definitions of human life. But herein also lies the menace: Is the identity real and genuine? Am I—are we—really like this? How am I or we to treat others, and, more importantly, do I/we-really want to be like this? It is for these reasons why the often-quoted words of Reinhold Niebuhr—given above—seems apt as a starting point. Most importantly, how we see each other in terms of our identities determines how we treat others.

Identities are peculiar and complicated mixtures of high hopes and cruel facts of life, of the surrounding world and our place in it. They are complicated also in the sense that the facts of life never fully or conclusively determine the character of the emerging identity.[1] Even if the circumstances where two people are born and raised were exactly the same in every relevant respect, these people will end up with completely different identities. In other words, in the creation, discovery, or emergence of identity, it is never really clear what are the undisputed facts of the world, and what the identity turns out to be, when interpreted through the framework of our hopes. These first items are referred to by literature as 'ascriptive facts', as something that the individual has not consciously chosen or selected, like one's hair color, ethnicity, or sexual preference. As a result, the central issue with identity is, as in the Serenity Prayer, that it is very difficult to say which are the things one can and one cannot change. All one can hope for is that one would have the wisdom to know the difference in the quest for genuine identity.

The central juxtaposition within the notion concerns then the extent identity seen as having emerged or been created. It is on the basis of this distinction that I will present three notions of identity. According to the first, identity is inextricably created or determined by circumstances, things such as history, heredity, genes, or upbringing. A pioneer of this thought was probably Baron de Montesquieu, who believed that natural surroundings have a permanent effect on human nature.[2] Today, the foremost theorists of this *archaic* or *traditional identity* are communitarian thinkers. According to the alternative view, identity is essentially a created one. The role of the individual volition is central, and the individual can create herself to be what she wants to be by freely choosing how she responds to the world surrounding her. The basic conviction of this *postmodernist identity* is that the circumstances of the world dictate or determine nothing: We are free to choose what and who we are; but most importantly, there is no permanent or fixed identity, but many selves and identities, which are not fixed but are in a continuous process of being redefined.

The middle ground here is covered by the *liberal identity*, which emphasizes the centrality of individual choice and voluntary choosing of memberships and commitments. It has, however, no clear stance towards the role of circumstances in identity, and in this respect it is clearly lacking.

The Archaic Notion of Identity

My starting assumption is that there is no real or genuine identity in the sense that it would be determined by facts of the world, such as the true nature or character of the human being or her group. This also applies to individual identity; there are no objective facts which would conclusively determine 'genuine' or 'real'. But neither, I claim here, is the individual fully free to plan or choose the identity that pleases her most: We are to a large extent the product of our environment, and this comprises limits to what our identity is and can be. With this stance, I am placing myself between the post-modernist, free-floating, choosing individual and the traditional individual, the creature of society, but I am also distancing myself from the liberal conception.

I will start my analysis from the traditional notion of identity. In real life, any attempt to determine and define what human identity is—be it individual or collective identity—is done in a social setting, under the influence of and in interaction with other people, who are also involved in a similar process of identity discovery, formation, and refinement. These inescapable social circumstances are also clearly present in the etymology of the concept: 'Identity' derives from post-classical Latin, meaning 'sameness', and as such it is operative only dialectically, i.e. in connection with its opposite, 'otherness'. Because of this dialectic, otherness is primary to sameness in the making of identity. When talking of collective identities, self-reference or self-image, 'oneness' and 'we-ness' is based on some 'origin' or basis, which is common to all its members. It has been thought to be, for instance, a common competence or task: the same language, similar work, a particular education, a specific insight, or possession of certain values. The notion addresses the 'we-ness' of a group, stressing the similarities or shared attributes of its members. People are seen as part and parcel of specific other people in a network of relationships, expectations, requirements, and affections, but also of a particular range and ordering of values,[3] determined conclusively by social and historical circumstances.

Traditionally these shared attributes are characterized as 'natural' or 'essential', as permanent features of the collective in question. They are thought to be persistently associated with the physiological traits, psychological predispositions, regional features, history, or the like of the collective. When the romantic seekers of the national identity of Finns at the end of the nineteenth century travelled through the countryside observing peasants and their habits, collecting poems, songs, and ancestral stories, it was such traits they were looking for: "collective's members were believed to internalize these qualities, suggesting a unified, singular social experience, a single canvas against which social actors constructed a sense of self".[4] This is the traditional or archaic notion of identity, which places great emphasis on tradition, moral authority, social order, hierarchy, and symbolic centres of power.[5]

These are essentialist and naturalist attributes, which have since been contested by a number of social theoretic approaches; literature mentions structuralist, postmodernist, primordialist, and relativist approaches, among others.[6] But this is not the direction I am heading to here. Instead, I will try to treat the notion of identity on its own terms, taking my cue from the recent work of Leonidas Donskis and in particular from his challenge of the relationship between identity and hatred.

From Identity to Hatred

The opening words of Donskis's excellent book *Forms of Hatred, The Troubled Imagination in Modern Philosophy and Literature* are shattering: "Odi ergo sum. I hate therefore I am. The nineteenth and twentieth centuries may well be described as the era of organized collective hatred".[7] Donskis's book analyses the history of ideas of hatred over the past two centuries, and links hatred in gripping way to areas with which it is not usually associated:

> [Hatred] proliferates its forms in the modern troubled imagination assuming such sophisticated forms of interpretation of the human world and of self-comprehension as the philosophies of history and culture, the comparative study of civilizations, literary scholarship, and fiction. Hatred of the modern world is manifest in myriad abuses of religion, spirituality, scholarship, and humanity.

The nineteenth and twentieth centuries—not to mention our own century—seem indeed to have been been eras of organised collective hatred, but at the same time they have also been centuries during which the liberal democratic societies have triumphed. And it seems that increasingly often these societies, boasting of open-mindedness and tolerance, impartial, and egalitarian institutions, the rights of individuals over groups, nevertheless allow identities, which are racist, sexist, or degrading, and involve bigotry, inequality, and oppression. This point is emphasized by Donskis: "It is assumed that hatred can be successfully generated only in isolation or in what we call 'closed societies'—which is true as far as religious and modern secular idiocracies are concerned—but it can flourish in a liberal democracy as well."[8]

Donskis raises an extremely important challenge to liberalism and modernity. He describes a situation where enlightened and educated people purposefully, on their own initiative, categorize others on bases that are often unfair and degrading. Such behaviour is further justified by what and who the others are; and this treatment may even be seen to be a duty or an obligation of the perpetrators. Such attitudes are seen as essential components of their own collective identity, and thus hating others becomes the basis on which their collective identity exists and is justified with.

From the perspective of our recent history and theorizing, Donskis's challenge hits hardest the already fraught battleground of liberal and traditional notions of identity: the ideal treatment of individuals versus established and traditional practices and assemblages. Donskis challenges what he conceives to be the empty normative ideals of liberalism and the not-so-admirable reality of traditionalism; in other words, our high hopes of individual moral responsibility which clash with the brute reality of the traditions of our world. So the question is, who are the dreamlike idealists here, the liberals with their trust in individual virtues or the archaists with their trust in stagnant social virtues? Which items in our human nature and the circumstances of the world are we able to change and which are we not?

Community-spirited thinkers have always tended to romanticize collective identity, seeing it somehow as more 'authentic',[9] and linking it to groups of people who are thought to be reliable, trustworthy and dependable. But as human history so clearly witnesses, it may just as well be the contrary. Often collective trustworthiness, reliability and safety are achieved at the high price of isolation, with prejudice and intolerance following in its wake. Collective identities often become narrow, dehumanizing and dangerous. This has the potential roots for a culture of hatred, as Donskis describes it:

> Ultimately, hatred implies that human individuality has no value, since good and evil are once and for all attached to some groups. It creates a kind of point-of-no-return situation: once we cross the line separating 'us' from 'them' or once we happen to belong to a group target, we cannot escape hatred. Neither our personality nor our individual history matters. Our moral choices, dreams and passions, remembrances and little secrets, confessions and discoveries, victories and failures—the whole content of

> our personality—can be instantly reduced to a single code word which designates our group or background. And that single word can be a warrant for hatred.[10]

We have always been acutely aware of the dangers of narrow collectivism in Western history; that has been a central constituent in the triumph of liberal ideology. But Donskis's challenge is not aimed exclusively at either liberalism or traditionalism. He claims that due to our archaic past *and* the more recent liberal aspirations, contemporary collective identities are increasingly often built on the foundation of hating others. And this suggests that liberal and traditional notions of identity are much closer to each other than we usually realize, and the canons would like.

Now why and how would liberal individuals, free, equal, and rational people, allow their collective identity to be built on such a basis? In more general terms the challenge is, whether it is possible for the modern individualism to create identities which are strong enough to be genuine and not be built on hatred. Donskis believes that individualism is too weak and problematic to serve as a basis for societal existence. Liberal-democratic societies run into trouble because they ignore the fact that societies are fundamentally holistic or hierarchic, that is, archaic, by nature. As a result, the development from traditional to liberal identity makes our present Western condition exceptionally vulnerable and fragile. It 'devalues old certainties', forces people into a state of rootlessness and uncertainty, and has created 'a ready market' for any movement, religious or otherwise, 'to provide or to renew certainty'.[11]

But how is such a development possible and is it an inevitable process? In order to answer these questions, we need to analyse more carefully the nature of liberal identity.

Identities as Ideologies

Personal identity is based on the self-image of the individual. Collective identity is similarly based on the self-image of the members of a collective. They are both built on observations and reflections of the world around us, constant comparing of oneself with others, and our society. During this process we evaluate, interpret and try to understand what we see, feel and experience and try to understand, how all that fits our conceptual frameworks and world visions. It is not that we first observe and investigate what the facts of this situation are, and then only deliberately and freely choose how we are to live with them. Quite the contrary, we perceive the world not only through our beliefs and hopes, but also through the habits and customs we have learned throughout our lives with other people, that is, our traditions.

This is what I meant in the beginning of this essay that our identities—be they personal or collective—are curious mixtures of factual circumstances and high hopes; what we are and what we wish to be, and how we are to treat others. They are ideologies[12] or worldviews, mixtures of facts and ideals. They contain, firstly, an empirical-scientific explanation of what humankind is like; of the world we live in and the causal or empirical laws that determine our behaviour. Secondly, they include normative judgements of the very same things: what is good or bad in human nature, what actions or states of affairs are praiseworthy or blameworthy; what the worthwhile goals of human life are, and what good society is like and how we are to raise our children. The problem is that we have no simple way of distinguishing between the facts of the world from these moral judgements and goals we have.

This also lies at the heart of Donskis's challenge to liberal modernism: by believing that the world is the way liberal theory claims it should be, and by acting accordingly, we have also made the world a liberal one in practice. This is the way ideals, principles, and norms become facts and are transformed into actual reasons or constraints for action. And it is in this light we should evaluate Donskis' challenge: What is it in liberal practices that enable or permit hatred to become such a central force in the creation of liberal identity?

The Liberal Normative Ideal

Part of the success of liberalism as a political theory and ideology is that it avoids making substantial recommendations concerning the goals of man and society. This is the essence of liberal individualism: it aspires to leave important life choices to individual people, to enable them to pursue their goals and values freely, as long as they do not harm others. This is institutionalized through the doctrine of neutrality, that is, the idea that government shouldn't favour any particular ideals existing in a society.

We need to be careful here in what liberals actually assert and believe and what follows. The crucial point is that their theory of the individual and her identity is *normative*; it is a justificatory theory that underlines the worth of all individuals; that is, it gives them a normative status.[13] Liberal theory sets limits how individuals may or may not be treated, what they are at liberty or have rights to do, and what they may or may not do to others. The fact that in real life people behave differently and do treat others badly does not refute the theory. Quite the contrary, it simply proves that we have even more reason to demand for such behaviour, since clearly it is absent.

This liberal commitment to the fundamental moral equality of individuals is also a universal ideal: it applies to all human beings and can be shared by all. The object of liberal identification, our 'primary collective identity', is the human race. What liberalism in fact says is "be whatever you like to be, as long as you are all liberals". Paradoxically, however, such an identity becomes empty, a mere negative description of humans co-existing: it has very little to say about the actual positive contents of life or worthwhile human goals—of social relationships, virtues, and lifechoices. The common liberal identity seems indeed to be, as Donskis and a number of communitarian writers say, 'weak and vague'.

Since defining human goods and their contents is clearly such an important question, why doesn't liberalism say anything about them? The reason is simply that we have never really agreed on what the universal human good is, despite having debated it since Socrates. Part of the liberal reluctance to define human good arises from these failures, and from the subsequent conclusion, that there are only particular goods and separate goods, and the individual is the best judge on which ones to pursue.

New Forms of Identity

Today, a new breed of diverse movements and groups have emerged. Gay movements, nationalistic groups, environmentalists, religious factions, even cyberspace assemblages have in their obstinate goal-settings and actual operation manifest disregard to traditional communities and roles, and historically- and culturally-fixed identities. All this takes place very much in a post-modernist spirit, as described earlier. This has brought along new sets of concepts and approaches, questions and problems anchored in identity and which are referred to as 'identity politics':[14]

> [I]dentity politics and new social movements suggest a special form of agency—a self-conscious "collective agency." Identities emerge and movements ensue because collectives consciously coordinate action; group members consciously develop offenses and defenses, consciously insulate, differentiate, and mark, cooperate and compete, persuade and coerce. In such a context, agency encompasses more than the control and transformation of one's social environment.[15]

Some of these new modes of existence, characteristics and purposes can surely be explained by the traditional as well as liberal notions of identity, but certainly not all. When traditional sociology studied identity through 'class', 'race' and 'sexuality', and liberal normativism emphasized free associating, these new movements are much more complicated mixtures and include a number of new elements. They are still, however, mixtures of hopes and facts, but with completely new conceptions of what the facts are and what we can hope for.

Noteworthy background for the new contemporary identities seems to be that during the past decades we have become convinced that very few things in our world count as hard facts for human beings. Global rapid changes around us—in technology, human physiology, and the environment—have had an immense effect: the old certainties of human life are truly gone. The traditional common goals and shared interests of society are increasingly often questioned, and there are increasing pressures to reflect and construct our identities, not only from the perspective of history, but from perspective of the future, that is, who we want to be. And at the same time the future seems more and more uncertain to us.

The Role of Science

We also need to acknowledge the role of culture and in particular that of science in the making of identities. I believe that Donskis is on the right track when he says that hatred assumes

> … sophisticated forms of interpretation of the human world and of self-comprehension as the philosophies of history and culture, the comparative study of civilizations, literary scholarship, and fiction. Hatred of the modern world is manifest in myriad abuses of religion, spirituality, scholarship, and humanity.

The crux of this sentence shows us, that the way our high hopes and the brute facts of real life clash, is to an extent guided by our culture and science. Hatred, although being a brute and tangible force, is also a much more elusive than we usually think, and is able to hide under very subtle guises.

The activities and functions of science and culture are many and versatile, and the need for a critical stance towards the thoughts, policies, and events of one's time is highlighted. It has long been debated, however, whether science may properly practice ideological and political criticism and advocatism. But politics and culture penetrate our lives as scholars deeply, and this is why we today have politically active feminist researchers and social theorists and advocators in environmental sciences, to name a few. These scholars believe that there is an inherent yet concealed political nature present in all enquiry, in which they are right: The facts of life, as science determines them, are not clear and undisputed in any straightforward manner. Yet when this emphasis is present in the cynicism of so many populist movements of today, it is twisted into a wholesale disregard to scientific inquiry and its results: Science cannot be trusted.

The notions of identity contain different and often contradictory methodological, ontological, epistemological, and normative or ideological presuppositions. They are tools purported to aid us to understand and conceptualize 'identity'. They encompass certain characteristics and features, which are conceptualized in scientific enquiry trying to reflect the real-life identities. Certain elements and characteristics are grouped together, depending on what is highlighted as the central element, whether it is the emphasis on community ties or individual choices or whether human nature is essentially seen as peaceful or aggressive, appropriative or altruistic, whether it can be chosen or is determined, etc. When some aspect of the notion is accentuated, a set of interlinked characteristics are correspondingly selected. Identity is not a clear-cut and forthright empirical phenomenon; it is that mixture of facts and ideals.

This is, of course, too large an issue to be dealt with here. What we can say, however, is that theoretical or conceptual work is of vital importance, and is bound to affect how we conceive of 'identity': What are these entities we refer to as collectives? Do they really exist, and, if they do, what follows from their existence? To what extent are they constructed or created as artifacts for political purposes? Is collective identity imposed on groups or does it evolve within the group? Why do people join in—to further their own interests or to promote contingent ideals? How far and how strongly do they motivate people and where does that force come from? And, finally, what consequences do collective identities have on individual rationality and morality? I believe that there is a dire need for philosophical analysis here and its central task lies in the clarification of questions such as these.

The disappearance of the unified, universal, or essentialist (traditional) conceptions of human nature has thoroughly changed the scene. Not only do we have a huge variety of actual identities on offer in our world, but we also have a huge variety of *concepts* of identities on offer.[16] It is considerations such as these that lead us to the postmodernist notion of identity.

The Postmodernist Idea

The postmodernist notion of identity[17] emphasizes, along with liberalism, the ideal of the choosing individual in the process of identity formation. The voluntary binding of oneself to a community is a way of developing one's individual identity, not subsuming oneself under some external authority or collective, which gives a readymade identity, as the traditionalist notion would want to interpret the situation. But instead of choosing your identity freely the liberal way, that is, in a sort of historical vacuum, with no earlier ties and commitments from one's culture and society, postmodernism passionately stresses that the choices individuals make necessarily take place under various pressures, coercive forces, and power structures. It is not an innocent procedure of voluntary choosing and fair exchange of interests, influences, or goals. As Karen Cerulo describes this process, it is "[i]n the spirit of Jean Baudrillard, Jacques Derrida, Michel Foucault, and Jean-Francois Lyotard, the postmodern-identity scholar deconstructs established identity categories and their accompanying rhetoric is an effort to explore the full range of 'being.' "[18] It is not only the active individual that is in the centre of postmodernist identity; it is the active individual struggling within the circumstances of power. Yet these circumstances do not directly dictate or determine what the identity will be like.

With this orientation, postmodernist theorists attack all classifications of identity which they consider essentialist, and examine categories such as women, gender, African-Americans, city experience, etc, concentrating on their internal variations. Through these they purport to reveal the "real, present day political and other reasons why essentialist identities continue to be invoked and often deeply felt."[19] Thus identity is fundamentally seen as 'dynamic', and 'place' (that is, to use my phrase here, 'circumstances of the world') as 'unbounded'. National makeup, ethnic origin, sexual preferences, or universal moral codes determine nothing; they are mere building blocks of identity, some usable in the circumstances one happens to be in, some not. But here we find yet another aspect of identity, which I believe to be vital in contemporary identities: struggle against those forces that we see as limiting our processes of identity building.

Conclusion

Contemporary identity building takes place in the cross-tide between the disappearance of traditions, the emptiness of the liberal vision, and the struggle against alienating and coercive forces. The fear of losing your traditions, the worries of the unpredictable future, combined with the distressing idea of having to choose your identity in a social-existential void, and under the mercy of hostile powers, create together the circumstances to which hatred may seem to be the appropriate response.

These are the three characteristics to which hatred is an easy solution: the empirical fact of the crumbling down of many of the traditional values and beliefs, the conviction that the individual is sovereign in choosing of her identity, and the existence of various powers restraining the identity building. In identities based on hatred, these considerations are often twisted into distorted reflections of the world: a crippling sticking to values, which are dear, and believed to be in danger; the belief that no justifications need be given in the choice of identity, and the need to get rid of those who are thought to restrain the realization of the chosen identity. Here the hopes are not high any more, and the facts of the world become truly cruel, they are those of survival. Further, these building blocks of identity as hatred are apparently often ignited by simple fears and simplistic explanations of the world.

As so often in philosophical enquiry, this essay raises more questions than it answers. Hatred has certainly been a central part of traditional identities, too. Was this hatred somehow different than the hatred present in the age of Enlightenment, Modernity, and our time? And if liberal identity is not strong enough to fend off hatred, is postmodernist identity able to do that, with its struggling against the forces of oppression? Experiences from the last few years show no sign of that; in fact, quite the contrary. Hatred seems increasingly often to be an integral part of contemporary identities.

Notes

1 The question of determinism naturally has relevance to the issues discussed here; also through the traditional question of responsibility and free will.

2 In *The Spirit of the Laws*, from 1748, Montesquieu explains how social systems and in particular laws should be adapted "to the people for whom they are framed… to the nature and principle of each government, … to the climate of each country, to the quality of its soil, to its situation and extent, to the principal occupation of the natives, whether husbandmen, huntsmen or shepherds: they should have

relation to the degree of liberty which the constitution will bear; to the religion of the inhabitants, to their inclinations, riches, numbers, commerce, manners, and customs". (1.3)

3 Loukola & Mustala (1997).
4 Ibid.
5 To use the words of Leonidas Donskis (2003).
6 See Cerulo (1997) and Snow (2001).
7 Donskis (2003, p. 1).
8 Op cit. 2.
9 The obverse of this notion is collective political identities built on propaganda, demagoguery, one-sided information or the like. 'Authentic' identity, in contrast, is something which is seen to evolve voluntarily, peacefully, and most importantly, 'naturally'. Needless to say, whatever these notions refer to would need to be thoroughly and carefully analysed.
10 Ibid.
11 Op. cit. 7.
12 This account of ideologies owes much to Gauthier (1977). See also Van der Burg (1997).
13 See for instance Carse (1994, pp. 187–188).
14 See for instance Kenny (2004).
15 Cerulo (1997, p. 389). See also Pettit (2001), and Loukola (2005).
16 As Snow puts it: "Although there is an extensive literature on collective identity, with considerable discussion regarding its conceptualization and sources, this literature has been relatively mute regarding variation in its form. The concept most often is invoked as if it is an invariant, uniform collective phenomenon. This is not the case, however, as collective identities can be multidimensional and be multi-layered within a specific locus, and they may also vary by type. The multi-dimensionality of collective identity is indicated by reference to its cognitive, emotional, and moral dimensions… The relative importance of each of these dimensions to the vitality and motivational force of a collective identity has not been elaborated, however. Presumably the presence of each of these dimensions yields a more robust and vital collective identity." Snow (2001, p. 11).
17 This emphasis in social theory is somewhat different from the political theory orientation I am mainly using in this essay. For instance, "constructivism" and "postmodernism" belong to the repertoire of social sciences, while "liberal individual" and "communitarianism" are concepts of political philosophy. The latter tradition has developed its central terms throughout centuries of thinking, while the methodology of social sciences has mainly concentrated on the problematic relationship between the use of empirical and humanistic research methods. This problematic relationship seems to be lurking behind most of the central concepts of social sciences. When we move to those 'interdisciplinary' concepts used in both paradigms such as 'identity', 'trust', 'environment' or 'sex/gender', the need for conceptual clarification becomes even more important.
18 Cerulo (1997, p. 391).
19 Calhoun (1994, p. 14).

References

Abadi-Nagy, Z., 2003, "Theorizing Collective Identity. Presentations of Virtual and Actual Collectives in Contemporary American Fiction." *Neohelicon*, 30.

Calhoun, C., 1994, "Social theory and the politics of identity." In C. Calhoun (ed.), *Social Theory and the Politics of Identity*. Cambridge: Blackwell.

Carse, A. L., 1994, "The Liberal Individual: A Metaphysical or a Moral Embarrassment", *Nous*, 28(2), 184–209.

Cerulo, K. A., 1997, "Identity Construction: New Issues, New Directions," *The Annual Review of Sociology*, 23, 385–409.

Donskis, L., 2003, *Forms of Hatred, The Troubled Imagination in Modern Philosophy and Literature*, Value Inquiry Book Series, vol. 145, The Netherlands: Rodopi.

Gauthier, D., 1997, "Social Contract as Ideology," *Philosophy and Public Affairs*, 6(2), 130–164.

Kelly, E., 2001, "Justice and Communitarian Identity Politics," *The Journal of Value Enquiry*, 35, 71–93.

Kenny, M., 2004, *The Politics of Identity: Liberal Political Theory and the Dilemmas of Difference*, Cambridge, UK, Malden, MA, Polity Press.

Kiss, E., 1998, "Saying we're sorry, Liberal Democracy and the Rhetoric of Collective identity," *Constellations*, 4(3), 387–398.

Kymlicka, W., 1989, "Liberal Individualism and Liberal Neutrality", *Ethics*, 99, 883–905.

Loukola, O. & Mustala, K., 1997, "Creating Identity: The Case of Europe." In *Memory, History and Critique: European Identity at the Millenium/Fifth Conference of the International Society for the Study of European Ideas*, MIT Press, (CD-rom).

Loukola, O., 2005, "The concept of collective identity and liberal theory," In O Loukola, ed. Changing, *Overlapping and Interacting Identities*, Acta Universitatis Latviensis, Ser, Political Science, Volume 680, Riga: University of Latvia.

Mason, A., 1999, "Political Community, Liberal-Nationalism, and the Ethics of Assimilation." *Ethics* 109, 261–286.

Pettit, P., 2001, *A Theory of Freedom: From the Psychology to the Politics of Agency*, Cambridge, UK: Oxford.

Polletta, F. & Jasper, J. M., 2001, "Collective Identity and Social Movements." *Annual Review of Sociology*, 27, 283–305.

Snow, D., 2001, "Collective Identity and Expressive Forms," Center for the Study of Democracy (University of California, Irvine), Paper 01/07, downloaded from http://repositories.cdlib.org/csd/01–07/ on 13.8.2004.

Trainor, B., 1998, "The Origin and End of Modernity," *Journal of Applied Philosophy*, 15(2), 133–144.

Van der Burg, W., 1997, "The Importance of Ideals." *The Journal of Value Inquiry* 31, 23–37.

Walzer, M., 1990, "The Communitarian Critique of Liberalism," *Political Theory*, 18(1), 6–23.

Chapter 10

Kotarbiński's Praxiology and the Analytic Action Theory

Piotr Tomasz Makowski

It is probably not a big exaggeration to say that contemporary philosophy of action (or: action theory), especially the one from the analytic tradition, has been shaped by the work of G. E. M. Anscombe and Donald Davidson. So, if we abstract from the Aristotelian, Humean, or Kantian roots and inspirations, it is rather plain that action theory does not have a long tradition. Nevertheless, I believe that it would be unjust oversimplification to say that Anscombe and Davidson were the only 'founding parents' of action theory. Among those who contributed to its development in no less degree is Tadeusz Kotarbiński. This is a bold claim. The name of this Polish philosopher—one of the most prominent figures from the Lvov-Warsaw School—is almost completely absent in the mainstream action theory.

My goals in this essay are two. Firstly, I would like to show the reasons why Kotarbiński's so-called praxiology is a philosophy of action which should be considered as no less important for the tradition of analytic action theory and for contemporary action-theoretical debates as the classics. Secondly, I shall try to explain why Kotarbiński's action theory—despite its incontestable philosophical value—has remained almost unnoticed in the mainstream for over half a century.[1]

In fact, the name of Kotarbiński does not exist in publications from the area of action theory. Thus, to fully reach the above two goals one would need to embark for a detailed investigation. I have proposed such investigations in Makowski (2017); here I shall try to approach this problem again in a more synthetic and summative way—with the hope for the elucidation of the most salient issues.

The structure of this essay is as follows. I start with a brief description of what praxiology is. Second, on the basis of selected examples, I try to show its most typical and attractive—from the perspective of classic and contemporary action theory—aspects and features. Third, I shortly sketch my answer to the question why Kotarbiński's praxiology in its original form has had to meet serious difficulties when it comes to its reception and interpretation. I end the essay claiming that the issue behind these difficulties not only veiled the classic character of praxiology and its contemporary attractiveness, but it also is responsible for its original shape as the Polish analytic action theory.

What Is Kotarbiński's Praxiology?

The term 'praxiology' usually rings a bell, but when one investigates its usage closer, people frequently cannot associate it with anything more than the name of Ludwig von Mises. Kotarbiński's praxiology certainly has a few things in common with the work of Mises (and it is something more than the name). Both of them were understood as general accounts of human action, both had wider 'scientific' ambitions to be grounding disciplines which study action from a theoretical perspective. Nevertheless, Kotarbiński's project is different from von Mises' praxiology—to keep things in order the latter has usually been spelled as 'praxeology' mainly for two reasons. First, it is much more philosophical, and therefore, conceptually more nuanced. Second, Kotarbiński's praxiological investigations have a different frame of reference. While von Mises' work is typically—and rightly—associated with theoretical basics of economy, Kotarbiński's project is broader, since it embraces any type of human action. So, Kotarbiński's praxiology is basically a philosophy of action or: a theory of action. What are its key features?

Put in a simplest form, the definition of praxiology highlights that it is a philosophy of action oriented towards human effectiveness. Undoubtedly, effectiveness, understood as successful purposiveness, is something especially salient in the case of human work. So, on the surface, it may be prima face related to the von Misesian project: The economy of actions on the market and the effectiveness of human work may appear as close allies. Again, this association is superficial: Kotarbiński's concept of work is rather a *metaphor* introduced to capture the fact that various human activities, considered from the angle of intentional *effectiveness*, are cases of a 'good job':[2] If your actions—especially the ones whose results are intersubjectively important—are effective and bring desired changes in the world, you hear that you do a 'good job'.

Thus, Kotarbiński's *Treatise on a Good Job* is a philosophy of human action which takes effectiveness as a *leitmotif* for its explorations. In explaining the scope of praxiological investigations, Kotarbiński frequently pointed to three issues which are its tasks. First, praxiology offers an analytic description of the 'elements of action'– it gives an account of the ontology of action. Second, it investigates 'the conditions on which the maximization of efficiency depends'—it shows the normative basis of human effectiveness. Third, it tries to study the progress in human efficiency. If one considers the latter task together with the fact that Kotarbiński often called his praxiology 'the science of efficient action', one easily sees that the ambitions of such 'science' were high. In fact, Kotarbiński wanted praxiology to be a broad field of scientific inquiry, something that is both justified epistemically and desired practically, due to its practical application and with regard to the possibility of amelioration of human practice. But such high ambitions were not anything surprising. They were present both in the work of von Mises and in various philosophical works, such as e.g. works on morality, beginning from Jeremy

Bentham.[3] We do not need to take them too seriously to undermine the content of Kotarbiński's project. And the content is basically and to a significant extent a philosophy of action.

Praxiology as an Analytic Action Theory

Reasons to understand Kotarbiński's praxiology as, primarily, an example of the philosophy of action are several. Some of them show that his work was concerned with the questions and problems which are typical for the classic accounts of action from the analytic tradition—call it *Classicism of Praxiology Thesis* [henceforth CPT]. Other reasons make the action-theoretical work of Kotarbiński a pioneering proposal which is still interesting for contemporary debates—call it *Modernism of Praxiology Thesis* [MPT]. One may stipulate that CPT and MPT define the biggest advantages of praxiology. Let us check this stipulation step by step.

To support CPT, one could discuss various issues introduced in the *Treatise*. Among other things, there are: an account of actions in terms of events (Chapter 3 of the *Treatise*), theory of collective actions and cooperation (Chapters 7 and 12), an account of choice explained with the aid of the *Buridan's Ass* (Chapter 5) or an account of basic action (Chapter 2). Here I shall focus only on the latter—as we shall see, Kotarbiński's proposal in this respect belongs to classic views to the bone.

The concept of basic action, presented in chapter two of Kotarbiński's main work is already implied by the idea of 'the elements of action', the 'analytic description' of which is taken to be one of the most important tasks of praxiology (Kotarbiński, 1965, p. 8). According to Kotarbiński, actions—complex activities—are built of 'simple acts'.

> Let us begin with examples. The pointsman moved the lever and the rails shifted sideways. The button was pressed and the lift started to move. The piano key was struck, and the sound was heard. What common and essential elements can be noticed in all these cases? First of all, some deliberate exertion of pressure on a thing—in the cases given, on the lever, the button, the key. Further, some subsequent event: that something which happened to some thing (since persons are things, too): to the rails, the lift, the listener. Finally, the causal bond: the subsequent event was an effect of that antecedent pressure and, consequently, that antecedent pressure was a cause of that subsequent event.
>
> (Kotarbiński, 1965, p. 14)[4]

'Simple acts' build human agency in the sense that they are 'atoms' of actions. Actions are complex, because they are made by something more basic. Philosophically, this strategy is very typical—in the most widely accepted versions it can be found, for example, in epistemology ('basic beliefs'—Aristotle, Descartes or Leibniz) and in the philosophy of language or the philosophy of logic ('elementary propositions'—Wittgenstein, 'atomic propositions'—Russell). All these versions fall under the heading of the so-called *foundationalism* and they share its worries. Before I make a few remarks about these worries, we should expand the presentation of Kotarbiński's approach. 'Simple acts' are explicable in terms of one of the most peculiar concepts in praxiology—'optional impulses':

> Let us now proceed to analysing the relation of agenthood—that is the relation between the agent and the result of his action. We obtain that relation simply by applying the concept of causality. The agent of an event is he whose optional impulse is a cause of that event. Shifting a lever, pushing a button, striking a piano key—all these are examples of optional impulses—in those particular cases, we may also say: optional pressures. But I prefer the term 'impulse' since it better covers those simple acts in which the behaviour of the agent... does not principally consist in any muscular exertion, such as when one makes an effort to recollect a forgotten name or to concentrate when carrying out a mental arithmetical operation. .... Every impulse is directional and intentional; it is an impulse aimed at something...
>
> (Kotarbiński, 1965, pp. 17–18)[5]

Optional impulses are devised to play two roles. On the one hand, they initiate action, in terms of causal generation, in a similar way *intentions* do.[6] On the other hand, they are actions themselves. That they can be actions and causes of action at the same time—it is possible due to the differentiation of simple acts from complex acts (basic and non-basic actions). One might immediately ask—are there acts which are not simple, or, in other words, are complex actions always reducible to some sets or clusters of simple acts?

This question has been raised by (putatively) the first modern author who investigated basic actions in more detail, Arthur Danto. Danto's responses—given about 10 years after the publication of Kotarbiński's main work—highlight different aspects of basic actions. Basic actions are conceived in the following way:

> "*B* is a basic action of *a* if and only if (i) *B* is an action and (ii) whenever *a* performs *B*, there is no other action *A* performed by *a* such that *B* is caused by *A*."
>
> (Danto & Morgenbesser, 1963, p. 435)

Danto's and Morgenbesser's attention was focused on the sensibility of the view that there are some actions which can be performed only if they are conceived as non-basic.[7] So, Danto and his collaborator responded negatively to the above question.

Later, Danto focused on the issue of performing such actions as moving one's arm "without someone or something causing it to move, without having to do anything to cause it to move." (Danto, 1965, p. 144). This is an interesting shift in comparison to the initial view (from 1963)—for several reasons. In a standard—call it Davidsonian—tradition such activities as moving one's arm require something more basic—some mental activity or attitude such as desire or intention which causes such movements. Danto did not enter this path and claimed that basic actions in a physical world are basic partially because they *are not* caused by mental states (although there are mental *analoga* of basic and non-basic actions).[8] Notwithstanding internal problems of Danto's view, it is also interesting in the context of Kotarbiński's notion of optional impulse. For optional impulse was apparently devised to deal with the issue of basic action in the context of the difference between mental actions ("carrying out a mental arithmetical operation") and activities in a physical world ("shifting a lever, pushing a button"). Much like Danto's basic actions, optional impulses do not require propositional attitudes that trigger them. Of course, there are significant dissimilarities. Danto's intuition concerning basic character of actions "which are not caused to happen by the man who performs them" (Danto, 1965, p. 145) highlights something different than Kotarbiński's simple act, but both Danto's basic actions and Kotarbiński's simple acts appear as equally foundationalist, reductive, and atomistic.

Foundationalism, in the present context, can be defined as the view that some actions (basic actions) must exist if other actions (complex actions, non-basic actions) are to be possible. Human agency requires foundation in the sense that it needs 'building blocks'. Danto says:

> A basic action is perfectly simple in the same sense in which the old 'simple ideas' were said to be: they were not compounded out of anything more elementary than themselves, but were instead the ultimately simple elements out of which other ideas were compounded.
>
> (Danto, 1965, p. 147)

Kotarbiński accompanies: "All work, all activity, and in general all active behaviour is fully built of simple acts…" (Kotarbiński, 1965, p. 14).[9] So construed, foundationalism is also a reductionism and atomism: there are no actions which would be non-basic—the universe of human agency is constituted by the atoms-simple acts to which complex actions are ontologically reducible. Simple acts build actions in the same way as pixels built raster images. Naturally, such atomism in the philosophy of action is susceptible to criticism. It is not only dubious that the 'element' described as a basic action should be considered as fully-fledged intentional action (see Lavin, 2013). One may also suspect that this approach has had far-reaching consequences for how we conceive human agency as such.[10] The tendencies of contemporary philosophy of action go towards *diachronic* understanding of human activities which highlights the role of temporal extension of actions together with their connection to an agent's life as a whole. This is a significant theoretical change. Nonetheless, foundationalism and atomism in action theory belong to its tradition and development. They make a classic standpoint which cannot easily be ignored.[11] The fact that we still consider this view—even critically—suggests, rather clearly, that CPT has a deep rationale.[12]

Given the fact that praxiology has been proposed over half a century ago, defending MPT may appear challenging. Still, there are a number of theoretical points and accounts in Kotarbiński's main work and in his minor essays that show the ongoing allure of his theory of action. His discussion of—to mention only a few issues—the concept of skills (Chapter 8 of the *Treatise*), practical error (Kotarbiński, 1964), automatic actions, or the so-called 'agglomeration of results' (both in Chapter 9 of the *Treatise*) plainly show that praxiology did not say its last word. According to the already used strategy, I shall discuss only one topic, mentioned at the end—the 'agglomeration of results'. In my opinion, this technical issue—seemingly of minor role—is sufficient to defend MPT, because it touches an important question for contemporary action theory and reveals the core of Kotarbiński's praxiology.

Begin with the passage in which Kotarbiński describes his account;

> in chess one can attack two figures by a single move of a single piece, or one can threaten to shoot at various persons in various directions (…). All these are examples of economies resulting from doing two different things 'at one stroke'. To generalize, an *agglomeration of results around a given mean* occurs if and only if the application of that mean ensures attainment of two goals which otherwise can only be attained separately, by applying two different means or by applying the same mean twice.
>
> (Kotarbiński, 1965, p. 109, my italics—PM)[13]

The agglomeration of results is a certain way of economizing actions. This principle may be considered as a theoretical analogue of the strategy which is metaphorically captured in such *dicta*: 'kill two birds with one stone' or 'keep several balls in the air'. The fact that such proverbs are common clearly suggests that the economizing strategy behind them may be (to a significant extent) rational. We should ask—under what conditions?

Except for the implicit intuition—a very important one in the context of the overall enterprise of praxiology—that such economizing strategies boost our effectiveness, because they prompt *more efficient* options, Kotarbiński left the idea of the agglomeration of results without further development.

The same situation obtains in Michael E. Bratman's account of the so called 'agglomeration of intentions'. Bratman introduced it in his critique of Davidson's action theory (Bratman, 1985) and later, in his widely discussed

1987 book (Bratman, 1987) as one of the norms governing distal (in his terminology: future-directed) intentions. He says:

> the notion of *rational agglomerativity*. Given the role of intentions in coordination, there is rational pressure for an agent to put his various intentions together into a larger intention. If I both intend to hit target 1 and intend to hit target 2, there will be rational pressure for me to intend to hit both targets'.
>
> (Bratman, 1987, p. 134)

Parallels between Kotarbiński's and Bratman's ideas are striking here. Both capture very similar issue, although describe it in a different conceptual framework. For Kotarbiński, this framework is infiltrated by his tendency to consider actions through their tangible aspects (results, materially understood means),[14] while the framework of Bratman's proposal is diachronic aspects of intending. The similarity is obvious because if one translates Kotarbiński's approach into the language of intentions, we get something like the following principle:

> *Intention Agglomeration* [IA]: If in one and the same time agent *A* intends φ_1 and intends φ_2, then it should be rational for A to intend both φ_1 and φ_2.

If you decide to achieve a few results 'at one go', you usually intend actions which lead to them in accordance with the above pattern.[15] Much like Kotarbiński, Bratman left this pattern without further development. Except for highlighting the role of rationality and coordination, the norm described by Bratman says even less than Kotarbiński's agglomeration of results,[16] because it does not underlie the pragmatic, effectiveness-boosting dimension of it. In my opinion, this is sufficient to defend MPT, but to fully understand why it can be so, we need a more explicit rationale of IA. In other words, we need to explain the thing noticed by Bratman, i.e. the rationality of IA.

Elsewhere (Makowski, 2015, 2017), I have proposed to develop IA with the use of two conditions. The first condition, already noticed in the praxiological approach, refers to economy.

> *Economy condition for IA*: intending in one and the same time both φ_1 and φ_2 is more rational than intending φ_1 and φ_2 separately, because of the limits of our mental and physical resources.

Rational agents agglomerate their intentions when possible, because this provides more parsimonious solutions. As the above condition states, such a parsimony is general and it refers both to our mental resources and physical assets. Take an example. You intend to go by car to the shopping mall. Before your departure, your friend is calling you because he needs a lift. He is staying close to your place and wants a ride to the area near the mall. So you intend to help him. But instead of intending to go to the mall and intending to give a lift, you agglomerate these intentions—you intend both actions: it is simpler, more convenient and more economical to intend to do these two options together. Notice that the failure to agglomerate these two intentions need not undermine the effectiveness of these two separate intentions. You may still reach what you want without intending both these actions *together*. You will spend more gasoline, more energy, and more time, but you will be effective in the sense defined by these two intentions taken separately. Nevertheless, such agglomerativity is frequently expected from effective agents. In other words, in many situations merely effective solutions do not exhaust our rationality. And this is at heart of the Kotarbińskian praxiological thinking of human agency: effectiveness sometimes presupposes economic solutions, i.e. is definable in terms of *efficiency*. But the economy condition for IA requires something else to be sensible—it cannot be considered mechanically as a flat calculus of the economy of available options.

Let us modify the above example. Suppose again that you intend do go by car to the shopping mall, called Murphy's. While preparing to go there, you receive a call from a friend—by coincidence, his name is Murphy. Murphy has overslept his train to another city where he has an important exam. Since you two are close friends, he decided to ask you for a lift. So, although he is staying in close proximity to your place, if you intend to give him a lift, the destination of the ride with him will not take you into the area near the mall. Far from it. Nevertheless, after a brief consideration, you intend to give him a lift—he is in need and you value your friendship. So, should you agglomerate your intention to go to Murphy's with the intention to give Murphy a lift? By mechanically applying the economy condition for IA, you should be positive: it appears as psychologically convenient and parsimonious to intend to go to Murphy's and to give Murphy a ride together. Obviously, this would be absurd. Except for additional modifying factors, IA does not apply here.[17] Intentions to be agglomerative—to make doing things 'at one stroke' possible—must meet another condition:

> *'Playing in the same game' condition for IA*: intending in one and the same time both φ_1 and φ_2 is more rational than intending φ_1 and φ_2 separately if the implementation of intentions to φ_1 and to φ_2 makes sense in one and the same planning scenario.

The metaphoric talk of 'playing in the same game' can be considered as a useful elucidation of the idea of doing things—as Kotarbiński would say—'at one stroke'. One might say: if someone can make a sensible plan out of two competitive intentions, assuming the economy condition obtains, then these intentions are agglomerative.[18] In the above example, the intention to go to the shopping mall and the intention to give a friend a lift to another city do not 'play in the same game'. Quite frequently, intending an action as giving a lift in the above example nullifies other intentions. Even if they are not nullified, their implementation frequently depends on devising an alternative planning scenario. If intentions do not play in the same game, there is no reason to agglomerate them.

Although some authors reject IA as a norm of rationality (cf. McCann, 1986, Sverdlik, 1996), it can still be considered as sensible and interesting. Why? It highlights the role of economic solutions in the context of human effectiveness. Also, since it is related to the idea of bounded resources, IA belongs to the model of resource-bounded agents which is at heart of contemporary social sciences. These issues are sufficient to defend MPT. The praxiological approach to IA clearly shows that praxiology has preceded in time the well-known Bratman's account. And the fact that the praxiological approach to IA is still attractive and competitive in the light of contemporary accounts, shows that the pioneering character of it is not the only virtue of praxiology.

Praxiology Out of the Mainstream

CPT and MPT, taken together, do not only allow to claim that Kotarbiński's praxiology is an example of analytic action theory. In the light of the above, this should be beyond discussion. CPT and MPT can be understood, reasonably, as constituting grounds for a very bold claim that praxiology is something important—both for the historical development of the analytic philosophy of action and for its contemporary condition. The issues discussed above provide warrants for this claim, but they do not remove the whole *onus probandi*. Why? If praxiology is so brilliant and contains so innovative ideas, then it should already be a part of the mainstream action theory—it should be *known*. But it is not.

So, how has it come that such a pioneering and interesting theory is almost completely absent in contemporary debates? This challenge is serious. Either CPT and MPT are false (and arguments provided for them are *much less* compelling than suggested), or there must be additional reason that praxiology has been remaining out of the mainstream of action theory for over half a century. Since I am still prone to defend CPT and MPT (assuming that arguments provided above are sufficient), the only way out of this difficulty is to attempt to disclose the reason why praxiology is almost completely unknown for contemporary action theorists. I believe that this is true: there are independent factors which made Kotarbiński's praxiology unknown.

These factors can be subsumed under another useful simple claim, *Idiosyncrasy of Praxiology Thesis* [IPT]: praxiology is peculiar to the extent that blocked its international reception. Here I shall only name the most central worries.[19] Let me enumerate them:

1 Praxiology, a theory about human practice, was published in the culture which remained under the influence of the Soviet Union. And the analytic action theory is typically a 'Western' tradition. So, it should not

be a surprise that a theory about human practice which appeared in the communist bloc was neglected by the Western World.[20]

2 Praxiology, as a theory anticipating the birth of action theory, is constituted by peculiar concepts, which are different from the conceptual apparatus characteristic for later classic (mainstream) proposals. The concept of optional impulse serves as a representative example here. Without sufficient knowledge of the conceptual scheme usual in the mainstream action theory, Kotarbiński's philosophy of action may be difficult to understand.
3 The peculiarity of Kotarbiński's concepts proposed in the *Treatise* (and other minor essays available in translations) has been strengthened—not decreased—in the English edition of the work. For example, Kotarbiński's concept of states of affairs, which also has a prominent place in the analytic tradition,[21] in the English edition of the *Treatise* has been translated as 'states of things'. If we consider the fact that peculiar Kotarbiński's concepts frequently received a peculiar translation, then the task of interpretation of his work is more than difficult.
4 The idiosyncrasy of the original language of praxiology is to some extent a cultural issue. Nevertheless, to a much more extent it is a matter of Kotarbiński's broader philosophical background—more specifically: his reism as an ontological-semantic view. Kotarbiński's reism (or: concretism, somatism) is the claim that only things, spatio-temporal concrete objects, exist. Reism is an analogue of classic physicalism defended, for example, by Rudolf Carnap or W. V. O. Quine (cf. Sinisi, 1965).[22] Although the explicit influence of reism on praxiology was limited, there are good reasons to claim that Kotarbiński's understanding of ontology had a tremendous impact on how he understood human agency and how he construed language suitable to describe its 'elements'. If reism highlighted the role of precision in giving descriptions of concrete things, being a protest against the use of language of *abstracta*, then its presence in praxiology must have shaped its language, too. It was not only responsible for the need of clarity in the analytic description of the praxiological foundationalist ontology and the need of seeing actions through the prism of their effects in the physical world. It affected the language of praxiology, having made it peculiar. It also obscured the role of intentionality (again, the concept of optional impulse may serve as an example).

This is a sketchy diagnosis, but it is rather clear that IPT refers to a complex issue. Such a complexity largely amounts to the claim about the peculiarity of Kotarbiński's language of action which, in turn, is the claim about praxiology being infiltrated by the reistic ontology. I take it that the influence of reism on praxiology is largely responsible for the fact that the interpretation of praxiology has not so far shown its true value. In other words, the phenomena behind IPT successfully masked many issues that support CPT and MPT. In consequence, praxiology, being no less important for the development of action theory as Anscombe's or Davidson's theory, has landed outside the mainstream of philosophy of action.

Besides such a negative impact, there is also interesting, positive aspect of IPT. Praxiology, as a 'theory of a good job', would probably not be possible without highlighting the role of *concreta*. Effectiveness and efficiency—rampant topics in the contemporary social sciences—can be understood as practical aspects of the reistically peculiar thinking about human actions. Effectiveness and efficiency matter for human agency much more than intentions and other mental states if the world-view behind the theory in which they are studied eliminates abstract entities and claims that only things exist. In a sense, praxiology as effectiveness-oriented philosophy is a theory of what can be done, made, or produced in in the world around us. Therefore, besides that IPT explains difficulties concerning the status of CPT and MPT, it also reveals the essence and distinguished character of praxiology as an action theory.

Summary

In this brief essay, I have proposed to read Kotarbiński's praxiology as a sample of the analytic philosophy of action which is no less important for its development than the work of Anscombe or Davidson. To defend this view, I have formulated three claims: that praxiology belongs to classic accounts of the analytic action theory (CPT), that praxiology still has the potential to enter contemporary debates in the analytic action theory (MPT), and that there are peculiar reasons which make the first two claims non-obvious (IPT). The last claim shows the extent to which praxiology is different from classic and modern action theories.

Notes

1 These two tasks are subject to a detailed investigation in my book (Makowski, 2016, esp. Chapter 2).
2 Kotarbiński used the term *robota*, which may be a semantic equivalent for economically understood *praca* (*work*), but this need not be so. In his utterance, *robota* has often very informal meaning, similar to English *job*. This informal use appears as especially salient in the combination with the adjective *good*. This phraseme has been used in the original Polish title of Kotarbiński's main praxiological work (Kotarbiński, 1965). Happily, the same phraseme is available in English—I translate the main praxiological work of Kotarbiński as: *Treatise on a good job*.
3 Ambitions among philosophers to establish the science for a given research field are present until today: cf. 'action science' (Prinz *et al.*, 2013).
4 If not marked otherwise, all quotations from Kotarbiński are in Wojtasiewicz's translation.
5 Translation slightly altered: 'optional impulse' for 'optional pressure'.
6 In terms of classic or modern causalism.
7 "(5) If there are any actions at all, there are basic actions. (6) There are basic actions. (7) Not every action is a basic action. (8) If B is an action performed by *a*, then either (i) *B* is a basic action or (ii) *B* is the terminal effect of a causal series the originating member of which is a basic action." (Danto & Morgenbesser, 1963, p. 436).
8 A good concise discussion of Danto's views is offered by Constantine Sandis (2010).

9 Translation slightly altered (in Wojtasiewicz's version: 'fully reducible to' instead of 'fully built of').
10 Michael Thompson claims that some "received conceptions of intentional action" result in "the tendency of students of practical philosophy to view individual human actions as discrete or atomic or pointlike or eye-blink-like units" (Thompson, 2008, p. 91) and he apparently refers to the atomistic approach to action.
11 Lavin's recent thoroughgoing discussion of the sensibility of basic actions proves that that the idea of basic action is something more than a history of action theory.
12 This outcome can be strengthened, since Kotarbiński's ideas on 'simple act' and 'optional impulse' significantly preceded in time Danto's account of basic action. Besides the elaboration of the distinction in the *Treatise* (1955), the first use of the idea of 'simple act' as distinguished from 'complex actions' appears in his 1933 essay titled *The Act*. Under the heading *The Uniwersum of Acts* Kotarbiński noted: "There are simple acts, such as collecting blueberries with one pull of bare hand, and there are extremely complex ones, such as the whole course of the process by which the personnel of a factory produces (…), with the use of machines, e.g. a series of cars" (Kotarbiński, 1933, p. 1138—in my translation, PM).
13 Translation slightly changed ('agglomeration' instead of 'accumulation', 'means' instead of 'measures', and 'goals' instead of 'aims').
14 It is related to the presence of the ontology of reism in praxiology. I shall turn back to this issue.
15 Here a comment for the initial quote from Kotarbiński is needed. When he says: "(…) in chess one can attack two figures by a single move of a single piece, or one can threaten to shoot at various persons in various directions (…)" (Kotarbiński, 1965, p. 109), we should note that these examples are not necessarily always examples of *intentions*. Perhaps there is no attack without intention to attack, but it seems convincing that we can threaten without intending to threaten. In this sense, 'agglomeration of results' cannot be translated mechanically into the language of intentions. Nonetheless, despite the peculiarity of the examples given in the *Treatise*, Kotarbiński's definition of 'agglomeration of 'results' can still be considered as an analogue of IA.
16 Minimal ambitions of Bratman's view have been noticed by various authors. See, e.g. (Yaffe, 2004, p. 512, Zhu, 2010, p. 90).
17 One can easily imagine that you intend to give your friend a ride to a different city, intending also to visit the shopping mall right after you will turn back from the city where Murphy has an exam. But this is not anything interesting in the context of IA. Equally well, you might reconsider your intention to go to the shopping mall and intend to go there tomorrow. The lack of agglomeration does not make you any less rational, although you see your goals clearly. Naturally, were additional circumstances in play, these two intentions should be agglomerated (suppose, for example that you really have to do the shopping today and the factor of time matters overwhelmingly).
18 Zhu's strategy towards IA relies on the idea of executive competition of intentions: "Two intentions are executively competitive if the execution of each of them will significantly decrease the resources (physical, mental or both) that are required for the execution of the other" (Zhu, 2010, p, 92). Although it does not explicitly highlight the role of economy in action, it is very close to my approach.
19 For the limits in space, a comprehensive discussion of this challenge cannot be provided in this short essay. I propose a full diagnosis of the problem in Chap. Two of my book.
20 This negligence appears as explicit in the work of von Mises who was very critical towards socialist economy and society. See (von Mises, 1949, Chap. XXV).
21 For example, in such classic authors as Wittgenstein or Russell (cf. Textor, 2016).

22 Inasmuch as reductive physicalism—infiltrating praxiology—is outdated, one might want to understand IPT rather as something as APT—*Archaicism of Praxiology Thesis*. I avoid this interpretation basically because it would be in tension with CPT and MPT.

References

Bratman, M. E., 1985, Davidson's Theory of Intention. In B. Vermazen & M. Hintikka (Eds.), *Essays on Davidson: Actions and events*, pp. 13–26, Oxford: Clarendon Press.

Bratman, M. E, 1987, *Intention, Plans, and Practical Reason*. Cambridge, MA: Harvard University Press.

Danto, A. C, 1965, Basic Actions. *American Philosophical Quarterly*, *2*(2): 141–148.

Danto, A. C. & Morgenbesser, S., 1963, What We Can Do, *The Journal of Philosophy*, 60(15): 435–445.

Kotarbiński, T., 1933, Czyn. In Z. Łempicki (Ed.), *Świat i Życie. Zarys encyklopedyczny współczesnej wiedzy i kultury*, T. 1, pp. 1137–1144, Lwów-Warszawa, Książnica Atlas.

Kotarbiński, T., 1964, Practical error. *Danish Yearbook of Philosophy*, Copenhagen 1, 65–71 [Bład praktyczny. Studia Filozoficzne, 2(1963): 17–30].

Kotarbiński, T., 1965, *Praxiology: An Introduction to the Sciences of Efficient Action* (transl. O. Wojtasiewicz,), Oxford, Pergamon Press/Warszawa: PWN [*Traktat o dobrej robocie*, Wrocław: Ossolineum 1955].

Lavin, D., 2013, Must There be Basic Action? *Noûs*, *47*(2): 273–301.

Makowski, P. T., 2015, Praxiology Meets Planning Theory of Intention. Kotarbiński and Bratman on Plans. In P. Makowski, M. Bonecki, & K. Nowak-Posadzy (Eds.), *Praxiology and the Reasons for Action*, pp. 43–71, New Brunswick, Transaction Publishers.

Makowski, P. T., 2017, *Tadeusz Kotarbiński's Action Theory—Reinterpretive Studies*, New York: Palgrave Macmillan.

McCann, H., 1986, Rationality and the Range of Intentions. In P. French, T. Uehling, & H. Wettstein (Eds.), *Midwest Studies of Philosophy* (Vol. X, pp. 191–211), Minneapolis: University of Minnesota Press.

Prinz, W., Beisert, M. & Herwig, A., (Eds.), 2013, *Action Science: Foundations of an emerging Discipline*. Cambridge, MA: MIT Press.

Sandis, C., 2010, Basic Actions and Individuation. In T. O'Connor & C. Sandis (Eds.), *A Companion to the Philosophy of Action*, pp. 10–17, Oxford: Blackwell.

Sinisi, V. F., 1965, Kotarbiński's Theory of Pseudo-names. *Theoria*, *31*(3): 218–241.

Sverdlik, S., 1996, Consistency Among Intentions and the Simple View. *Canadian Journal of Philosophy*, *26*: 515–522.

Textor, M., 2016, States of Affairs. E. N. Zalta (Ed.), *The Stanford Encyclopedia of Philosophy*, https://plato.stanford.edu/archives/win2016/entries/states-of-affairs/.

Thompson, M., 2008, *Life and Action*, Cambridge, MA: Harvard UP.

Von Mises, L., 1949, *Human action. A treatise on economics*, New Haven: Yale University Press.

Yaffe, G., 2004, Trying, Intending and Attempted Crimes, *Philosophical Topics*, *32*(1&2): 505–532.

Zhu, J., 2010, On the Principle of Intention Agglomeration. *Synthese*, *175*: 89–99.

Chapter 11

New Areas of Research in Praxiology

Piotr Masiukiewicz

Introduction

Praxiology as a metatheory can and should constitute a base for further development of management theory and practice. This requires identification of new research areas and establishing new paradigms in the light of contemporary trends in business. T. Kotarbiński thought that "praxiology is simply the most general branch of organization and management science, the initial or the final one, depending on whether we want to deductively deliver the theses of this science, starting from the most general and proceeding to more detailed ones or we want to deliver them inductively, starting from relatively detailed reasoning and aiming at the most general level" (Kotarbiński, 2003, p. 403). After the international subprime mortgage crisis, changes take place also in management science (Krugman, 2009).

What's important in contemporary research on enterprises' functioning is noticing their multidimensional activities as they operate in several spaces—both real and imagined as well as those created by humans. Research on activities in multiple business areas has to be correlated with their specific character.

The aim of the paper is to analyse the research necessary for theory and practice of praxiology in a multidimensional space of contemporary business management. Analysed areas have been limited to several chosen aspects of enterprise management.

Research in analysed areas can create fundaments for significant enhancement or even revaluation of a praxiology branch concerning managerial actions (decisions) at the level of an enterprise, holding, and conglomerate.

Spaces of Enterprise Functioning

Economic activity of humans in the broad sense is realized in the following spaces: regulatory, temporal, psychological, tangible, intangible (also financial) and digital. Every human activity is performed in regulatory, temporal and psychological area; the rest of them have facultative character (Figure 11.1). Those spaces overlap and they can restrain each other (for instance, passage of time limits natural resources).

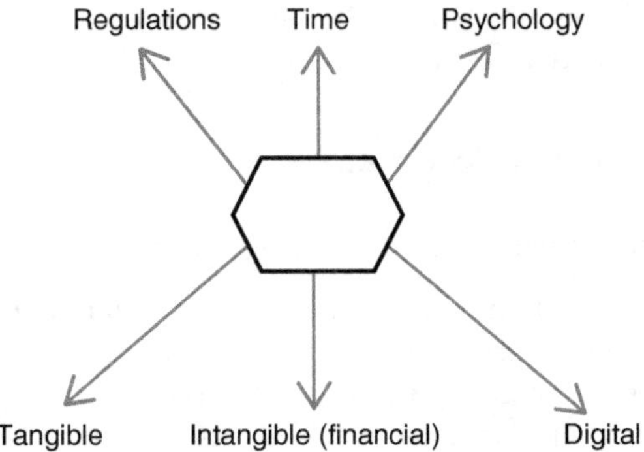

Figure 11.1 Spaces of Business.

Societies create economic rules in the form of legal acts, which become obligatory for market participants; including consumers and state authorities. Ignoring the regulations and functioning in grey market leads to criminal, civil, labour law, or financial liability of the participants of economic operations.

Time period and its role in economic activity (as Karl Marx had written before) is underestimated in economy (time of decision-making, work effectivity, debt payment deadline, etc.). Time has its limits; it is not repeatable; it has its costs; time passage can be also destructive. Efficient and effective use of time seems to be a significant problem in enterprise management.

Psychological space means processes occurring in human minds, like internalized value systems, ethical and religious norms (vide Islamic finance), criteria for rationality of actions, behaviours, decision-making processes, self-evaluation, etc. It's here where the frames of responsible business are created (Biznes, etyka, odpowiedzialność, 2013).

Tangible space concerns manufacturing of material goods, natural resources and their protection, distribution, and consumption. Similarly, the space of intangible services; but it also contains institutions, procedures, and financial operations—providing significant infrastructure for the economy. Also, state social services could be included here.

Digital space enables economic activities in other, dematerialized processes, simultaneously to other spaces; it facilitates globalization and lowers the costs. It also increases workers' responsibility.

Green revolution, the theory of intelligent economic growth, innovation management, economy of time, economy of crisis, ethical economy, compliance theory, and anomie theory (R. Merton) are new economic theories that will in future determine programs for economic development, globalization levels, and changes in enterprises management in those six described above business spaces (Fucks,2013).

Increase of requirements and responsibility of managers and their ancillary role in economy—described by J. Taft—seems to show a real direction change in management practice (Taft, 2012, part 3).

New Areas of Praxiological Research

Regulatory Processes in Economy versus Compliance

Predicting all the situations of enterprise managing in legal regulations is neither possible not necessary and the literature contains more and more pleas of overregulating the economy. Even good law is not efficient if it's misapplied by judiciary system or if there is a weak observance of the law in business. There has been a breakthrough in literature devoted to economic regulations because they are not treated solely as an instrument of removing or toning down market mechanisms' failures but they are also thought to be an efficient instrument of gaining competitive advantage (Kasiewicz, 2011, p. 9).

Legal systems of many countries are characterized by instability and by ambiguous and inconsistent regulations while regulatory decisions are dictated by political conditioning rather than by reliable costs and benefits balance (Kasiewicz, 2011; Masiukiewicz and Morawska, 2015a). That's why some regulations become ineffective; they also favour grey market activities. The shape of legal and political culture is still influenced by positivistic concepts; for instance, the law forms a system independent from ethics in such a sense that a correctly established norm is in force even if it's apparently unfair, irrational, or not in line with other extralegal regulations.

Regulatory processes in the whole economy and also at the level of individual enterprises stumble on a number of problems: (Masiukiewicz and Morawska, 2015a)

- Inefficiencies and dysfunctionality of legislative procedures for the economy, a need of a new paradigm for economic and administrative lawmaking
- Poor law culture in certain societies
- Regulation arbitrage of large corporations
- Problems of poor morals of MPs and the administration applying the law
- Lack of efficient and effective models for economic analysis of the law; for instance, European Commission in its Better Regulations statement obliged member states to a reliable assessment of consequences of ex ante regulations (Masiukiewicz and Morawska, 2015b)
- Phenomena of overregulating the economy, ignoring the principle of proportionality of regulations
- Lack of compliance risk management in enterprises

Compliance means the risk of activity ill-suited for internal regulations of an enterprise, domestic, and international legislation. Compliance risk can translate into high costs for an enterprise and managers' responsibility (Compliance i funkcja compliance w bankach, 2015).

In conclusion, the thesis (requiring further research) goes like this: Regulating of the market requires a new approach to this process, based on the following concepts: the principle of purpose and proportionality, economic analysis of law, public consultations, and praxiological principles (Masiukiewicz and Morawska, 2015b).

Risk Management Efficiency

In praxiological approach the risk can be defined as predictable events, which, if they come through, can disturb planned decisions and actions in an enterprise. Every economic activity has an element of risk. Since the time of fundamental monography by A. Damodaran many theories explaining the risk in business and risk management were created (Damodaran, 2009). They concern among others: stock market investing risks, risk of digital economy, financial crisis risk, risk of bankruptcy, risk of large corporations, compliance risk, risk of inefficiency of risk management models.

In one of the chapters of his work T. Kotarbiński writes about the values of efficient practice. The author ponders on a value, which he names 'bold acting'. He writes about objective boldness, which "could be an asset but can also be a defect, and then sometimes it is characterized as reckless risking, adventurous behavior etc."

> … boldness of a deed is essentially connected to risk, i.e. to objective uncertainty of acting. Larger or lesser risk stands in inverse relation to probability of effectiveness of means, but always, if the deed is bold to a certain degree, it has to be risky, hence the objective uncertainty.
>
> (Kotarbiński, 1982, p. 127)

Risk in business can be researched in the following the business spaces: tangible, intangible, digital, and psychological. Risk can be also analysed in the context of reasons for an enterprise's losses, crisis, or bankruptcy.

Risk (external or internal) coming true often leads to enterprise crisis (Krugman, 2009). Hence, many research questions appear; among others: (Gajda, 2014)

- How to identify risk in business operations; what's the efficiency of stress-tests in this area
- What are the areas of dysfunctional market management in enterprises and how to limit them (Hacker, Huber, Rehm, Schlesinger, and Valetta, 2010)
- How to create an effective network of financial safety in enterprises and financial institutions (Masiukiewicz, 2013)
- How to suppress managers' appetite for risk (Brousseau, Driver, Hourihan, and Larsson, 2006)

- How to turn crisis into an enterprise's success, whether the preference of restructuring procedures in an enterprise over bankruptcy is the right way
- How to manage marketing and public relations in crisis
- How to create efficient and effective models for crisis management in an enterprise

Size and complexity constitute nowadays a specific area of management science. In recent years, many publications were devoted to the negative role of large corporations in creating risks for financial stability of the economy and in causing crises (Masiukiewicz and Dec, 2013; Olszak, 2012). Managing large organizational structures obviously creates numerous problems for top managers and for corporate governance systems (Brousseau *et al.*, 2006; Drucker, 2004). Is creating huge holdings and conglomerates in the interest of sustainable development? Do they not threaten competition and implement a concept of corporate social responsibility? (Carroll, 2006; Entrepreneurships Values and Responsibility, 2009) The following research questions arise:

- What are the benefits or dysfunctions in huge corporations, including the costs of complexity of institutions
- How to manage huge corporations, how to make decisions in an effective and efficient manner
- Whether limitations of huge corporations growth is justified (also, in the context of green economy theory and the Liikanen report for European Commission, proposing compulsory segmentation)
- How to improve ethics level in managing those corporations (after-hours, low wages in the developing countries, tax squeeze, etc.)

Examples of actions taken up by governments and international organizations were: giving up on the 'too big to fail' principle after the subprime mortgage crisis and limiting growth of Systemically Important Financial Institutions (SIFIs) upon implementation of the Dodd-Frank Act in the USA and the CRD/CRR Directive in the European Union (Sorkin, 2009; Olszak, 2012). Recovery and resolution regime for large banks included in the UE directive aims at avoiding sudden bankruptcy of large banks at the cost of the tax payers. Taxes actually paid by huge corporations are effectively lower than in other businesses. It's also a problem of poor ethics of liabilities payments. So, the effective solution that was for instance discussed in Belgium would be implementation of a so called 'fairless tax' for huge corporations.

In summary, efficiency and effectiveness of risk management in an enterprise that means its limitations and not letting the risk come through has to take into account such components as predicting phenomena, monitoring different risks, measuring potential consequences, creating financial reserves, effective and efficient crisis management according to the procedures prepared beforehand (such procedures have been obligatory for years in financial institutions).

Parallel Digital Economy

Enterprise management on the Internet is connected to the specific character of this economic space. Precise sequential acting, lesser time limits and lack of spatial limitations, creating flat, multinational and international corporations, possible simultaneous operations, speedy action copying, lesser costs—all that creates new possibilities for business development. Web 2.0 technologies promote ideas of freedom, liberty in the virtual space, even certain own norms, but these values, ironically, are addressed rather to the machines than to humans.

Negative phenomena in digital economy mean first of all growing digital risk. There's also a problem of cannibalism of sales offer on the internet and in real economy, tax evasions by some online platforms that play an intermediary role in services, creating bitcoin (own money) as well as economic crimes.

The phenomenon of parallel reality, created on the net with the features of emergence and multi-process systems is used in economic activity via the Internet (it is a mechanism researched and defined in physics, e.g. works by A. Einstein). Higher parallelism usually brings an enterprise higher value than better organizational efficiency. New concept of enterprise parallel activities possible with the network utilization, explains this mechanism. (Masiukiewicz, 2015b).

The risk of acting in digital space is still rising nowadays in three areas:

- The risk of IT programs, including the risk of applications for Internet security
- The risk of Internet users
- The risk of cyber-attacks by hackers and Internet offenders

There are a few economic areas in which Internet crime thrives—for instance, in the bank sector (financial pyramids, black market loans), HFT transactions on the capital market, on the insurance and intangible services market, in the area of gambling and recently in organized immigrant-smuggling (Masiukiewicz, 2015b). The Internet facilitates connections between legal and illegal operations; money laundering, penetrating legal structures, continuation of enterprise in legal business, etc. (Schneider, 2010). Hackers' activity reaches not only enterprises but also banks and governments; for instance, in 2016 in Poland there was a simultaneous cyber-attack on 17 commercial banks and 240 cooperative banks; thankfully, these attacks failed.

Enterprises' activity on the Internet seems to be an important area of praxiological research, as well as research on the ethics of those activities.

Sharing Economy—Efficiency and Effectiveness

Sharing economy is a phenomenon dynamically developing all over the world although it's still poorly researched and described. Does it pose competition for traditional economy? According to R. Fucks with the spread of digital models

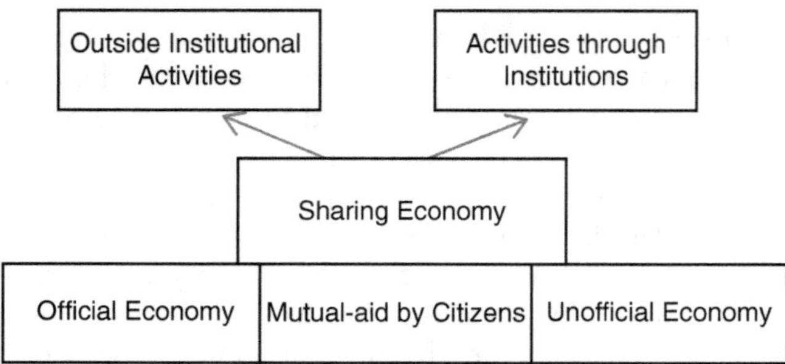

Figure 11.2 Position of Sharing Economy.

of exchange like hire, rent, or exchange, new forms of transactions based on trust have been created. It means saving money, energy, and resources. Thanks to virtual stock exchanges on the internet the idea of common use is becoming more and more popular; for instance, in Germany in 2009 three students launched a garment exchange market Klederkreisel—three years on, it had 360,000 users (Fucks, 2013, pp. 374–375).

However, when the communities of users turn into corporations, they usually don't respect regulations applicable to entrepreneurs and that can lead to unfair business competition and tax evasion (Domaradzki, 2015). A necessary condition for sharing consumption is close relationships between people. When this closeness is missing, the relationship stays purely commercial (Figure 11.2). A demand of implementing legal regulations for the new model of exchange of goods and services, e.g. in taxation and consumer protection principles, seems controversial.

Global revenue from sharing economy will come to $335 billion by 2025 (Ekonomia współdzielenia to szansa dla Polski, 2016). Internet services based on the idea of sharing that offer among others,in road transportation or accommodation, gain popularity also in Poland: They are actively used by 26 per cent of the population. The sharing economy provides a significant development potential for European economies.

The sharing economy requires research both in real and digital space, as well as in regulatory space.

Decisions and Managers' Responsibility

Every decision bears both legal and moral effects and consequences. The praxiological approach to decision-making can be found in W. Gasparski's and P. Drucker's works (Drucker, 2004; Gasparski, 2002, 2013). These issues are discussed again in the light of the lesson learned due to subprime mortgage crisis (Gajda, 2014; Krugman, 2009; Masiukiewicz, 2015a). Within the framework of praxiological cycle: deed (decision)—effect—assessment—responsibility—consequences many theoretical and practical problems of responsibility occur. According to T. Kotarbiński, the notion of responsibility constitutes iunctim with perpetration—only the doer can be responsible for a deed. W. Gasparski points out that in praxiological sense the doer is held responsible, which means he is liable for the course of action consistent with the praxiological (universal) form" (Gasparski, 2002). A manger can be held responsible because of a guilt or a risk and the experience of subprime mortgage crisis indicates to ignorance of the latter area. In the issue of ethics, P. Drucker underlined that social responsibility is one of the main tasks of corporation management. "A free enterprise, operating in the conditions of economic freedom can't exist only because it's good for business; sense of its existence is based on the fact that the society needs it" (Drucker, 2002, p. 34).

In theory there are models of decision making and responsibility, with a possibility of three different approaches: rational-normative, based on logical norms and rationality; descriptive-explanatory, defining real decision making processes; cognitive-explanatory, which analyses policymakers' behaviours and rationalization of decisions.

W. Gasparski introduced a notion of qualified responsibility, i.e. liability defined by regulations and integral with the essence of the actions and decisions. He gave an example of responsibility connected to certain jobs (like, for instance, a lawyer's or a manager's job) (Gasparski, 2002).

Acting in accordance with principles of rationality should limit effects of managers' responsibility; but is it always possible? Especially that the law in force is not always rational. V. L. Smith has devoted many of his works to rationality of economic decisions; however, rationality criteria change in different societies which creates an always present research problem (Smith, 2003, 2008, 2013; Taft, 2012).

Exemplary research problems in the area of managers' responsibility:

- Criteria of economic rationality
- Managers' moral gambling, focus on short-term profits
- Rationality in different management cultures
- Principle of unlimited right to errors in managers' decisions
- Limits of manager's responsibility and corporate governance
- Types of managers' responsibility
- Financial responsibility popularization of clawback principle (no financial bonuses for managers in case of losses, as recommended also in a CRD/CRR directive) etc. (Masiukiewicz, 2015a)

It's important to research value systems of managers in different management cultures as they constitute a base for their actions and decisions (Zarządzanie respektujące wartości, 2016).

In summary, managers' decisions, sometimes of huge importance and concerning even millions of clients plus risk appetite on one hand and the right to errors on the other, high remunerations, and bonuses as well as weak corporate governance justify financial liability for managerial errors and tightening of the criteria (also the moral ones) for selecting managers.

Conclusions

Praxiology as a metatheory can provide important support for the development of management theory and practice. There is a justified need of praxiology theory development in the context of entrepreneur's functioning in many spaces of economic activity, and especially the need of further research on market management, sharing economy, digital economy, responsibility of managers for their decisions, and regulatory systems. Contemporary management practice provides many research topics; what the paper tried to present.

New praxiological tools for supporting effectiveness and efficiency of enterprise management should be looked for; for instance, 'Ockham's razor' should be used to verify organizational structures, production processes, and information systems of the management and decision-making systems.

Also institutionalized actions are needed, like the popularization of the annual *Praxiology* as a forum for exchanging experiences and new ideas, organizing scientific conferences, and creating a praxiological research database on the Internet.

References

Biznes, etyka, odpowiedzialność. 2013, (ed.) W. Gasparski, Wydawnictwa Profesjonalne PWN, Warszawa.

Brousseau, K. R., Driver M. K., Hourihan G., and Larsson R., 2006, Jak doświadczeni menedżerowie podejmują decyzje, Harvard Business Review PL, wrzesień.

Carroll, A. B., 2006, Corporate Social Responsibility: A Historical Perspective, in: *The Accountable Corporation*, vol. 3, (eds.) M. J. Epstein and K. O. Hanson, Praeger Publishers, Westport.

Compliance i funkcja compliance w bankach. 2015. www.bis.org/publ/bcbs103.pdf?noframes=1, access 15.11.15.

Damodaran, A., 2009, Ryzyko strategiczne. Podstawy zarządzania ryzykiem, Wharton School Publ, Akademia Leona Koźmińskiego, Warszawa.

Domaradzki, K., 2015, Oszczędzanie czy kantowanie, www.forbes.pl, access 04.05.15.

Drucker, P. F., 2002, Myśli przewodnie Druckera, Wydawnictwo MT Biznes, Warszawa.

Drucker, P., 2004, Od czego zależy skuteczność menedżera, Harvard Business Review PL, Wrzesień.

Ekonomia współdzielenia to szansa dla Polski. 2016, www.forsal.pl, access 6.05.16.

Entrepreneurships Values and Responsibility, 2009, (eds) W. Gasparski, L. V. Ryan, S. Kwiatkowski, Praxiology, vol. 17.

Fucks, R., 2013, Intelligent Wachsen, Die grune Revolution, Carl Hnaser Verlag.

Gajda, J., 2014, Chosen Aspects of Crisis Management in the Organization's Activity, Theory and Management no 7.

Gasparski, W., 2002, Forma i treść odpowiedzialności, Prakseologia no 142.

Gasparski, W., 2013, Teorie oraz dylematy etyczne i prakseologiczne, in: *Biznes, etyka, odpowiedzialność*, (ed.) W. Gasparski, Wydawnictwa Profesjonalne PWN, Warszawa.

Hacker, J., Huber, G. A., Rehm, P., Schlesinger, M., Valetta, R., 2010, Economic Security at Risk, Findings from the Economic Security Index, The Rockefeller Foundation, New York, July.

Kasiewicz, S., 2011, Nowe regulacje—instrument równoważenia konkurencyjności i stabilności sektora bankowego, in: *Zarządzanie ryzykiem—reakcje i wyzwania pokryzysowe*, (ed.) L. Kurkliński, Wydawnictwo BIK SA, Warszawa.

Kasiewicz, S., 2016, Teoria i praktyka zarządzania ryzykiem regulacyjnym, Alterum, WIB, Warszawa.

Kotarbiński, T., 1982, Traktat o dobrej robocie, Ossolineum, Wrocław.

Kotarbiński, T., 2003, Postępy znawstwa dobrej roboty, organizacji i kierownictwa. Prakseologia, Część II, Zakład Narodowy im. Ossolińskich, Wrocław.

Krugman, P., 2009, The Return of Depression Economics and the Crisis of 2008, W. W. Norton Publ., NJ.

Masiukiewicz, P., 2013, Management of Financial Safety Net in Poland, in: *Management Trends in Theory and Practice*, Scientific Papers, Faculty of Management Science and Informatics, Institute of Management by University of Zilina.

Masiukiewicz, P., 2015a, Models of Financial Responsibility of Management Board, Journal of Applied Management and Investments, vol. 4, no 4.

Masiukiewicz, P., 2015b, Przestępczość zorganizowana—w stronę internetu? Kwartalnik Nauk o Przedsiębiorstwie, no 4.

Masiukiewicz, P., and Dec, P., 2013, Dysfunctions and Risks of Big Financial Institutions, Business Systems and Economics, Research Journal, no 3.

Masiukiewicz, P., and Morawska, S., 2015a, Proclaim Rules of Economy Law. Need of New Treatment, Theory of Management, no 8.

Masiukiewicz, P., and Morawska, S., 2015b, Regulacje rynku finansowego. Aspekty prakseologiczne, Finanse i Zarządzanie, no 3/1.

Olszak, M., 2012, Procyclicality in Banking and Bank Size? A Review of Empirical Evidence, in: *Kryzys finansowy. Przebieg i skutki społeczno-gospodarcze w Europie Środkowej i Wschodniej*, vol. I, Katolicki Uniwersytet Lubelski, Lublin.

Schneider, F., 2010, The Influence of Public Institutions on the Shadow Economy: An Empirical Investigation for OECD Countries, Review of Law and Economics, vol. 6, no. 3.

Smith, V. L., 2003, Constructivist and Ecological Rationality in Economics, American Economic Review, no 93.

Smith, V. L., 2008, Rationality in Economics. Constructivist and Ecological Forms, Cambridge University Press, New York.

Smith, V. L., 2013, Racjonalność w ekonomii, Wolters Kluwer, Warszawa.

Sorkin, A. R., 2009, Too Big To Fail, Allen Lane.

Taft, J. G., 2012, Stewardship. Lessons learned from the lost culture of Wall Street, J. Wiley & Sons Inc., New Jersey.

Zarządzanie respektujące wartości, 2016, (eds). A. Herman, T. Oleksyn, and J. Stańczyk, Difin, Warszawa.

Chapter 12

The Praxiological Lifeworlds and the Design Universes

Tufan Orel

Introduction

A previous collective work called Designology was undertaken with the intention of encouraging, as Professor Gasparski formulated, a "tendency" for "the gradual unification of various currents of design studies into a unified discipline" (Gasparski & Orel, 2014, p. 7). In the same work I also argued on the term 'design stuffs' (p. xvi) in the sense that, since there is no *Weltstoff*—primitive substance—out of which all the design objects or products are obtained, the design operations are oriented to different substances: such as social design, intelligence design, industrial design, etc. In this paper my intention is to draw attention to the strong relations between the varieties of *design stuffs* and the *praxiological lifeworlds*.

In one sense, we can consider a praxiological lifeworld as the context or the environment of an action. This context can shelter some ad-native elements of action such as agent, activity, work, etc. but furthermore the 'internal circumstances' of a context can contain (1) realization and execution, (2) evaluation and decision making capacities (Gasparski, 2000, p. 374). But such a concept of environment also implies an exterior world. In this paper, I will try to show that it is also possible to consider actions taking place in relatively autonomous and parallel environments. In this case, the relation of an action's environment is not necessarily with an undetermined 'outside' (or determined by some selected 'factors'), but different contexts, with strong coherence of their ad-native elements, can evolve next to each other and can be attracted to each other by their specific bonds. So, we can talk not only about an 'intra-weaving' of the components of action, which creates *ipso facto* a special environment of an action—what I will call a praxiological lifeworld—but also about the 'inter-weaving' of praxiological lifeworlds between them.

One of the scholars who has worked thoroughly on the idea of lifeworlds, Alfred Schutz, insisted on two different methodologies for the study of lifeworlds. On one hand, it's possible to speak of 'provinces of meaning' and, on the other, the subject of study can be the analysis of the ontological structure (or the sub-universe) of these lifeworlds (Schutz, 1982, p. 230). Although these approaches are highly reasonable, I will nevertheless give an opportunity, in the following pages, for the consideration of a 'historical' approach. I will try to trace the footprints of some of the important components of action, from their Greek origins to their constitution as theories of praxiology (or praxeology) in the nineteenth and the twentieth centuries. Through this approach, I will try to show not only how it's possible to talk about 'lifeworlds' in the framework of praxiological theories, but also how it can be done concerning today's practices. I will suggest some propositions focusing on the complex relation of design stuffs and their reception and usage in different praxiological lifeworlds.

A Short Analysis of Human Action: An Aristotelian *Ouverture*

Practical Wisdom (Phronesis)

In a very broad sense praxiology can be considered as a reflection or a methodology on whatever genre of knowledge is related to action or to its result (*oeuvre or work*). One of the ancient Greek words that indicates this relation of knowledge with action is called *Phronesis* (*prudence* in Latin), which is generally translated as 'practical wisdom'. But how does one understand practical wisdom? What is its specificity? When we talk about *phronesis* we should first of all underline the fact that it's related to *human* action, with all its hazards, adventures, and obligations. This view is very well illustrated by a modern commentator of Aristotle, Pierre Aubenque. In a synoptic way, (i.e. with a compilation of important passages of *Nicomachean Ethics*) he writes:

> Gods are not just, they are not courageous, not liberal, neither temperate because they do not live in a world where they have to sign contracts, face dangers, distribute sums of money or to moderate their desires. So the gods don't live in the world of relations, of adventure and needs like humans.
>
> (Aubenque, 1993, p. 65)

It is correct to speak not only of *Human* Action, but also of *Human* Wisdom. This wisdom should not be automatically assimilated to the 'philosophical wisdom' (*sophia*) nor to the 'total wisdom' or *cosmic competence or knowledge,* like the wisdom of King Solomon, for example. Human wisdom is not given, once and for all, in a perfect state, but it can evolve and can be perfected through time.

Way of Life (Bios)

To stay in the Aristotelian universe of action, we should also take note that, according to Aristotle, *phronesis* takes place in a special context of human experience, which he calls *praxis or* politics. What is the difference between *praxis* and other contexts of experiences of man? Here, we must refer to the idea of *bios*: form of life. In his *Ethics*, Aristotle refers, on the one hand to the three ways of life: Life of Enjoyment (*bios apolaustikos*), the Life of Politics, and, third, the Life of Contemplation (*Nic. Eth., 1095b*) and on the other hand, he specifies that "action and production are different (kinds or ways of life), since making aims an end distinct from the act of making, whereas in doing, the end cannot be other than the act itself" (*Nic. Eth., 1140b*). In most of his writings, Aristotle mainly talks about three major Ways of Life: *praxis, theoria* and *poiesis*. These 'Ways of Life' are in priory related to commitment to different genres of living: *bios theorètikos* is a contemplative attitude to life; whereas *bios politicos or bios praktikos* is related to doing right or obtaining a good life (*eudaimonia*). The main aim of *poiesis* is the production of material or artistic work.

Activity (Energeia)

We can consider that one of the most important elements of action theory is 'activity' (or actuality) and one of the most important elements of activity is its efficiency (*apodotikótita*). It can come into play with deliberation: choosing methods, means or instruments. The efficient cause, according to Aristotle, is "That from which the change or the resting" occurs (*Metaphysics Book V, 2*). Concerning the efficiency of instruments, we can for example ask this question: Can we cook a cake with the utensils of carpentry? The choice of instruments will be reasoned on the basis of timing and agility. But also, we should take into consideration not only the activity, but also the *efficacy* of its final end (*ergon*). Let's say that the obstacles of the instruments were overcome in the act of cooking, but there can still remain this other question: did we obtain a good cake? Now, the first case corresponds to a mechanical problem, which is *efficiency* (in modern terms it will be called a ratio, between the useful work done and the energy expended), whereas the problem of *efficacy* is related to a successfully cooked cake. Besides efficiency and efficacy there is also the issue of *eupraxia* (right conduct or the *effectiveness* of a conduct). *Eupraxis* in itself can be a more complicated aspect of human activity, since it can be considered as an adequate act regarding an objective rule (*nomos*), or it can be viewed as a result of good action (for example, helping others, or acting to obtain happiness) hence, in this second sense, it constitutes the content of a specific theory of ethics (*eudaimonia*). Yet, we must admit that good action and justness of an action (*ortho-praxie*), are not easy to separate from each other. On this particular case, J. L. Ackrill makes a very important point by saying that:

> How can an action could be good in itself if it's valued as a means to *eudaimonia*? Secondly, how can action be something done to bring about an outcome and yet be distinguished from a production because done for its own sake?
>
> (Ackrill, 1980, p. 93)

The content of ethics is good life (*eudaimonia*), but what interests us in this study is rather the relation of the formal aspects of action (*energeia*, ergon, usage, etc.) to knowledge and cognition. Therefore, we will leave aside the issues surrounding the ethical problem (good action) or the science of morals in our study.

Work (Ergon)

According to Aristotle, in its most general meaning *ergon* is a 'function', a 'task', or a 'finished work' (*oeuvre*). The function of each entity is to do its job in its own way. The function of the knife is to cut, the function of the eye is to see and the function of the human being is to fulfil its function: his function is to do well, when he is in an activity. But the end products (results of an activity) can still have a big variety, if we take into consideration the cognitive element, as well as the ways of life in which it is produced. By the help of *technè*, for example, an activity can produce (or create *poiein*) an amphorae or a drama [originally the word drama comes from *dran* which means 'thing done' and *poiema* means 'thing made']. But here, the work *(ergon)* is not related to using (final cause, purpose), it's always related to functioning or the result of an efficient activity. So how did Aristotle see the purpose or usage dimension of an *ergon*? On this we can suggest the idea of *hexis*, having or wearing, on which he says:

> "Having" *(hexis)* means a kind of activity *(energeia)* of the haver and of what he has—something like an action *(praxis)* or movement. For when one thing makes and one is made, between them there is a making.
>
> (Metaphysics, Book 5, Chapter 20)

The idea of purpose (final cause, or the teleological issue) is not attached to the idea of *ergon* by Aristotle (see Orel T., 2016a). But also his definition of *hexis* does not completely fulfil the idea of usage. Usage can be considered as a process rather than a fixed state: like having. We will see in the next paragraph how the idea of usage takes a more profound meaning in the discourse of the Sophists.

Technè, Poiesis, and Praxis: Conflicts amongst Greek Schools

The Aristotelian chart on *praxis* should not conceal some conflicting views about action and its cognitive components among some other Greek philosophers before Aristotle's time (the fifth century BC). One of these views belongs to the Socratic school, the other one is the Sophist's view. The Socratic school, not only considers human action as something functional ("doing the job, the profession of being human"), but this functioning is explained by the help of analogies taken directly from the sphere of technology. For example, to understand how Man should act in everyday life, Socrates refers to the competences of the pilot, the carpenter or the musician (Boutroux, 1989, p. 58). Hence, every professional knows the basics of their profession and in a similar way, the just man should know justice. But this fundamental *knowledge* or what Socrates calls virtue (*arretè*) was interpreted in two different directions by the modern Greek scholars. According to the French philosopher of Antiquity Pierre Hadot, "the manners of living of Socrates is not only to obtain pure wisdom (*sophia*) but it is at the same time 'A way of Life': it is a 'realized ethics', it is an applied knowledge of the sciences of morals" (Domański, 1996, p. 11). Whereas for Collingwood (1982), the reasoning of Socrates illustrates perfectly a technological (*technè*) thinking. After proposing the definition of *technè* (or craft) as "The power to produce a preconceived result by means of consciously controlled and directed action", (p. 15) Collingwood considers that "Once the Socratic school had laid down the main lines of a theory of craft [*technè*] they were bound to look for instances of craft in all sorts of likely and unlikely places" (p. 17).

The position of the Sophists on the relation between *technè* and everyday life activities seems clearer. The Sophist considers human language, as it's used in action, as a *technè*. And the one who uses the language in a technical way is a professional like an artisan. According to a myth attributed to Protagoras, knowledge of the techniques (or technologies), needed to undertake joint actions in society, was shared fairly among all the gods. Whereas in the Human World, the knowledge of technology was necessary to carry on trading, hence it was not required to all; that is why "the arts (instead) were divided so that one man, an expert in the art (eg. Medicine) is sufficient for many laymen" but the "cities cannot be formed if only a few have a share of these (social arts) (Plato, *Protagoras*, p. 322, c.d). The principle which guided Protagoras throughout the use of this myth was the want to highlight the original affinity between techniques (technologies) necessary for a trade, and technologies required for each man to live in society. But at the same time, he considers that these technical skills should be thought through the efforts of experts (sophists) of the social life. These experts can hence ensure the transmission of this technique to ordinary people, for the sustainability of human society (see also on the sophists Orel, 1993).

There exist two other important facts in the Sophists teaching, as it was well remarked in Plato's writings. One of these facts is about the importance of techniques of usage (or the 'acquisitive arts'). In other words, technological action is not considered as directly related to production, intention, agent, project, instruments, rationality, etc., but it's about the procedures and attitudes (cognitive as well as emotional) in front of an already created product (natural or artificial). On the philosophy of usage Plato writes: There

> exists the whole class of learning and that of acquiring knowledge, (like money-making, combat, and hunting) none of these people are workmen,

> by deeds or words, they subdue existing or created things and look to not being subdued themselves; on account of these things especially, all together they would stand out as being called the *acquisitive art*.
>
> (Plato, *Sophist*, p. 219c, emphasis added)

The second important reflection of Plato is on the cross fertilization of Ways of Life by the help of *technè* (Plato himself has a tendency to consider *episteme* sometimes as a *technè* according to Hintikka, 1974, p. 31). Concerning the cross fertilization of the Ways of Life, we can refer to one of the famous judgments of Plato on the Sophists: for him the Sophist philosophy consists of the "Interweaving together of classes or ideas (Forms) with one another" (Plato, *Sophist*, p. 259e), (for the other possible interpretations of this famous phrase see Noriega-Olmos, 2012). In this 'interweaving' we should, of course, also take into consideration the 'semantic shift' of *technè*: *technè* is no longer an instrumental (material) action, but it's the action of human language. So with the help of the information gathered above, we can represent in the following schema (see Figure 12.1) the crossing over of *technè*, from one *bios* (Way of Life) to another, as it is conceived by the sophists.

Before finishing our analysis of *technè* and *praxis* in Ancient Greek philosophy, we should also refer to the direct influence of Greek culture and language on the action theories. In his comments on the study of Emile Benveniste, concerning the two major Indo-European suffixes found in Greek language, i.e. *-tor and *-ter, Jean-Pierre Vernant (a historian of Ancient Greece) draws our attention to the difference between 'being inside one's action', and action as a realization of something outside the agent. In the first sense action is functional, the agent and their function are not different entities, i.e. doing one's action is not producing something new; it is realizing what should be done. And here, activity in its function is more important than the Agent (Vernant, 1979, p. 88 & 91). So, this cultural heritage of Ancient Greece can enlighten us on the two levels of acting: acting as an *immersion* with one's

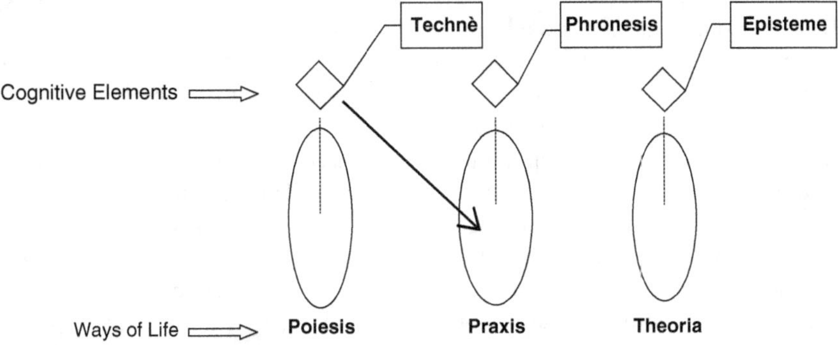

Figure 12.1 Ways of Life and Their Cognitive Modes.

ergon (spontaneous action), where there is not yet an objective knowledge of action, and acting with the knowledge of action, either to follow the rules of action or to know the end result in a deliberate manner.

Elements of Action in Modern Philosophies of *Praxis*

Since the the nineteenth century, the modern theories of action have appealed to most of the 'primitives' (or the major elements) of action theory, as we have inherited from Greek philosophy. Now it is time to verify; which are the elements that were integrated directly without any questioning; which ingredients have undergone a slight or radical change during their process of integration; and during this process, which changes are semantic in nature and which ones are more substantial; and finally, which elements were neglected either due to a misunderstanding or due to a lack of interest? In the subsequent paragraph, I will investigate the four major ingredients of the action theory in the following manner:

1 The nature of cognition in action theories (problem of *phronesis*)
2 The theories on activity (*energeia*)
3 The universes or the matrices of action (the problem of *bios*).
4 The usage: the cognitive and the emotional reception and acquisition of everyday objects (the problem of *ergon*).

The Status of the Cognitive Elements. Perhaps the most distinguished aspect of the modern theories of action is their preference for the concept of *Practical Reason (logos)*, rather than the 'practical wisdom' (although some theories of *praxis* seem to overcome this 'Kantian prerogative'). As for the idea of Wisdom *per se*, it seems to be accepted in the twentieth century as the sense of a universal cultural element and sometimes as the 'popular wisdom of the people'. Among the intellectuals who have contributed the most to this special meaning of wisdom, we can mention Count Keyserling, who in his efforts to promote a planetary culture (i.e. beyond nationalism and ethnocentrism), founded the School of Wisdom in Darmstadt, Germany, in 1920. However, the aim of the school was spiritual and not praxiological. Another important factor is that the word 'wisdom' seemed to become an emotional concept in the twentieth century. For example, it has helped to criticize the emerging information society, as we can see in the saying of the famous American poet T. S. Eliot: "Where is the wisdom we have lost in knowledge? Where is the knowledge we have lost in information?"

Now how about the role of practical wisdom inside the theories of praxiology?

Before taking into account the fundamental contribution of Kotarbiński (1886–1981)—one of the eminent founders of praxiology—to the principle of activity, we can already remember that, for him, practical wisdom is a result of a constant interaction between a stock of cultural knowledge (or popular wisdom) such as maxims, proverbs, and sayings and the evolutionary and creative aspect of knowledge. Concerning the transmission of this wisdom (or excellence) he says: The predecessors perform partial improvement, the disciples appropriate them at lower cost, because they have only to learn a knowledge which is already constituted. They use, in turn their creative energy to think and realize new partial improvements in transmitting to their successors their knowledge and skill of any previous generation.(Kotarbiński, 2007, p. 238, p. 197 in the original manuscript)

The Status of Energeia. We have already encountered in the Greek philosophies the tension between *technè* and *praxis*. In the social theory of Karl Marx the tension which is accentuated is the contradiction between the *theoria* and *praxis*. With this consideration, Marx takes *praxis* not only as a Way of life (*bios*), but above all, as an activity (*energeia*): as a *transforming* force of nature and society (or history). On the resolution of this contradiction Marx says:

> We see how subjectivism and objectivism, spiritualism and materialism, activity and suffering, only lose their antithetical character, and—thus their existence as such antitheses only within the framework of society; we see how the resolution of the *theoretical* antitheses is *only* possible in a *practical* way, by virtue of the practical energy of man (*praktische Energie des Menschen*). Their resolution is therefore by no means merely a problem of understanding, but a *real* problem of life, which *philosophy* could not solve precisely because it conceived this problem as *merely* a theoretical one.
>
> (Marx, 1844, p. 47)

Here *praxis* represents more than the classical conception of *technè*. In the Aristotelian sense, *technè* is almost complementary of nature: *technè*, either imitates nature or intervenes where nature cannot do its job by its own dynamics. But in the case of Marx, *praxis* ceases to be a mechanical force, it becomes rather a 'chemical' force, because the final aim of *praxis* is to 'transmute' the existing order of things, on the material, as well as the social level.

Although Marx was one of the first theoreticians of *praxis*, the birth of the discipline praxiology (or praxeology) is generally attributed to a French School of social sciences, amongst which we can mention Louis Bourdeau and Alfred Espinas. Bourdeau is considered to have coined, for the first time, the word 'praxéologie'. For him, this new discipline is the 'science of the functions' and it should study the somatic (corporal) as well as the psychic functioning of Man (Bourdeau, 1882, p. 17 & p. 81). But with a closer look at his theory, we can realize that the preoccupation of Bourdeau was not directly about 'action' but it was more concerned with motion or 'movement', notably the body movements. *This* tradition of 'praxéologie' seems to be continued by the French anthropologist Marcel Mauss—especially with his theory of 'techniques du corps'— and the Dutch anthropologist and physiologist Frederik Buytendijk (see on this Orel, 1983).

As for Espinas, praxeology was considered to be an equivalent of 'General Technology': which means that (1) it's an analytical description of the arts or all kind of techniques (technologies) (2) according to which they have their rules and their efficacy, and finally (3) praxeology should be the study of the future of these elements of technology; their progress or their regress (Espinas, 1897, p. 9). Concerning the idea of practice Espinas says:The word practice… can easily be taken as a concrete substantive (practice, practices); it is suitable for all collective manifestations of the will, to those who are *spontaneous* as to those who are *reflective*. It provides an excellent term to the science of this order of facts, which is *The Praxéologie* (emphasis added, p. 8).

> We can also include Louis Weber to the French school of Praxeology. As a theoretician of Social technology, he said that language "is the tool of *social technology*, as well as the punch, the club, the arrow are the tools of the material technology".
>
> (Weber, 1913, p. 140)

'Spontaneous' and 'reflective' action, a Greek heritage, reappears again in the the nineteenth century. But what is maybe new in praxiological theories is that an activity can carry a 'therapeutic action': besides being objectively efficient, an action can also, subjectively, bring relief to a state of 'unease' (or an 'irritation') of an Agent. As one can notice, our present study is not directly focused on the Agent or the Doer—it's the User-Ergon relation that interests us the most. Nevertheless, we can emphasize that in Aristotle's theory of action, 'relief' is not related to an activity, but to the reception of the result (ergon) of an activity, like the reception of a play (drama = thing done) to the spectators, what he calls *catharsis* (relief). Aristotle mainly studied the *catharsis* question in his *Politics*. Whereas in his only study concerning craft or technology—*Poetics*—he pointed out the importance of the craft of representation (*mimesis*).

In modern times, the 'therapeutic action' theory made its first appearance in the philosophy of John Locke ("The incentive that impels a man to act is always some uneasiness") and was later on developed by C. S. Peirce, (the founder of pragmatism), and finally we can see its continuation in the praxeology theory of the economist Von Mises (1881–1973). For Von Mises, besides the fact that a human being is an intentional agent, the acting man wants to substitute a state of affairs satisfying, with a state of affairs less satisfactory. Following this principle of therapeutic action, Von Mises establishes the idea of exchange, the substitution of a state of things more satisfying to a state of things less satisfying is the price paid to obtain something different. In the terminology of economy, the difference between the value of the price 'paid' and the value of the result can be called its profit or loss (Von Mises, 1985, p. 17).

Now to come back to the contribution of Kotarbiński to praxiology we should remind ourselves of his systematic study of efficient (*sprawny*) action. Many eminent specialists of Kotarbińsky have already, and in an intense way, studied this aspect of his theory, so without pretending to be exhaustive on this subject, I will briefly mention three important aspects of his conception of 'activity'. (1) First of all, Kotarbiński integrates his theory of human activity inside a system theory, but not only that, he also anticipates the 'open system theories', or what is called today the 'principle of order out of noise (disorder, chaos)'; (2) second, he analyses in every minute detail the unity of acts: the building blocks of an activity are the acts-impulses, obeying to the law of causality; and this analysis is not only limited to the context of production (factories), but extends to all social actions in the global society; (3) third, Kotarbiński, stays faithful to the Aristotelian principle of *eudemonism*, which means that his theory of activity is developed alongside his 'ethical' engagements (Kotarbiński, 2007). This aspect of his theory of acts distinguishes him fundamentally from the position of Von Mises, for whom "praxeology is indifferent about the ultimate ends (i.e. ethical values) of action" (Von Mises, 1985, p. 17).

Multiple Universes or Matrices of Action. Kotarbiński has already attracted our attention to the social and economical contexts of action, whereas some other modern *praxis* theories have proposed to establish some significant taxonomies, by taking into consideration the effect of *techne* (technology as cognition) on different genres of human action. Among those, we can notice, for example, the taxonomies of the economist F. von Gottl-Ottlilienfeld (Ropohl, 1984) and the philosopher Mario Bunge (1968, 1983). Their taxonomies especially underline four universes of technological action. Mainly (1) the 'individual technologies': as in techniques of meditation or physical education, now more commonly called 'body techniques'); (2) the 'Social technologies'; (3) the 'intellectual technologies' (e.g. like today's informatics), and; (4) 'Real world technologies' (like industrial design or what we can call the 'material technologies').

Finally, the most recent efforts to illustrate the different universes of action belong to Michel Foucault. He considers that there exists four types of technologies which each correspond to a specific 'matrix of practical reason' (as contrasted to Speculative Reason). They are:

> (1) technologies of production, which permit us to produce, transform, or manipulate things; (2) technologies of sign systems, which permit us to use signs, meanings, symbols, or signification; (3) technologies of power, which determine the conduct of individuals and submit them to certain ends or domination, an objectivizing of the subject; (4) technologies of the self, which permit individuals to effect by their own means or with the help of others a certain number of operations on their own bodies and souls.
>
> (Foucault, 1988, p. 18)

Taking into consideration the views of Michel Foucault on the plurality of practical action, I have also proposed (Orel, 1984, 1987) three universes or matrices of action which are: (1) 'game' against nature, or the world of instrumental action; (2) 'play' or communication between people, or the world of symbolic action; and finally (3) the universe of the individual action, which can be characterized by action towards oneself: here the effectiveness (or the efficacy) of techniques does not aim to achieve mastery or sovereignty over Nature or Men, but on the contrary unto oneself in order to change, to control and to transform oneself. (Orel, 1984, p. 31) Talking about this last type of action—the individual action—we can add that it does not aim at a (economical) production, nor at a social action (human organization), although these actions can be elsewhere productive strictly for the individual in the sphere of consumption.

So we may ask, what is the advantage of recognizing these different praxiological lifeworlds for design studies?

It can be helpful in the following way: by recognizing three distinct praxiological lifeworlds we can, for example, make a sharp and unambiguous distinction between two types of social design. (1) The social design that is active inside a symbolic universe, like social planning. (for more details on this see Orel, 2016b, chapter XII) (2) The social design that envisages producing everyday objects for a collective use (for example, like the *Vélib system in Paris*, a self-service *bike system*, available twenty-four hours a day for the Parisians). Besides that, the recent dazzling development of the Fablabs and 3D printings enables the individual to participate in the industrial world as a (lay) designer, without being a part of its structure and its organization: i.e. 'acting-on' a machine at distance and without necessary 'acting-with' the co-workers or colleagues of a factory. For the representation of these Three Universes of Design or the praxiological Lifeworlds See Figure 12.2.

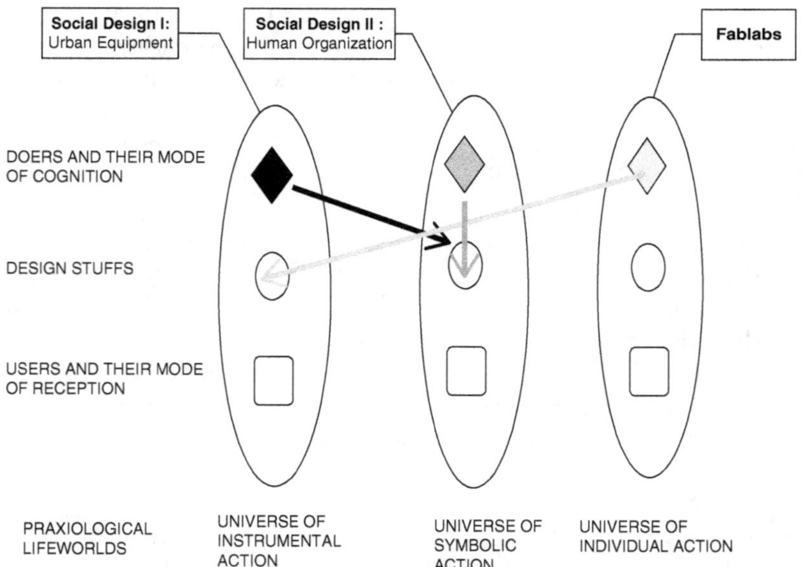

Figure 12.2 Three Universes of Design Productions.

Ergon, Reception, and Usage

Ergon

In general the 'usage' dimension of the designed objects is studied by a special discipline that is called ergonomics. More precisely, this discipline studies the relation of man with his 'tools'. Furthermore, in many respects, the preoccupations of ergonomics and praxiology coincide, as it is very well shown in an article that I have previously quoted (Gasparski, 2000).

But, nevertheless we can still question whether the idea of ergon (in ergonomics as well as in praxiology) corresponds completely to the idea of 'usage'. We have already mentioned that for Aristotle, *ergon* is related to the efficient cause (related to production) and not to the final cause (purpose) or usage. But, having said this, we should not neglect other attempts made, throughout history, to reconsider ergon as purpose. Often *ergon* was considered as something static (whereas *energeia* being something dynamic). This crystallization of *ergon* as an object was also brought closer to the idea of 'thingness'. In the metaphysics of Avicenna, (980–1037) *shay'iyya, 'thingness'*, (shay in arabic = thing, object, or *x* in algebra), is what makes a thing a thing, and it is considered to have a primordial final cause, prior to all the other causes, including the efficient cause. In this perspective, the essence of all things (natural or artificial) is for an end, for a purpose. (For the original phrase of Avicenna see Wisnovsky, 2003, p. 161).

In his theory of the 'commodity fetishism', Marx (Capital, 1867, Chapter I, Section 4) views produced objects as losing their connection with *energeia* (working), it is 'as if' the products pretend, imagine, and fantasize that they are connected to each other, on the basis of their use-value (market value). But concentrating his analysis on the relation (or rather the 'alienation') between *energeia* (production) and *ergon* (work), Marx neglects somehow the complex relation between *ergon* and *usage*. (Here I consider 'usage' different than the use-value or the market-value, as I will explicit more in the following lines).

As for Kotarbiński, while recognizing the importance of Aristotle (and his four causes) as "a precursor in analyzing reality in the terms of general praxiology" (Kotarbiński, 2007, p. 59, p. 31 in the original version), he considers work (dzielo) not always as a frozen function or a fixed concretion, but sometimes as a 'changing' substance. In an important chapter of his book (Chapter III, pp. 49–60), he proposes to codify work, on one side, as a 'continuity' and on the other, as a 'permutation'. And finally, according to their positive or negative characteristics works can be classified as constructive/destructive and as conservative/preventive (p. 51) But again, we can remark that in this text of Kotarbiński the 'bonds' that the ergon have with energeia (the main factor of change) are considered much stronger than the bonds that it might have with the usage.

From Ergon to Usage

In one sense, the shifting of perspective from *ergon* to usage can be considered as something which already exist in architecture; post occupancy evaluation; in industrial design 'user centered design' theories; in engineering, monitoring, and evaluation of innovations; and more recently, the Control of Bug-tracking in the Informatics industry. Maybe the best generic name that we can give to these examples is 'assessment'. What is said for architecture, design, engineering, and informatics can also be said for the artistic universe. On this, we can highlight the contributions of John Dewey and Valery. Dewey considers that in each productive action of man there is an emphatic artistic-aesthetic experience (Dewey, 1981, p. 567). Which means, "The doing or making is artistic when the perceived result is of such a nature that its qualities as perceived have controlled the question of production" (p. 566). So the relation of action and the reception of the finished work is what makes the experience circle complete. The French poet and philosopher Valery (1871–1945) has also attracted our attention to the issue of 'reception' of artistic works. For Valery, in a similar manner to Dewey, next to the study of poetic-artistic production there should exist a study of aesthetic 'reception': "Producer and consumer analyze and judge an artistic work from completely different points of view" (Blüher, 1979, p. 114). In a way, the theory of reception of artistic objects is also to guarantee that we can have a meta-point of view while we are receptors. On this Valery says that the literary critic should not only be a reader but he should be a *witness* (be a "Monsieur Teste", the name of Valery's book on the artistic reception) of reading, he should observe himself reading and have emotions at the same time (Blüher, 1979, p. 119).

In spite of all these interesting contributions, what seems to have escaped observation is not only that every praxiological lifeworld has its own **intra-weaving** of doing and using (i.e. perception of an ergon and its usage), but also that there exists an **inter-weaving** between the praxiological lifeworlds, which can modify the initially in-built principles of usage. If the concept of usage that I speak about is correctly understood, then we must admit that, the logic of reacting to an object (*ergon*) can take different values from the different perspectives of praxiological lifeworlds. In the concrete technical world of engineering or designing, the aim of the object (or the product) that is received is not to give satisfaction, but it is to be evaluated on the basis of objective engineering criteria. We can also envisage that, in each praxiological universe, usage has its own hidden cognition, a cognition that is necessary before having (hexis), before manipulating, and before consuming. One of the rare analysis of this hidden dimension of usage knowledge was well studied in the classical work of the American philosopher C.I. Lewis: (1883–1964) "An Analysis of Knowledge and Valuation". Lewis makes a distinction between intent (or intention) and purpose:

"In particular instances the purpose and the whole intent may coincide. More often, however, there will be some part of the expected result of action to which the doer is indifferent" (Lewis, 1962, p. 368). To underline another case of possible disequilibrium between intend and purpose he remarks: "It would be possible to apply the phrase successful act in cases where a specific result expected is realized, although the anticipation of value in this result should be disappointed" (p. 370).

However what is more important is that, for Lewis, a form of knowledge always precedes usage in every different context of human experience with (everyday) objects. Of course, the engineer has to proceed with some professional knowledge for assessment. But this is not totally different concerning a consumer: "Even to 'know what one likes' is a form of knowledge" (p. 372) says Lewis. So it will not be wrong to recognize that, in some way, all usage is preceded by some "undisclosed knowledge"—yet not identical with the well-known "tacit knowledge" (Polanyi) that is active for doing, making or producing.

The Three Principles of Reception

Now based on this idea of users' knowledge, in the most general sense, the knowledge dimension of usage for the universe of an engineer or a designer can correctly be called the *Principle of Evaluation*. For example, to find out what is really innovative concerning a product, a designer can react to a finished work, in order to *prove* its objective qualities. If it's the case of a new chair, after examining the backrest, the seat, the knee-high, and the self-supporting structure, they must know what can be added or improved in terms of ergonomics, materials, shape, or form. The perception of the designer will be constantly sharpened when they will incorporate new meanings of the chair into their previous experiences. In other words, *proving* the existence of new elements is users' knowledge, not the doers' knowledge, but of course, eventually this knowledge can enrich the future productive know-how of the designer.

In a completely different way, we can see a 'reaction' to an *ergon* (or objectively speaking, 'reception' of a product) from the social world. We will call the usage principle at the base of this reception *The Principle of Legitimacy*. After all, all reaction/reception is not only on the basis of the criteria of efficiency: an object has to be published or to be released as a 'Success'. Success is a type of fulfilment of a purpose. The image of consumers queuing in front of the smart phone stores shows that the object is *approved*. On the other hand, the innovators themselves can also be actively involved as a leader of opinion, hence not only will they *prove* the technological excellence and quality of the products, but their *ideas* (and sometimes their 'personnel-myths') can accompany the product. A professional *approval* or *disapproval* of an innovation may also have heavy consequences. For example, a bio-medical equipment like a Holter monitor has an application on smartphones. But some cardiologists need the old, heavy, and big device as the 'power symbol' of their profession: it is very likely that for a conservative cardiologist the smartphone application will be considered a 'toy' and not a 'device'!

In the world of engineers or designers, an innovation either IS or IS NOT, whereas in the symbolic world, the user claims what SHOULD and SHOULD NOT be an innovation. As for the sphere of the individual user, it is a question of intimate *experience:* a product is either AGREEABLE or DISAGREEABLE, in other words, the dominant rule of their universe is the *Principle of Promise of Satisfaction* (or *Happiness*). (The three distinct receptions of a product by the praxiological lifeworlds is schematized in Figure 12.3.)

Before finishing my paper, I would like to come back to the two main concepts that I have used in this essay: lifeworlds and the users' knowledge. In order to avoid all misunderstanding on these concepts I will insist on the fact that, the first one should not be confused with the idea of lifestyles, and the second, with the content of knowledge management.

The study of lifestyles in the consumers research can well detect tendencies for social prestige or for hedonism, as the principle motivations in buying a product. But all this research is about the 'market'! As we have seen in this paper, it's difficult to enter the sphere of individual lifeworlds into consumers research. Today it would not be false to talk about the birth of a non-commercial individual action sphere, yet not in the sense of D.I.Y. products (popularized

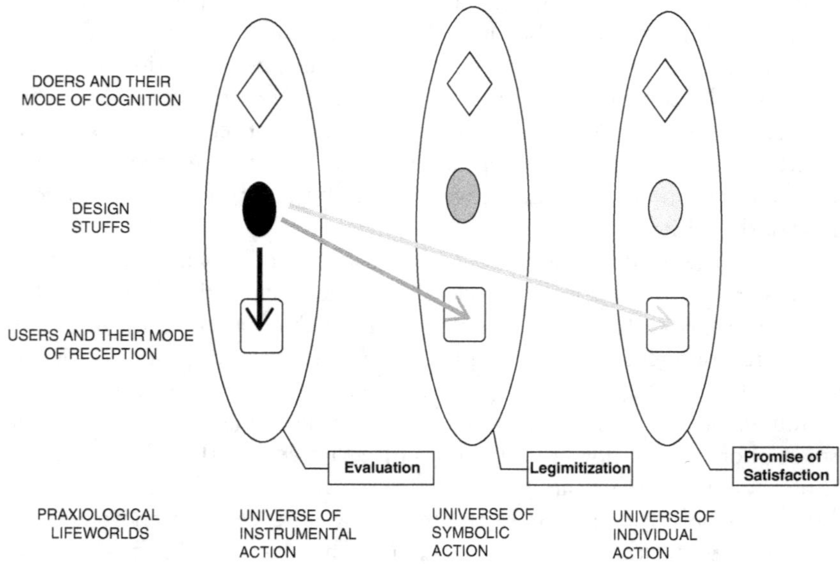

Figure 12.3 Three Different Receptions of Design Products.

long time ago by the theories of Toffler, Gershuny, Gorz, etc.), but as a real autonomous lifeworld, which can be better understood on the basis of praxiological analysis than on economical ones.

As for the users and their knowledge, our approach should not be confused by the theories of knowledge management. Knowledge management is a view concerning the production, the storage, and the use of knowledge in a most efficient fashion in the industrial and service sectors. In our text we have not talked about 'knowledge use' but about the 'users' knowledge'. Essentially this knowledge does not intervene directly in actions for doing and producing, it's a knowledge of a second cycle, which checks; which confirms or rejects; which likes or dislikes a work done (ergon). But nevertheless, in spite of the variety of their manifestations, these cognitive attitudes can be recognized as a genuine form of knowledge. Taking this into account, 'Management of Points of View' maybe a better name for our study, because after all, it is a matter of recognizing the multiple praxiological Lifeworlds, or the multiple design universes: it's through the reflection or the filtration of these universes that a design stuff becomes something familiar to us.

Acknowledgment

I would like to thank Peter Miller (M.A.) for reading the manuscript of this paper and providing me with some valuable remarks which helped the readability of this text.

References

Ackrill, J. L., 1980, Aristotle on Action, in Essays on Aristotle's Ethics (ed. A. O. Rorty), University of California Press, pp. 93–101. P., 1993, La prudence chez Aristote, Quadridge/Press Universitaire de France, 1st edition1963.

Aristotle, Metaphysics, trans. by W.D. Ross, Retrieved from http://pinkmonkey.com/dl/library1/gp010.pdf.

Aristotle, Nicomachean Ethics, trans. by H. Rackham, Retrieved from www.perseus.tufts.edu/hopper/text?doc=Aristot.+Nic.+Eth.Aubenque, P., 1993, La prudence chez Aristote, Quadridge/Press Universitaire de France, 1st edition 1963.

Blüher, K. A., 1979, La fonction du Public dans la pensée esthétique de Valery, Cahiers du 20e Siècle, No 11, Klincksieck, pp. 105–128.Bourdeau, L., 1882, Theorie des sciences, Librairie Germer Baillière, Paris.

Boutroux, E., 1989, Leçons sur Socrate, Editions Universitaires, Paris (transcriptions of Courses on Socrates (1878–79 and 1880–81).

Bunge, M.,1968, Towards a Philosophy of Technology, in Civilisation technique et Humanisme: Colloque de l'Académie Internationale de Philosophie des Sciences, Beauchesne, Paris.

Bunge, M., 1983, Epistémologie, (trad. J. De Gramont), Editions Universitaires.

Collingwood, R. G., 1938, The Principles of Art, Oxford University Press, London, (15th edition) 1982.

Dewey, J., 1981, The philosophy of John Dewey (Two Volumes in One), ed. J. J. Mcdermott, The University of Chicago Press.
Domański, J., 1996, La philosophie, Théorie ou Manière de Vivre? (Préface par Pierre Hadot) Ed. Universitaires Fribourg Suisse.
Espinas, A., 1897, Les origines de la technologie, Félix Alcan, Paris.
Foucault, M./Martin, L. H., *et al.* 1988, Technologies of the Self: A Seminar with Michel Foucault. London: Tavistock. pp. 16–49. Retrieved from http://heavysideindustries.com/wp-content/uploads/2012/02/Michel-Foucault-Technologies-of-the-Self.pdf
Gasparski, W. W., 2000, Ergonomics and Praxiology, Theoretical Issues in Ergonomics Science, vol. I, No 4, pp. 366–377.
Gasparski, W. W. & Orel, T., (editors) 2014, Designology: Studies on Planning for Action, Transactions Publishers, New Brunswich, USA.
Hintikka, J., 1974, Knowledge and the Known: Historical Perspectives in Epistemology, C. Reidel Publishing, Dortrecht/Boston.
Kotarbiński, T., 2007, Traité du travail efficace, trad. du polonais coordonée par Jean-Luc Dumont, Press Universitaire de Franche-Comté.
Lewis, C.I., 1962, An Analysis of Knowledge and Valuation, Open Court Publishing Company, Illinois.
Marx, K., 1844, Economic-Philosophical-Manuscripts. Retrieved from: www.marxists.org/archive/marx/works/download/pdf/Economic-Philosophic-Manuscripts-1844.pdf.
Marx, K., 1867, Capital (vol 1). Retrieved from www.marxists.org/archive/marx/works/download/pdf/Capital-Volume-I.pdf.
Noriega-Olmos, S., 2012, "Plato's Sophist 259E4", Journal of Ancient Philosophy Vol. VI, Issue no. 2.
Orel, T., 1983, L' étude du corps dans les rituels, in Cahiers Internationaux de Sociologie, janvier-juin, PUF, Paris.
Orel, T., 1984, A propos des techniques d'autofaçonnage, in Sociétés, vol 1, No 1, Éditions Masson, Paris. pp. 32–33.
Orel, T. 1987. De l'acte aux ouvres et l'acte d'autofaçonnage, in Technologie, Idéologies, Pratique, vol VIII, No 1–4, pp. 109–121.
Orel, T., 1993, Une philosophie des techniques pour la formation des ingénieurs, in Deforge, Y, De l'éducation technologique à la culture technique, ESF Éditeur, Collection Pédagogies, Paris. pp. 121–150.
Orel, T., 2016a, Eclat Precedes Form: The Ontology and The Perception of Designed Objects, in Radical Designist, Retrieved from: http://unidcom.iade.pt/radicaldesignist/eclat-precedes-form-the-ontology-and-the-perception-of-designed-objects/.
Orel, T., 2016b, Écrits sur le design, Éditions L'Harmattan. Paris.
Plato, Protagoras, Translated by H. N. Fowler, Retrieved from www.perseus.tufts.edu/hopper/text?doc=Perseus%3Atext%3A1999.01.0178%3Atext%3DProt.
Plato, Sophist, translated by H. N. Fowler, Retrieved from www.perseus.tufts.edu/hopper/text? doc=Perseus%3Atext%3A1999.01.0172%3Atext%3DSoph.
Ropohl, G., 1984, La signification des concepts de « technique » et« technologie » dans la langue allemande, (trad. J. P. Chrétien-Goniet Ch. Lazzeri), in Cahiers Science, Technologie, Société, Éditions du CNRS, Paris.
Schutz, A., 1982, On Multiple Realities, in The Problem of Social Reality, collected Papers 1 by Alfred Schutz, (ed. And Intro. By Maurice Natanson) Martinus Nijhoff Publishers, pp. 207–259, First publication 1962.

Vernant, J. P., 1979, Categories de l'agent et de l'action en Grèce ancienne, in Religions, histoires, raisons, Petite Collection Maspero, Paris, pp. 85–95.
Von Mises, L., 1985, L' action Humaine: Traité d' Economie, trad. Raoul Audouin, PUF, Paris, 1st edition 1949.
Weber, L., 1913, Le rythme du progrès: Étude sociologique, Felix Alcan, Paris.
Wisnovsky, R., 2003, Avicenna's Metaphysics in Context, Cornell University Press, Ithaca, N.Y. Retrieved from www.academia.edu/8194863/Avicennas_Meta-physics_in_Context.

Chapter 13

Praxiological Reflections

Introductory Remarks[1]

Gunnar Skirbekk

> Teaching which is not meant to apply to anything but the examples given is different from that which *points behind* them.
>
> —Ludwig Wittgenstein, Philosophical Investigations, § 208

In our day-to-day world, each one of us has to know quite a number of things, depending on the varied activities we engage in. There are so many things, for instance, that a traditional housewife (or a modern family father) *may* know about; but given a certain set of housing conditions and a certain pattern of family life, there are things she must know in order to be a housewife in that particular society. She *must*, for instance, know how to get hold of food, how various dishes are prepared with the equipment at her disposal, how these may be served up to the members of her family, and how to clear the table and wash up in readiness for the next time around. Here we have one type of operation with clear temporal and spatial boundaries—one kind of day-to-day world for one species of housewife.

The housewife we have in mind doesn't necessarily know where the food—or even the money to buy it—comes from, still less the exact chemical composition of the cheese. What she knows is what has to be known if her job is to get done; and, be it noted, in terms of the concepts built into the performance. The handle is what-you-get-hold-of, butter is what melts in the pan, the knife what you cut bread with, and so on.

Things crop up as playing their role in that activity, and this applies both to what we work *with* and to what we operate *on*, what is in process of becoming a finished product. The human body, too, like the space in which it operates, enters the picture as a function of what is going on. We can no more account for the things independently of the activity than we can describe the activity independently of the things. The housewife's knowledge—the knowledge that is essential to her function—can likewise be described only in terms of things and operations to conceive.

To do her work, the housewife must be aware when each included operation is complete—just when, for instance, the cream has reached the required stiffness for breaking off the whipping process and switching to the next step (such as spreading the cream on the cake). She must know, too, when the job is finally finished—know the proper start-and-stop routines. And this means she must have a conscious identity—a certain self-awareness through time—which comprehends the process in its entirety and enables her to switch from activity to activity.

It is assumed here that the *agent* is aware of what she is doing (in this case, that the housewife is aware of what it is her work requires her to know). We assume, moreover, that *we*, reporting on this activity, share that insight with the agent.[2]

What we are looking for are those features of day-to-day activities without which those activities could not retain their identity. We are thus in search of something quite different from an empirical review of diverse activities or the subjection of some theory about such activities to an empirical test. Our concern is with the basic structure of these activities. Or, if you please, features seen as constitutive—as a *sine qua non*—of the activities in question.

The use we make of examples is not intended to lend empirical support to theories or to illustrate concepts already acquired. Our examples, already given shape by our preconceptions concerning what is as issue, provide us with a basis for acquiring and testing the categories best suited for getting to grips with the matter in hand.

We could therefore in a sense be said to be engaging in phenomenology, an attempt to spell out the constitutive features of phenomena by taking activities within well-defined life-environments as illustrative examples;[3] indeed, a sort of transcendental phenomenology, though such terms yield in themselves no very precise information.

What emerges as we describe the housewife's activity and function is the *point of view* it constitutes—the close encounter with things and processes, with spatial and temporal dimensions, with one's own body and one's own identity, as well as with other individuals for whom things are done and with whom dealings go on.[4] And the more exhaustively the activity is specified, the finer the distinctions, of which the point of view, that emerges, admits.

The agent in characteristic action affords us double access to the process of concept formation via two interlocking fields of association, viz. those of grasping and of seeing. If we are not to get hold of the wrong end of the stick, we must first focus right, while a good grip on things helps us get them in focus. The one field lies open through getting a hold and manipulating, the other through sighting and focusing, and the two merge in the operation, the activity. The concepts by which we get to grips with an activity's components are at one and the same time definitive of and determined by what is grasped. It might be put like this: point of view and object in sight, means of comprehension and thing comprehended, are conditional upon each other—just as the activity as a whole and its constituent acts and objects are mutually definitive. It is these two fields of association—visual and manual—that afford joint access to the dialectic of concept formation. The notion of an operation-dependent view thus encapsulates an understanding essentially rooted in activity.

Our aim in describing such activities and the views they incorporate is to bring out more clearly what we already know about our own and other people's activities. We want to bring both our own and other people's way of looking at things into better focus. Failure to realize how other people are 'making out' is very possibly a more common reason for gratuitously imposing upon or offending others than any real wish to do them an injury. Just think of the problems children can face and of which grown-ups are quite unaware simply because adults are taller. Or think of the ways we unconsciously exploit other people, where an effort to put ourselves in their shoes could awaken us to what we are doing. Key phrases in this connection are 'bringing to consciousness'[5] and 'confluence of horizons',[6] and the keynote is struck wherever different individual agents, classes, age-groups, sexes, or periods can find no shared viewpoint, no common perspective.

Gaining recognition is, we might say, getting oneself seen as a person, one consequence being that others begin to *see the point* of what one is up to; anyone who remains 'unseen' in this sense simply doesn't belong to a community, and suffers all the consequences this must have for a person's sense of identity. There is a kind of unimaginativeness which leaves a person imprisoned in his or her own narrow vision, with very little idea of what it is like for the various other people they rub shoulders with. And this stunted awareness of others brings with it a stunted awareness of oneself. For how can I know what I myself am really about unless I have an adequate picture of the dealings of those around me? The housewife's daily doings mesh with those of the rest of the family, as well as with those of the shopkeeper, the bus driver, the teacher, etc. and thus with the whole community in which she lives.

What a person does (and what gives an adequate picture of that person's doings) is thus seen to be correlative with what other people do (and with what gives an adequate picture of *their* activities). These is no understanding an activity (along with the agent's view of things and of herself) in isolation, for self-understanding is understanding oneself-and-others within a common framework.

Deciding what a person is about when engaging in a particular activity—forging horseshoes, say, at the anvil with a hammer—depends in addition on the actions that *precede* and *follow*. In order to discover whether the man doing the forging is a smith, we don't just keep on watching what he does; we take a look at what he does along with the result. It is selling horseshoes to make a living that identifies him as a blacksmith.[7] If, instead, he goes on to exhibit his handiwork to a class of schoolchildren, he could well be a metalwork teacher or an expert on arts and crafts rather than a smith. Thus the greater totality to which the activity belongs, and from which it gets its identity, has its own *temporal* setting.

As we are already aware, then, the identity of an activity is never to be determined in isolation, but only with reference to a wider scheme of things to which it belongs, one involving other people via division of labour and complementarity of occupations, besides the other activities of the agent himself as time goes on.

A blacksmith is a blacksmith within a division-of-labour patterned community while at the same time, simply as human, having both immediate and more remote bonds of kinship. (The smith may be said to have his place within both a productive and a reproductive sphere, whereas the traditional housewife is, as it were, permanently housed in the realm of reproduction.) By just picking on one function—the smith in his smithy, the wife in her kitchen—we are left with loose threads right and left: connections not to be coped with via a single function, but linking inexorably with other roles in a pattern of life. In a given integrated socio-historical setting, this immanent carry-over from function to function culminates in a variety of typical life-cycles.[8]

The stable, self-sufficient, self-governing community is in this sense a sort of minimal operational whole, and *ipso facto* a minimal overall perspective. Such worlds compact in their time, were perhaps the tribe, the city-state, and the village.

Yet here, too, we encounter diverse agents, each with a 'station and its duties' and the viewpoint that goes with them. Can there be found anywhere a bearer of that conspectus, that overview, in which the wholeness wins its own perspective? Each individual view shades over into others, and so into a totality, but how can the individual, from one confined perspective, reach over into comprehensiveness? Once we admit that the view is bound up with the agent, and that the social sum-total finds no agent identity, we seem at a loss to make the total overview do any real work.

Even if the various activities, each having its own perspective, may be said to culminate in a single operational totality—the self-sufficient local community—there is no one agent who acts out the totality role and to whom we can attribute the overview. The comprehensive agent-subject is a composite of things communally done by a multitude of agents.

Religious leaders have no doubt been taken to be bearers of the real conspectus. But how can we think of them as 'agents'? And haven't just such claims been under bombardment ever since the Enlightenment?

The idea was once current that the absolute monarch—in full sail—simply *was* the functioning community as overview-endowed agent. We all know how this claim has been unmasked.

The words of the poets no doubt make the world we live in present to us, but what is there to give them agent status? Admittedly, our vision can be poetically sharpened and revised, too, for that matter. But how is poetry qua poetry to *authenticate* its would-be synoptic vision?

The diverse members of a community surely do, in a sense, assimilate it in its entirety. Just as the individual's functions fall in with and have reference to a whole communal network of intermeshing operations, so does the individual's view of things somehow mirror the aggregate's power of seeing. Through the learning of a language, and by being trained to carry out specific operations and to identify with them, each individual is impregnated with a vision in which the corporate overview is, so to speak, printed off at a specialized location. Seen in this light, the transparent society is one in which everyone sees the point of what everyone else is up to.[9]

By no means is everything we do straightforward 'agent-activity', a one-way traffic in the processing of concrete objects. Our way of looking at things, our notion of what we are and the sort of things we latch on to—all this takes shape, to no small extent, in the course of the varied dealings we have with others: conversing, passing on information, showing affective concern, putting a whole viewpoint on display through artistic creativity. Our points of view are, then, not fully represented in the notions of agent-and-things-done: there must be this carry-over into the dialogue of social and cultural interchange. Accounting for the black-smith in his smithy is not enough. Our picture must take in the putting of children to bed, the ritual, the festivity and artist's innovation.[10]

But in what sense may the agents in such cases be said to 'know what they have to know in order to do what they do'? And in what sense are the agent's outlook and our own coincident? It is now that we really come face-to-face with the validation issue, as concerns both the agent's outlook and our own. Questions of truth and rightness come up naturally for the agents when their actions and interactions run into problems. Doubts and dissensions can then be dealt with in a variety of ways: force majeure or ritual, careful inquiry or counting votes. But in describing the agents and their actions we ourselves face the same issues, for we implicitly claim for ourselves the relevant insight, and thus claim to have gained the necessary vantage point. To make this claim good, we are bound to validate our own account of things—if we can.

It may be worthwhile supplementing these programmatic sketches of a phenomenological approach with an attempt to put our validation problem in its historical setting.

In the Greek city-state, a conspectus was still fairly feasible. Aristotle was therefore on the whole content to describe the good life and the good community, so attaining a model perspective as a guide to action and an elucidation of what every inhabitant knew. Otherwise, he assembled data about various city-states and assigned them to classes. Nothing more seemed to be needed. A little reflection and observation sufficed for a man to know what he was doing when he took action, and the consequences of an action were plain for all to see.

In the larger post-Renaissance societies, with their propensity for continual change, the conspectus has been harder to come by. Shared reflections and simple observations are no longer enough if we want to know what we are doing, and each man's deeds are swallowed up in a vast theatre of action no man can survey. Indeed, to the extent that we *are* what we do, not knowing what we are up to means not knowing who we are. It is quite apparent that actions not uncommonly have unintended consequences, or even bring about the very opposite of what we meant. Agents, in short, have all too often lost touch with what is really going on, and the sum-total of all the separate acts points sightlessly in a direction none foresaw. The opaque society has no observation window from which it may be steered.

All this leads to a greater need for systematic scrutiny of what is really afoot, and in the wake of the natural sciences empirically oriented social sciences emerge and take shape. What the traditional housewife never glimpsed from her functionally restricted viewpoint, economics, sociology and psychology can open her eyes to. Enlightened by the sciences, we see more clearly, act more effectively; they pave the way from the microcosmic to the macrocosmic perspective. And as they acquaint us with their overview, much that is obscure in our everyday picture is more deeply and sharply illuminated.

The comprehensive overview comes to be identified with the scientific perspective, the outlook shared by scientists as agents who represent the common quest of the questioning community.

Phenomena like economic crisis, unemployment, and climate change are things which no one seems to have aimed at and which cannot be comprehended from the functional viewpoint of the traditional housewife or blacksmith. The attempt is now being made to get to the bottom of such problems through the sciences, and hopefully to get them under some control through political institutions that turn to the sciences for assistance.

This makes the community of researchers, taken collectively as investigators in joint action, into the agent-subject endowed with an overview. At the same time, the social embodiment of science in the form of expertise available to employers and administrators has transferred the principal overview-directed agent roles to political and financial leaders. As Max Weber has it, the world has undergone 'scientization': supposedly rational management and ideological concord are in the driving seat. Presumably, the sciences tell us the way things are, and how the various means available are more or less well suited to attainment of this or that objective. Yet the ends in view, the values to be served, are beyond the scope of science—final justification is not a scientific issue, and values may be chosen, not factually established. Decisionism is a watchword here, not rational consensus based on argumentation. Value questions can be decided by the largest vote, not by the strongest argument, and it is in free elections and representative political institutions that the various stands on value find a voice.

These views concerning science and politics are, however, questionable to say the least. In the first place, the sciences present themselves as particular disciplines, each defined by its specific concepts and methods and, indeed its own view. How the one Truth is to emerge as an all-embracing synthesis of these dissimilar approaches is no small problem. And how might the variants within socio-economics, sociology, psychology, etc. be harmonized or unified? Is some categorial frame of a higher order to be found, some mate-science, or is intertranslatability at a given stage the most we can hope for?

Supposing these problems to be solved, what sort of organization is needed to ensure that this total view of things takes control over society? Presumably one that restricts the exercise of power to political institutions and places the comprehensive overview at their disposal. Which would, of course, mean putting such spontaneous mechanisms as the market pretty well out of commission. Yet this would call for a multitude of administrative structures serving to ensure access to crucial insights and to consolidate control, surely just the mechanisms that would again fragment both the perspective and the overall control we were after.

Now let us suppose that these problems, too, are out of the way, and that a unitary collective agent-subject, bringing comprehensive insight to bear, controls and governs everything. What sort of society do we end up with? An optimally enlightened oligarchy, it would seem, in which the privileged few have total insight and total power, the rest being left devoid of either. The Platonic state ideal springs to mind.

We have admittedly got this far on very much of an *ex hypothesi* basis: We have envisaged both a unitary agent at the political level and a synthesis of disciplines yielding scientific unity. A fully Platonic position further requires, in the last analysis, the subsumption of all particular viewpoints and interests under the one overview and the interests common to all—a synthesis comprising not just the view-points of the several sciences, but even in the last resort each and every functionally localized view, whether of class, occupation or individual citizen.

We might call this the God's-eye view, and find no finite eye to behold it. Let us turn in our tracks and look the way we have come.

Suppose, then, a conflict has arisen about building a nuclear power station. How can the problem be tackled in a way that will finally lead to a sane overall perspective and a rational and reasonable programme of action? Various disciplines can throw light on the issue, and the corresponding experts must be called in: technicians, economists, lawyers, ecologists; and all these submit their reports to the authorities, whose subsequent decisions should reflect the values expressed by the electorate. Presumably the special forms of expertise tell us the way things are, leaving no room for disagreement where the facts are concerned. But when we turn to asking what is wanted and what needs to be done, there is no expert consensus to draw on. This is where the counting of votes might take over.

But who is expert on what sort of experts to call in? Each discipline furnishes truths about the matter, derived from its own peculiar concepts and methods, but how are we to decide, in a scientific way, who are the relevant experts on a given issue? The answer would appear to be that none of the particular disciplines in question—physics, sociology, economics, and so forth—can settle the matter. Are we to conclude, then, that there is no rational way of hitting on the right choice of experts, so that there is only decision-making to fall back on—as many contend is the case with values and purposes generally? And does this really imply disagreement on just what is at issue?

However—it was, after all, these disciplines that put us in the picture! What are we in fact doing when *we* take it upon ourselves to bring all this up for *discussion*? What sort of expertise and rationality do we lay claim to, and how are we to validate our own pronouncements?

Well, even admitting our lack of any such meta-discipline as we were canvassing, we have at least succeeded in reflecting on the problem-complex involved. Despite our still having arrived at no criterion for selecting the rightful expert, we have succeeded in focusing attention on this multiplicity-of-experts problem. And if we go on to ask by virtue of what sort of insight we do so, the answer that suggests itself is: through reflective understanding of what is at issue and how the various disciplines relate to it. The whole complex of problems is sharply illumined through a reflective interchange among persons with a genuine commitment to penetrate deeper.

We are thus invoking the possibility of an interpretative hermeneutic and essentially interdisciplinary procedure. The insight which thus emerges owes its credibility to the way arguments stand up under constant challenge—though only, we may add, where arguments win on their own merits, and gratuitous disturbing factors are eliminated. Such ideal conditions, where only the rationality and reasonableness of the participants is allowed to count for anything, must at least be approximated if a resulting consensus is to be accredited. And, needless to say, the free exchange of views here envisaged promotes the formulation of diverse particular viewpoints and thus a wider recognition of them.

In light of this, the overview is now attributed, not to the individual experts or to the powers that be, but to the communion of participants in open, public debate—in an ongoing, emancipated interchange between all those concerned: expert, politician, and layman alike.[11]

Are we drifting again into the fanciful, the Utopian?

Let us resume our former track. We must ask whether the very fact that we engage in talk and dialogue about the building of a nuclear power station does not in itself involve us in the presupposition that our own comments are true and correct, inasmuch as, even if we cannot make good what we say there and then, we at any rate count on being able to do so in a fair debate (where the best argument is bound to win). Surely the very person who plays up the irrational elements in human actions and opinions in order to discredit the notion of such an ideal fellowship-in-disputation is bound to make just such a claim about his own protestations. To the extent to which this is always being taken for granted, the ideal communion of fellowship of arguers is already there and in action—if only as an operative presupposition.[12]

This being so, why then should there be such a decisive distinction between 'is' and 'ought', between assertions on the one hand and imperatives and value-judgments on the other? No doubt there are differences in the way we go about backing these different kinds of claim to validity; but might it not very well prove possible to meet normative validation requirements in the course of such continuing discussion, and here, too, arrive at rational and reasonable agreement?

In so far as the facts are shaped and indeed constituted via a social practice or institution, there will in principle be nothing to block an immediate transition from institutional facts to norms. Granted, for instance, a lifepattern which includes the institution of borrowing and paying back, the *obligation* to repay under certain circumstances is already ensured. This we can take account of without ourselves underwriting the institution, so that the point really at issue is to what extent we can find institutions (having norms built into them) to which there is no real alternative. For a kind of universal validity could in this way be claimed for the built-in norms. Yet is not the optimally argument-decided discussion to which we implicitly appeal in claiming to validate our assertions and actions just such an indispensable 'institution'? However much we may protest that this publicly paraded rationality is a historically conditioned phenomenon, that it is vulnerable, imperfectly realized and easily undermined, do not our own utterances and actions somehow presuppose that we hold ourselves answerable to such an ideal standard? And doesn't the very notion of arguments being judged on their own merits entail the presence of inbuilt norms—regulative principles—such as freedom, equality and universality?

Once more, we find ourselves propelled toward the overhead lighting, and recoil, dazzled. From our humble and down-to-earth start, picturing the doings of blacksmith and housewife, we repeatedly soar to vantage points at which our sight grows dim.

Yet as we rest and reflect, rubbing weary eyes, a certain after-image will not go away—that of reason as a reflected-upon and continuing argumentative coherence due to the joint efforts of agent-subjects in pursuit of honest agreement.

Notes

1 This is a slightly revised version of a text published in Gunnar Skirbekk, *Rationality and Modernity*, Oslo/Oxford: Scandinavian University Press/Oxford University Press, 1993: 18–38. Translated from the Norwegian by Kenneth Young.

2 Cf. Jakob Meløe, «The Agent and His World», in Gunnar Skirbekk, ed., *Praxeology*, Oslo: Norwegian University Press, 1983: 13–29.

3 One of the background philosophers here is Martin Heidegger in *Sein und Zeit* (*Being and Time*), §§ 12–34.

4 "As individuals express their life, so they are. What they are, therefore, coincides with their production, with what they produce and with how they produce it." Karl Marx and Friedrich Engels, *German Ideology*, 1845–1846 (MEGA 175, pp. 10–11).

5 Alluding to Hegel.
6 Alluding to Gadamer.
7 Professional titles tell us what people do and must know, and what *we* can do together with them.
8 The viewpoint essential to a traditional industrial worker in his job may be more limited that that essential to the traditional housewife who reproduces him—or that of a self-supplied peasant. Cf. the gap between the viewpoint essential to an industrial worker in *Modern Times* and that essential to an organized and politically active worker who wants to realize the forces behind the events and take part in constructive changes.
9 Cf. the difference between «coming up through the ranks», e.g. from deck boy to captain, and being given a job directly after school. This leads us to the topics of 'professionalism' and 'educative society'.
10 On praxeology and art, cf. Jakob Meløe, «The Picture in our World», in Gunnar Skirbekk, ed., *Praxeology*, Oslo: Norwegian University Press, 1983: 89–93.
11 This transition from act-oriented praxelogy (Wittgenstein) to universal and transcendental pragmatics (in Habermas and Apel) is a main topic in Skirbekk (1993).
12 Alluding to Apel and Habermas.

Chapter 14

Praxiology

A New Approach

Mirosław Sułek

Traditional praxiology was on the lookout for general principles of crucial actions—which is in line with the intention of Polish praxiologist Tadeusz Kotarbiński—in all domains of human activity from farming, military defence, and healthcare, from the judicial system to education. In this article, I put forward the following theory: Further development of praxiology as a study of efficient action requires a thoroughly new approach to the notion of human activity. The approach is based on the division into three distinct types of human action in society. According to the adopted terminology, these include: cooperation, struggle, and rivalry. These actions are described within the domains of economics, the art of war, and political science, which have their equivalents in the practical domains of management, command, and politics. The efficiency of action in each of the domains is based on different logic—a different understanding of outlay and effects, as well as the efficiency calculi. The division mentioned above suggests that there is general praxiology and detailed praxiology.

Nature of Interpersonal Relations

Humans, as part of social organism, live and act in a competitive environment, i.e. in the world of limited resources (the so-called scarcity of goods), where they primarily struggle to *survive*, and subsequently *develop*. For this purpose, they create *social systems of action*. Scarcity of goods can only be handled in two ways: either through voluntary *cooperation*, or *struggle*. In game theory, cooperation is a positive-sum game (all parties involved benefit from it); while struggle is a negative-sum game (all parties involved incur losses). In reality, there is no pure cooperation, or pure struggle. There always exists a mix (hence, the relationships between countries can either be friendly, congruous, tense, or hostile). In the course of their activity, people must make decisions related to the direction and proportion (intensity) of cooperation/struggle. This form of action shall be called *rivalry* (which is a zero-sum game). Survival and development in the conditions of scarcity of goods force people to maximize their potential (wealth, power, force, glory, fame, prestige, recognition, authority).

These aspirations are synthesized in a concept of power developed by Bertrand Russell. In his view, "the fundamental concept in social science is Power in the same sense in which Energy is the fundamental concept in physics".[1]

There are three types of human action: cooperation, struggle, and rivalry. *Cooperation*, as a positive-sum game, is characterized by the fact that all of the parties involved benefit from it. Considering states, a good example is a market economy. Company–client cooperation, as well as company–company cooperation, is beneficial for both entrepreneurs and their clients. What is more, the success of an enterprise is not determined by another enterprise's elimination; quite conversely—the development of a specified group of enterprises requires the development of other enterprises. Even enterprises directly competing with each other obtain benefits (through an increased focus on the development of innovation, the flexibility of action, etc.). And even if one of them fails (as a result of insufficient cooperation with society or the fact that they have stopped their cooperation), the entire society benefits, as the released resources are transferred to more efficient entrepreneurs, which in turn means that they can be utilized in a better way.

Economy falls within the theory of cooperation (it can be called economy of cooperation, or even civil economy). On its foundations emerges an applied science-management. Cooperation is based on trust and truth, and therefore on informing. It is characterized by the ethics of cooperation, or economic ethics, understood as ethics of calculation, ethics of reason and prudence, and accompanied by economic aesthetics, directed towards creating order and harmony in the economic system.

Struggle (as a negative-sum game) means that all the parties involved incur losses. Struggle understood like this can be observed in various areas. Considering countries, the best example is an armed conflict, i.e. life-and-death struggle. Struggle is all about victory and either destruction of the opponent, or inflicting injury to the opponent so as to make him harmless.

The art of war falls within the theory of struggle (which can also be called the economy of struggle or simply the military economy). It constitutes a foundation for the applied science of leadership. The art of war is based on deception, deceit, surprise, and misinformation. It goes with military ethics, which protects unity of leadership and action, as well as the spirit of fight. It is accompanied by military aesthetics, which is reflected not only in the elegance of military uniforms and drill, but also in military operations.

Rivalry (as a zero-sum game) means that one party's gains are the other party's losses of the same extent. This is the nature of aspiring to power nationally or globally, power always equals 100 per cent, and individual units organized into different social groups struggle for the biggest share they can secure. It is evident on the international arena—individual countries aspire to as much power as they can reach, or the biggest share in global power. In this case, power cannot be shared, and particular parties have completely opposing interests.

Table 14.1 System of Human Action

Sphere of Reality		*Sphere of Regulation*
Cooperation	*Struggle*	*Rivalry*
Logic of cooperation	Logic of struggle	Logic of rivalry
Theory of cooperation	Theory of struggle	Theory of rivalry
Economy	Warfare theory	Political science
Management	Command	Politics
Positive-sum game	Negative-sum game	Zero-sum game
Truth	Deception	Hypocrisy (double-dealing)
Information	Misinformation	Propaganda
Ethics of cooperation	Ethics of struggle	Ethics of rivalry
Aesthetics of cooperation	Aesthetics of struggle	Aesthetics of rivalry

As rivalry ranges across cooperation and struggle, it is based on double-dealing, which is mainly reflected in propaganda. Depending on the level of tension between the rivals, propaganda leans either toward the truth, or toward deception. It all complies with the ethics of rivalry (ethics of politics), supported by the aesthetics of rivalry. Rivalry is a basic element of social life—ruling over the subsystems of cooperation and struggle. One might even say that rivalry is the essence of social life.

This reasoning is illustrated by Table 14.1.

The three aforementioned types of action constitute a uniform social system of action, which consists of spheres of reality and regulation. Cooperation and struggle belong to the sphere of reality, whereas rivalry belongs to the sphere of regulation. The reality sphere is where matter and energy are processed, while the sphere of regulation is where information processing happens. Information processing is aimed at controlling people's action.

Areas directly relating to praxiology include: economy and management; the art of war and leadership; political science and politics. Based on the traditional division, it may be assumed that economy, the art of war, and political science belong to descriptive sciences, while management, leadership, and politics belong to applied sciences, i.e. to praxiology, as such.

Key Concepts

The above considerations enable a division into general praxiology, which is compatible with its traditional definition, and detailed praxiology, referring to the three systems of action—cooperation, struggle, and rivalry. Praxiology is, by definition, an applied science. However, it is certainly acceptable to distinguish descriptive praxiology. In this article, I consider exclusively applied praxiology. The following definitions are proposed.

General praxiology is a study of efficient action, i.e. of efficient management of limited resources. Scarcity of resources is common to cooperation, struggle, as well as rivalry. Praxiology is actually a study of decision-taking: optimal *method* of exploiting the *resources* (means) available for the purpose of achieving intended *goals*. Most textbooks use definitions of this kind, yet they refer to management, and not praxiology, consequently missing the issues of politics and leadership.

Praxiology is thus a study of strategies of achieving goals by means of the available resources regardless of the type of action. This approach is, in principle, compatible with the traditional approach. While Tadeusz Kotarbiński was concerned with the technique of struggle (negative cooperation), he was not fully consistent with the issue. He also failed to consider the struggle for the balance of power (opportunity) as a natural axis of human action, which comes down to maximizing power. On the other hand, Ludwig von Mises wrote of war, yet he mentioned it in passing, virtually equating praxiology with economics.

Considering the three types of action, one may distinguish respectively—in terminological terms—three branches of praxiology: management, command, and politics.

The following definitions shall be assumed.

Management (the sphere of mainly market action, i.e. based on exchanges) is a process of decision-making, referring to the methods (strategies) of achieving goals by means of the available means (resources) within the system of positive-sum game.

Command (sphere of mainly military action) is a process of decision-making, referring to the methods (strategies) or achieving goals by means of the available means (resources) within the system of negative-sum game.

Politics (the sphere of governance, i.e. domestic and international politics) is a process of decision-making, referring to the methods (strategies) of achieving goals by means of the available means (resources) within the system of zero-sum game.

The first parts of the definitions presented are identical, the only difference being the type of the game being played. However, it has major consequences in the methods of efficient action. Every type of the action mentioned requires use of different principles (not merely technical, but also ethical and aesthetic ones), different efficiency calculus, distinct knowledge and skills, as well as different personality traits. Therefore, principles of the kind of economic principles (principles of cooperation) should not be transferred to the battlefield or generally to the armed forces. And vice versa, the economy should not be militarized in the times of peace. However, such attempts have often been made. The well-known PPB (planning, programming, budgeting) system introduced at the beginning of the 1960s in the United States at the time of automobile business executive

Robert McNamara's term as secretary of defence, was based on thorough economic analyses, subject to "civil" logic. The system in question did not recognize the different principles of management in the armed forces. On the other hand, socialist economics, especially in the initial phases, was highly militarized, which resulted in mismanagement, wastefulness, and finally its collapse.

For dozens of years, in western literature (mainly in the US), there has been a tendency toward referring to the works on the theory and practice of warfare in the study of organizations, management and formulation of recommendations for entrepreneurs. Interestingly, propagators of the application of warfare principles in business hailed the work of a Chinese strategist from 2500 years ago as its holy book. It is obviously *The Art of War*, attributed to Sun Tzu (also referred to as Sun Tsu, or Sunzi). There emerge publications concerned with 'the art of war in business', 'the art of war on executives', etc. This trend continues.[2] Not surprisingly, the propagators of Sun Tzu's work include the Chinese. The author of one of the books writes:

> Of course, in the context of this book, war and business activity are synonymous with each other. Both war and business are human activities with a well-defined objective or objectives. (...) Although Sunzi was talking about military issues, its strong generality, the vast time and space span of his theories and principles make it totally applicable to any type of business activity.[3]

This view is based on a misunderstanding. The foundations of economic activity include complex structures of cooperation, which contribute to the general increase in wealth, while struggle leads to destruction and impoverishment. Undoubtedly, 'business is not war'. Opposite statements which sometimes occur, emphasizing the intensity of struggle in economic competition, are no more than a generally acceptable literary metaphor.

"Business and war may share a number of common elements, yet they will always differ in the unique nature of forces which trigger them, and in the results they produce."[4] This is in line with my theses, which are based on a simple truth that the logic of actions and the efficiency calculi in cooperation and struggle are entirely different. Economic (market) activity belongs to the sphere of cooperation, not struggle. Both cooperation and struggle are spheres of human activity and for this reason, they have certain common characteristics. Yet, this does not justify the interchangeability of principles used in the two disparate systems. In the light of the presented reasoning, an approach like this is unwarranted.

Efficiency Calculi

Principles of Efficient Action

Being an applied science, praxiology aims to provide recommendations and cautions, i.e. certain principles and norms of behaviour.

As previously mentioned, cooperation is a positive-sum game—it is based on a community of interests. The study of economics was not focused on a provision of principles of efficient action following those of the art of war, but it proposed what can be called "the principles of economic analysis"—this issue will be skipped here. It would seem that the study of management should be aimed at codifying the principles of efficient management (action), but the list of these is hard to find. I believe that the attempts to formulate the principles of cooperation make sense; the proposed provisional set contains the following principles: freedom of choice; mutual profit; openness; accuracy; trust; gradual arrangements (negotiations); solidarity; incrementalism (evening of end profits); empathy.

These principles refer to so-called pure cooperation. Real life is, however, richer, e.g. in commercial exchange, some forms of struggle occur, yet they do not interfere in the general logic of cooperation.

The principles of the art of war are historically determined rules of preparing and conducting military operations, which constitute a foundation for rational activity of commands and armies in the tactical, operational and strategic areas. It is noteworthy to mention a disputable issue of the invariability of warfare principles. It seems that most authors consider warfare principles to be constant, which is what I am also inclined to believe. However, the undoubtedly changeable struggle conditions, mainly impacted by technology (forces and means of armed struggle), but also by the political aims of war, highlights or weakens the significance of particular principles, which, however, does not render them variable.

As was already mentioned, struggle is a negative-sum game. While it is connected with conflicting interests, there is a common element too—both parties incur losses! Hence, struggle is more honourable in nature than rivalry. The art of war is based on principles known for centuries, or even millennia, and in nature—for millions of years. Hence, its principles do need to be not so much discovered as deciphered from the experience of the animated world. The best-known treatise on the art of war is Sun Tzu's *Art of War* (approx. 2500 years ago). He identified numerous principles of the art of war, emphasizing the strategy of surprise and deception of the enemy; "Try to deceive your enemy"; "War is based on deception"; "Create numerous fake military operations" etc.[5]

Nowadays, there exist many various lists of the principles of warfare; many of them are similar to each other, while the other ones significantly differ from the traditional approaches. Their number ranges from a few to a dozen or so, which shows that there still remains a large area for research. Here is a typical list: offensive, concentration, security, unity of command, manoeuvre, surprise, simplicity.[6] Polish General Franciszek Skibiński, World War I and World War II participant, mentions very similar principles: aim, concentration, economy of force, manoeuvre, simplicity, offensive, surprise, freedom of action (guard), and unity of command.[7]

As was already mentioned, rivalry is a zero-sum game, which means that it is connected with entirely conflicting interests. There is no shared element, which occurs in the sphere of cooperation, or even struggle. The following principles will be stipulated, which are clearly noticeable in the sphere of international relations: constant aim (results from striving for maximizing one's power); hypocrisy (results from a combination of the principles of cooperation and struggle—the more cooperation, the more truth, and vice versa); tenacity (zero-sum game!); instability (agreements, alliances)—also resulting from countries aspiring towards improving their positions; seizing opportunities—it seems that it is a general principle of reasonable action, but it is especially worth recommending in the sphere of rivalry.

All of the mentioned principles of cooperation, struggle and rivalry are principles of efficient action. An attempt at their inclusion into inappropriate field, e.g. warfare principles to activity based on cooperation, is a misunderstanding. Similarly, principles of cooperation (economy) should not be applied to activities based on struggle.

Profits and Losses in the Sphere of Reality (Cooperation and Struggle)

Every organized action involves people entering into various types of relations, which are connected with certain benefits (profits, gains) and outlay (costs, losses). In the light of the opinions presented here, they depend on the type of system of action and the balance of power (potential), i.e. the state of balance or imbalance. Cooperation is beneficial for both parties, yet it should be emphasized that the relative profits of the weaker (less-developed) partner are bigger. In struggle (where losses prevail), it is the opposite—the stronger party incurs lesser losses (absolute and relative ones). This reasoning is presented in Table 14.2.

Table 14.2 Profits and Losses Depending on the System of Action and Balance of Power (Potential)

Balance of Power (Potential)	*System of Action*	
	Cooperation	*Struggle*
	Profits	*Losses*
Balance	Balance of profits (proceeds)	Balance of losses (human and financial ones)
No Balance	Weaker party gains more (less-developed)	Smaller losses borne by the stronger party (better-developed)

The content of Table 14.2 is often misunderstood. In literature, contrary statements can be found. International economic exchange, liberalization—is seen as more profitable for countries which are economically stronger than for those which are weaker. This view is obviously wrong. Proponents of an expansion of economic cooperation as part of integration argue that benefits will be obtained by the less-developed countries, or even highly-developed, but small ones more commercial opportunities arise, turnover from international trade grows, transfer of technology increases, more educational opportunities arise etc. International relations experts often indicate China and India as the countries which have significantly benefited from globalization.

Competition is also often misinterpreted as allegedly serving the stronger party. First of all, competition (the so-called fair competition, in line with the prearranged rules of the game, supervised by the judiciary) is a form of cooperation, therefore it serves both parties (and at the same time—whole society), but to a larger extent—the weaker party. It turns out that in the times of globalization, the rich defend from competition of the poor, and hence the weaker ones. One cannot fail to acknowledge that, "the contribution of the USA into the growth of GDP in China is undoubtedly bigger than the contribution of China into the growth of GDP in the USA. The conclusion: as global economy progressed, peripheral countries reaped more benefits than the central countries. Economies which remained behind global capitalist economy incurred losses".[8] This thesis is supported by successes of giants like China, India, or Brazil, but also of relatively smaller Asian and African countries.[9]

To sum up, voluntary economic exchange serves both parties, but it is the less-developed economy that gains more. One can refer to the teacher—student analogy. The teacher can also undoubtedly learn from the student, but it is the student who is the main beneficiary of this cooperation. A totally different situation occurs in struggle—it is the stronger one who incurs lesser losses, inflicting respectively higher losses on the opponent.

Profits and Losses in the Sphere of Regulation (Rivalry)

Rivalry, which is a zero-sum game, concerns power, in which case the profits mainly mean an increase in power, while the losses entail its decrease. It is clearly noticeable on the international area, where countries compete for an extent of national power, or their share in 100% of global power. An increase in one country's power results in a decrease of another, and vice versa. In other words, while some grow, others will fall. A significant increase in the power of China and a considerable increase in that of India (and other countries) happened at the expense of countries such as Japan, the USA, or the majority of EU countries. It is notable that the end results of the competition on the international arena depend on more than just the effort of a given nation, but are a function of the changes in the entire global system.

Two major approaches can be adopted while calculating national power formal models and expert assessments. The theory of international relations offers several dozens of methods of assessing and measuring national power, however, this issue is only discussed in a few countries, mainly current superpowers and countries aspiring to a superpower status. The most extensive research of this type is conducted in the USA, Russia and China, and less so in Japan, India, Iran, Turkey, Poland, Germany, and Brazil. Expert assessments can be used independently of formal models, yet the best results are yielded by a combination of the two approaches.

Summary

Praxiology has been going through a crisis for dozens of years. The reason for this is the exhaustion of possibilities for finding general principles of efficient action valid for all areas of human action. A new approach, based on the division of praxiology into three branches, corresponding to the three types of human activity—cooperation, struggle and rivalry, can offer a new opportunity for praxiology to further develop. The three branches differ in their logic of action, their understanding of outlay, and their distinct efficiency calculi. Therefore, it seems justified to distinguish between general praxiology (similar to traditional praxiology) and detailed praxiology, composed of—as I propose—management (the sphere of cooperation, positive-sum game); leadership (the sphere of struggle, negative-sum game) and politics (zero-sum game). Management is primarily based on the developments of the economics, leadership—on the developments of the art of war, and politics—on the developments of the theory of politics.

The art of war seems best developed of the three, the least developed one being the economics (as in its mature version, it emerged no earlier than the emergence of market economics), while wars have been with us for hundreds of years. Politics emerged a long time ago, when people started organizing themselves into larger agglomerations, based on hierarchy and aspiration to power.

Calculations and any efficiency calculi in management, leadership or politics are focused on their key values, which include, respectively: economic value (prices, wages, profits), military value (military ability, military readiness) and the political value (e.g. power, force, influence).

There undoubtedly exist general principles of efficient action, but they have a limited practical usefulness. The true colour of praxiology is reflected in its three branches and the respective principles of efficiency.

Notes

1 B. Russell, *Power. A New Social Analysis*, Routledge, London and New York 1996, p. 4.
2 See e.g.: Becky Sheetz-Runkle, *The Art of War for the Small Business. Defeat the Competition and Dominate the Market with the Masterful Strategies of Sun Tzu*, Amacon 2014 (Ebook); Mark Mc Neilly, *Sun Tzu and the Art of Business. Six Strategic Principles for Managers*, Oxford University Press 2012 (revised edition) and other.

3 M. W. Luke Chan, Chen Bingfu, *Sunzi on the Art of War and its General Application to Business*, Fundan University Press, Shanghai 1998, p. 6–7.
4 T. von Ghyczy, B. von Oetinger, Ch. Bassford, *Clausewitz o strategii*, The Strategy Institute of Boston Consulting Group, Polskie Wydawnictwo Ekonomiczne, Warszawa 2002, s. 23. (Tiha von Ghyczy, Bolko von Oetinger, Christopher Bassford, *Clausewitz on Strategy*, The Boston Consulting Group 2001).
5 Por. Sun Tzu, *Sztuka wojny*, Wydawnictwo Przedświt, Warszawa 1994, passim.
6 Por. V. H. Krulak, *Organization for National Security*. A Study, Washington D. C. 1983, s. 105.
7 Por. F. Skibiński, *Rozważania o sztuce wojennej*, Wojskowy Instytut Historyczny, Warszawa 1972, p. 441–559.
8 J. Hryniewicz, "Globalizacja—rachunkowość geopolityczna", *Przegląd Organizacji* 2009, no. 3, p. 19.
9 See results of the report: M. Sułek (ed.), *Potęga 2015. Międzynarodowy układ sił w procesie zmian*, Polskie Towarzystwo Geopolityczne, Kraków 2015.

Chapter 15

Ethical Measure of Authorship by Tadeusz Kotarbiński's Conception of Action

Andrzej Sztylka

A great deal of significant attention has been devoted by Professor Kotarbiński to problems of authorship. His famous "Treatise on Good Work" speaks volumes on that subject. The ethical measure of authorship is comprised in the professor's considerations, see:

I. "The Tasks of Praxiology", V. "The Possibility to Act" or VI. "The Compound action and its Kinds". The problems can also be seen in Appendix 15, entitled "The Problem of Authorship Essence", presented in the edition of the Treatise mentioned here…[1]

In Chapters II–IV, Professor Kotarbiński carries on the analysis of such elements of acting as the author of an action, the optional impulse, the purpose, the material, the substance, the work, the instrument, and the way of acting, the method, and the result of acting.[2] Professor Kotarbiński also takes up questions of getting conditioned. All this goes to make extensive material to consider. The significance of this material is not expressed in the number of text pages but in the very thorough and close analysis of the subject. In those considerations the ethical measure of authorship is shown in many points and aspects. And so acting, e.g. considering its value, is drawn up doubly, as itself for itself, autotelically, and for its outer aim. Thus, in spite of the causative relation inherent in any action, our attention should be paid at the same time to the teleological aspects of acting. By Kotarbiński's statement, the reason for acting doesn't always refer to things on the outside but directs our attention to the personality and inner life of an author of an action. Ethical questions can be found in many other points of the carried on analysis, as much as character (content) of an optional impulse defined by 'being' itself or by knowledge; in the notion of a motive while considering the differences between the purpose and intention which results in the question of task understood as the tactical aim… Visions of actions depending on personal development of an acting subject as well as on hard occurrences (historical, biographical) can define equally in both cases the ethical measure of authorship. In Appendix 15, the ethical measure of authorship has been taken up, so to say, in three areas, and all of them refer to the problem of making definite choices by an author of an action. They are as follows: (1) examining, stating, creating conditions for optional acting; (2) selecting necessary means; (3) suitable application of them. The present writer analyses the question of fortunate or unfortunate action.[3]

Questions of differences between efficiency and causativeness thought in normative way are important while studying the problem of ethical aspect of authorship. Creating new beings—as the result of acting always brings some ethical risk. And the causative subject's attitude towards itself is a matter of importance. Not only does efficiency become significant but also the rightness of a carried action. The praxiological analysis would have to be crossed diversely by ethical diagnosis of definite causativeness. It's not possible for the present writer to address, even superficially, those questions here. And still so little has been written on the social and cultural aspects of the problem. Here, while taking up the question of character (process) of selecting the action means, we should pay attention to the human beings' morals based on efficient realization of intensions, whereas the customs (habits), grounded on their causative importance, pass over into the sphere of social morals being real components of people's social living. Professor Kotarbiński himself was believed—independently of his remarkable praxiological clear-sightedness—to be very sensitive to normative problems of moral philosophy of authorship; however, he used to claim that *he'd rather give priority to the co-researcher than to the propagandist.*[4] Still, the normative problem of moral philosophy of authorship is a kind of space that can't be passed by even by technically-orientated praxiologist. Therefore his consideration—significant in this measure—in *The Main Problems of Art of Living* and *Problems of Independent Ethics* was published in a famous little book entitled *Meditations on the Equitable Life*.

By the 'art of living' Professor Kotarbiński means the ability for rational selection and the way of acting by any individual. We meet with opposition to such ability, *when someone, as it's said, has wasted one's life.*[5] Thus occurs a very important question of causativeness of acting. In Kotarbiński's opinion, every act, even the most complicated activity, is a compound of one-subject simple actions. And here Kotarbiński introduces the notion of optional impulse, so crucial for the whole conception of causativeness. It's *the strain of the living individual being at the same time some sort of "me", so as to make something happened in definite way and not otherwise.*[6] The action resulting in some way from the said impulse can be directional, and so to present the direct reason of the given result, but it can also be teleological in nature: as professor says, taking the intentional state of things into account, quite remote sometimes from the initial state. The second directive tendency making its way towards the chosen aim, distinguishes the action from among all sorts of events.[7] And so, straining to make something happen, the causative 'me' senses its own optional impulse not as a common sequence of events belonging to the age-long natural course but as something that wouldn't have come into being without it as the causative subject and what couldn't be most certainly foreseen by anyone else. In this way the not-natural act of contemplation originates and this contemplation—through this act—gets an insight into the the core of our actions. And thus occurs *the philosophical deficiency which can be sensed in the face of actions as the components of being.*[8] The causative 'me' detects the perspective of various possibilities left for its choice. So it's necessary to contrive the rational choice to answer the question of what to do to behave sensibly—following professor Kotarbiński's words. But it's just that reflection which introduces the acting being into the reality of human values because *to specific wonders of action belong paradoxes of responsibility.*[9] We realize that the results of our and not-our actions go beyond the sphere of intentions and irrespectively whether the causative act succeeds or not, it's followed by *large number of side effects.*[10] Thus, the causative subject, aware of its own and the others' responsibility, becomes not only a glorifier of possible actions, a fan of the problems, but also at the same time their slave. Being in need and seeking for other, wiser people's help, the said subject gets experience which proves that no one can replace us as far as our own acting and responsibility is concerned. And yet one has to act and manage in this area.

Tadeusz Kotarbiński's masterly reflections on ethical measure of authorship are shown by the **threefold analysis of conception of action**. And so the **first** goes the ***causative action technics*** and two action qualities: efficiency and economic management, that is to say, *concern about protecting strength.*[11] It's necessary to organize energy. In wider sense it means that the author of causation is ready to restrain from expending anything indispensable to achieve aim. However, such intention may overstep the limits of the strength resources of the acting subject. In a more narrow sense, one acts efficiently who shows at the same time some knowledge of one's own energy resources and uses them while performing an action and along the way enabling successful accomplishment of intention. The use of a necessary input of energy resources in the whole may be joined with the suffering of acting 'me'. And here the strictly ethical thread occurs: *that one works in an energetic way who doesn't restrain from distress of one's own wearying effort in case if that effort is necessary to achieve the intended result—says professor.*[12] Energy of acting makes the basic condition of its efficiency. However, Professor Kotarbiński declares that energetic acting meant in this way doesn't mean the primitive, coarse aggressiveness or constraint. Finally, such a kind of energy *becomes negation of real energy facing complicated, long-distanced rules requiring thorough discernment, gentle catch, moving along serpentines of detours.*[13]

While economical, we're going to call the sort of acting that expends just as much energy as is needed to achieve the aim, but not the whole possessed store, to be used.

What does the ethical measure of energetic acting consist in? Its contradiction is the sluggish messing around just like the thriftlessness in contradiction to economical management. Apart from energetic acting the technics of efficient acting comprises the minimization of intervention process. Ethical sense of such acting lies in the sort of causation, according to which events develop spontaneously corresponding however with the acting subject's intensions.

An important way of such minimization is so called potentialization—a step used in martial arts. Instead of attacking just threatening with an attack. *It happens that a bank refuses to lend money to a firm but offers the warrant of getting the loan by the firm in case of trouble and the warrant itself, much less expensive than taking the loan, is quite sufficient to support the firm in satisfying way.*[14] Such actions comprise an element of a game and a game means education. Following the professor's words: *when you're playing, then play well… it's in my opinion a sensible way of acting because it's instructive.*[15] It's an organizational instruction. *For in games of that kind models of simplified practical situations are being realized.*[16] Applying the metaphor of good game to the conception of organizing, Tadeusz Kotarbiński defines it as *the most efficient and most economical choice and system of compound action, i.e. the entanglement of actions.*[17] And it's important to say at this point that *the compound action as a whole should come off as most economical and most efficient as possible. Order of the following movements is of importance here.*[18] And there's the problem of game and at the same time of education and moral philosophy of acting: A *bungler… will try to spend possessed trump cards as soon as possible* and loses because later on he hasn't got anything to enter the further game. *An experienced player will behave the other way round*: he (she) will keep his (her) trump cards until their adversaries get rid of their values and become weaker in comparison with the might of an experienced player.[19] Professor Kotarbiński emphasizes here not just the fact of winning itself but rather the *significance of the competent organization in the whole huge area of activity trying to be rational.*[20]

Second—*happiness* and ***unhappiness***. *Good work can be equally harmful as well as helpful says* professor.[21] In definite cases, 'do well' means one thing and in some other ones 'do good' means something different. And here we follow Kotarbiński's significant words: *In any case the technics of efficient activity must define its behind-technical reason, must define its attitude towards someone's welfare.*[22] Thus, we're getting into the area of the second—besides the technics of efficient activity—constituent part of conception of action. The first call in this respect reads: if we want to be happy, let's protect ourselves from unhappiness. The analysis of good work proves here that the point is to go by the hierarchy of importance while undertaking tasks. More important yet is *what removes a bigger harm or what the bigger harm prevents.*[23]

And sensible is the one who carries out documents and not the waste paper from the house on fire.[24] In human acting always exist different but often simultaneous, forced situations. The only things which change are their kind and graduation. The existing structure of relations puts the acting subject before the alternative: The professor says—either *you strain your strength and resist evil choking and lurking to make a hostile jump or you'll surrender and repay with your suffering for your negligence.*[25] And here goes the second call: *woe betide the reckless one who's trusted the appearances of absolute security.*[26] And what does the conception of effective acting say on this? The priority of economy over the ornaments. That postulate has got far-reaching ethical consequences.

And so the material protection of carried life should be valued higher in hierarchy than entertainments. And so the real doing of definite good, as *how to save the beloved person from distress, to spare keen annoyance to someone nice, to contribute in killing a disease epidemics in the germ and so on—are valuated higher in hierarchy than the passion of finding an outlet for one's own energy.*[27] Tadeusz Kotarbiński says that *passions are not equal to each other and that passion doesn't make the sufficient reason to be privileged just because it is passion.*[28] We come here across the 'soft' problem of common features and differences between need and desire. If the 'need' results from an objectively existing lack, deficiency, then 'desire' is a subjectively sensed longing for some less or more conscious satisfaction. The objectively existing need (e.g. some lack of important vitamins in the body) may be expressed by the desire to be satisfied but it doesn't have to be so. Someone may enjoy a diet without those vitamins and this can cause further worsening of one's body condition. It's similar with education. Someone may have some basic educational lacks, but regarding oneself as a well-educated person, might not desire having one's education completed. Next, someone may have desires not proved in objectively existing deficiency, the desires stimulated heterogenically by e.g. dishonest or just strongly suggestive commercials. One more problem within the discussed question are needs and desires resulting of some dysfunctional individuals' conditions as well as of the dysfunctions of social communities. As the examples can serve here: need and desire of some sort of drag in an addicted person and the need of a Leader in the community being on the level of heteronomical regress. Professor Kotarbiński himself doesn't discuss those problems in such a précised way, yet his profound ethical feeling makes him not to stay indifferent towards the discussed questions. *Away with the slogan as the leading one, promoting living in the full to find an outlet for one's energy*—he writes. *It would have been an illusive happiness guide-post for its practical adherents... But let's consider: beside fancies there are needs... There are needs without fancies and giving up one's own specific fancy may be necessary for defending the others against the elementary defeat...*[29] What ethical conclusion comes out of that? Here is *the household which has to state the most preferable actions* as long as the basic needs are not fulfilled.[30] Restrain then is supposed to direct the impulse. It should be remembered that an action, basically successful always results in numerous side effects among which also appear the undesired ones. Its required then—explains professor—to *take present reality as the starting point since one can exist in it somehow.*[31] And in the present reality the only warrant of the possibility to accomplish the intention is a successful test for its actual execution. Here is just the practical realism. Still, *the bearable state of affairs, well known anyway as general principle of the grown up human being*, is hard to stand especially against threats and ill.[32] The moral sense of practical realism is here, however, the rejection of the stoic standpoint. We can't stay indifferent. *I accept the suggestion of activation*—says Tadeusz Kotarbiński. *I ask a question to myself: what to do?* And if there is anything he cares about and what depends on his acting, he takes it in hand.[33]

Fighting against something that makes one unhappy, he acts according to the hierarchy of importance of things; making choice he reckons the proved range of possibilities and chooses minor ill; he doesn't care about his own satisfaction in a straight line and directly—it's not the purpose of his acting but may follow its results. Saying generally, in ethical problems regarding human happiness and unhappiness it's the joy which weighs most and may occur *if you devote yourself to the matter worth to be loved following the estimation of your heart.*[34] Obviously, it happens that the action doesn't attain the conceived aim. But even the greatest loss can't be, in Kotarbiński's opinion, the pretext for taking the stoical attitude *of getting completely independent of the run of events beyond our control.*[35] As only the self-annihilation is able to bring us to it altogether. And that is an ethically reprehensible attitude. At the end of the second analysis of conception of action in sense of ethical measure of caution, let's quote the following Tadeusz Kotarbiński's credo: *Protection from such fate—the broadness of heart. The one whose love is not focused on just one distinguished something, doesn't die along with what's dying. The one bids the lost right and directs one's own thinking and work towards possible rights requiring the one's care.*[36]

Third—the ***question of conscience***. In the conception of action by Kotarbiński there is the profound relation between protection and conscience. In demands: *don't be a bad man; don't be a coward; don't be deceitful; don't be a slut*—occurs the conception of a 'dependable guardian'.[37] We want to emphasize here that it is an ethical-praxiological conception and not just a charitable demand. It doesn't result from 'wishful thinking' but from the postulate of rationality inspired by the heart's demands. An understanding of the essence of ethical estimation is necessary here but insufficient. The choice can be easy when the situation is simple. But it hardly ever is simple. One *should know then what and when should be done and what shouldn't in the given specific situation.*[38] Referring to the already discussed nuances of compound action and to its always specific and repeatedly unique conditions, it's necessary to emphasize that the acting individual by helping someone may hurt the other one at the same time… So if you decide to take responsibility for the right of possibly everyone under your care, *it's necessary to seek strenuously for some ways of justice which always requires some sort of equality from one side, and from the other side it requires some preference choice.*[39] The problem is practically insolvable on the base of ethics—professor Kotarbiński ascertains. But you can try to solve it pedagogically: *having no knowledge how to behave in order to get things rightly, you can arouse and strengthen the motivation of dependable guardianship* in *surrounding individuals* and *choose masterfully one thing keeping to it, as it's better to live in accordance to some order than to stay in confusion.*[40] Such ethical standpoint leads to an attitude by which the main value of seriously treated life problems is joined with ability *to enjoy the independent charms of whiles in the full.*[41] Action, acting are a serious thing but it shouldn't stay at variance with brimming with joy over the surroundings. One should work on developing one's *own inner sunshine*—maintains professor Kotarbiński. *After all, forced* *situations, serious tasks, fixed plans and undertakings—make the framework... through which colours of all possible kinds, harmonious...savoury surprises... are percolated. Catch them on the way and sow them by yourself.*[42] Such attitude—if it's supposed to be commensurable with successful and happy causation can be realized in independent ethics.

And what is the estimation gist of ethical and moral value of behaviour? The autonomy of values and treating them in an unselfish way. Such attitude—says Kotarbiński—unites *decent people of different ideologies.*[43] This idea leads us to the reflection, that real ethics is the ethics of causation itself, that it's independent of philosophy, of philosophic outlook on life. Its indications remain invariable in the area of common sense. *The only thing necessary here but very necessary*—emphasizes Tadeusz Kotarbiński—*is protection against trumped up statements used while motivating opinions.*[44] Thus, the standpoint of practical realism is presented, as far as ethical acting, i.e. causation is concerned.

By the same professor defends the importance of causation in aspect of choice and responsibility of the author of action declaring himself against automatism and indifferentism of convictions and human attitudes; against standpoint of the type: *everything will happen in its time, anything which is supposed to happen—will happen anyway, and if it's going to happen in the future, there'll always appear someone who will do it...* The professor thinks that the gist of ethical causation lies *in the sphere of people's practical relations towards co-members of social communities.*[45] In that meaning the attitude and acting which prove that the given individual has no qualifications for a dependable guardian—deserves of contempt. Professor asks however whether the moral duty is trying to be the possibly most venerable man? Disagreeing on such ethical maximalism, he assumes the attitude of practical realism: *I think that our conscience is not that exacting... It doesn't require records but reliability. It's sufficient if one hasn't deserved of disgrace.*[46] Obviously, just like in production, art, or sport—in the sphere of ethical opinions—great achievements are also possible. And yet, appreciating *leaders in ethics, let's not require leadership from anybody.*[47]

The autonomy of values and disinterested way of treating them enables, to some extent, joining of ethical causation with striving for happiness. Professor says: *Instead of the question, what's more respectable, arises the question: what will you feel better with.*[48] And that one who lives in agreement with one's conscience—feels the best.

And yet the obviousness of such answer may be disquieting. Because reality is not that simple. Therefore if more respect deserves someone with predominating emotionality feature, symptomatic for people devotedly taking care of the other ones,[49] arises the question: how to behave to satisfy the requirements of such motivation. Following the point of view presented by practical realism the question reads: how is an ethical man supposed to behave in disharmonious environment?[50] Then the conscience of kind and brave people faces the dilemma. If, while helping the ones, they're harmful to the others, they can't be satisfied with the quantitative criterion according to which one should stand by the majority even if the minority were to be wronged quite troublesomely.

From the authorship's point of view the most important thing is to do what is right in the best possible way. And if we are able to comply with this condition while facing some serious vital dilemma, *one is supposed to bring oneself to the act of choice and to stand in with some basic circle standing up for it firmly in case of antagonism towards subjects out of the circle.*[51] Yet none of the sides of such dilemma can be neglected by an acting subject. Therefore—one should be aware of the main direction and decide the executory questions in the substantial way fully and taking into account the individual character of each specific case, every human individual.

And this act of ethical crossing of the real causation has a humanistic capacity; that is, namely, ProfessorTadeusz Kotarbiński's immanent humanism. Expressing such methodological option Kotarbiński concludes: *And therefore it's impossible to teach ethics as a branch settled in its details… For it's impossible to replace one's own voice of conscience with someone else's.*[52]

That's what Tadeusz Kotarbiński's appeal of humanism looks like: modest, simple, and profoundly human.

Notes

1 T. Kotarbiński, Treatise on Good Work, fifth edition, Wroclaw-Warszawa-Krakow-Gdansk 1973, Publishing House "Ossolineum", pp. 7–24; 62–92; 542–549.
2 Ibid., p. 25–61.
3 Ibid., pp. 542–549.
4 T. Kotarbiński, Meditations on the Equitable Life, third edition, Warszawa 1976, Publishing House "Wiedza Powszechna", p. 148.
5 Ibid., p. 149.
6 Ibidem.
7 Ibid., p. 150.
8 Ibid., p. 151.
9 Ibidem.
10 Ibidem.
11 Ibid., p. 152.
12 Ibid., p. 153.
13 Ibid., p. 154.
14 Ibid., p. 156.
15 Ibidem.
16 Ibidem.
17 Ibid., pp. 156–157.
18 Ibid., pp. 157.
19 Ibidem.
20 Ibidem.
21 Ibid., p. 158.
22 Ibid., pp. 158–159.
23 Ibid., p. 159.
24 Ibidem.
25 Ibidem.

26 Ibidem.
27 Ibid., p. 160.
28 Ibidem.
29 Ibidem.
30 Ibidem.
31 Ibid., p. 161.
32 Ibidem.
33 Ibid., p. 162.
34 Ibidem.
35 Ibid., p. 163.
36 Ibidem.
37 Ibid., pp. 163–164.
38 Ibid., p. 164.
39 Ibid., p. 165.
40 Ibidem.
41 Ibid., p. 166.
42 Ibidem.
43 Ibid., p. 172.
44 Ibid., p. 173.
45 Ibid., p. 175.
46 Ibid., p. 176.
47 Ibidem.
48 Ibid., p. 177.
49 Ibid., p. 178.
50 Ibidem.
51 Ibid., p. 180.
52 Ibid., p. 183.

Chapter 16

Market Fundamentalism versus Responsible Economizing

Laszlo Zsolnai

In the early twenty-first-century capitalism is at a crossroads. Ecological data show the unsustainable way our economies are functioning. Inequality is record high in our societies and also globally. The legitimacy of capitalism became questionable in many respects. The moral foundation of capitalism should be reconsidered and renewed. I am convinced that *business ethics* and the *future* of *capitalism* are strongly connected. If we want to sustain capitalism for a long time we certainly have to create a less violent, more caring form of it.

Market Fundamentalism and Its Critiques

George Soros (1997, 1998) has developed a strong argument that *laissez-faire capitalism* undermines the values on which open and democratic societies depend. His argument is more relevant today than ever before. While national capitalism was socially constrained and politically regulated, present-day global capitalism is basically unconstrained and unregulated. Soros calls the underlying ideology of global capitalism as 'market fundamentalism'. Market fundamentalism is a belief system according to which all kind of values can be reduced to market values and the free market is the only efficient mechanism that can provide rational allocation of resources.

Harvard philosopher Michael Sandel (2013) argues that the invasion of market into all spheres of life inevitably destroys the intrinsic value of human activities by corrupting them. There are two interrelated aspects of corrupting human activities. (i) Introducing extrinsic motivation (especially money) for doing activities may crowd out intrinsic motivation of actors which in turn leads to decreasing quality of the output of activities. (ii) Measuring the success of activities in one dimensional, money terms may distort the goal of activities and results in socially and ecologically degrading activities. The market is a powerful *evaluation mechanism* which has inherent deficiencies. First of all, there are stakeholders that are simply non-represented in determining market values. Natural beings and future generations do not have the opportunity to vote on the marketplace. Second, the preferences of human individuals count rather unequally, that is, in proportion to their purchasing power; the interests of the poor and disadvantageous people are necessarily underrepresented in free market settings. Third, the actual preferences of the market players are rather self-centred and myopic; that is, economic agents make their own decisions regarding short-term consequences only.

The inherent deficiencies of the market mechanism imply that free markets cannot produce socially optimal outcomes. In many cases market evaluation is misleading from a social or environmental point of view. The market is not a sufficient form of evaluating economic activities. Alternative evaluation mechanisms (e.g. environmental and social reporting, accounting, and auditing) are also needed. Since both market and alternative evaluation mechanisms are fallible the simultaneous application of them is needed in providing a fair and accurate picture about the value of economic activities.

Global capitalism does need countervailing forces. Both *international politics* and *law* as well as *transnational civil society* have a role to play in correcting the deficiencies of market fundamentalism. Soros predicted that the instabilities and inequalities of the global capitalist system could feed into nationalistic, ethnic and religious fundamentalism (Soros, 1997, 1998).

German philosopher, the late Peter Koslowski (2002) noted that three structural features can characterize capitalism as an economic order, namely private property of the means of production, profit and utility maximization as basic motivation for economic action, and co-ordination of economic activities by the market mechanism. Modern capitalism is *disembedded* from the social and cultural norms of society. The capitalist economy can show the individuals the relative prices of resources but cannot relieve them of the choice between goals and values.

Koslowski (2002) argues that from the perspective of ethics the goals that individuals in a society set for themselves are as important as how these goals are to be fulfilled. One must ask about the reasonableness of the goals as well as the optimal allocation of resources for those goals. Pareto-optimality cannot define social or ethical optimality beyond the economic viewpoint of allocative rationality. Ethics requires considering and balancing the *totality* of *aspects* and not making evaluations and decisions solely on the basis of individual preferences.

Market does not properly deal with certain values of vital importance (public goods, cultural goods, and the environment). A society that bases the pursuit of its goals on the economic principle only is not able to realize the good. There is a need for re-embedding business, the market, and economic motivation into ethical and social norms. Capitalism should be *re-embedded* in the ethics and culture of *society* (Koslowski, 2002). The economy is necessarily based on *meta-economic values* that are beyond and above economic efficiency. Business ethics is not a luxury for advanced economies but a source of the wealth of nations (Mlcoch, 2002).

Italian economist Stefano Zamagni (2002) argues that societies of success enable people to undertake co-operative ventures for mutual advantages. In such societies the so-called *social capital* is well developed. This means that an efficient network of non-profit and voluntary organizations functions to provide public goods of various kinds. *Reciprocity* plays a vital role in the functioning of advanced economies. Reciprocity may increase the outcome of the economic interactions either by stabilizing the co-operative behaviour of the agents or by altering endogenously the preferences of the agents themselves.

Zamagni (2002) believes that the most detrimental effect of the self-interest doctrine and the culture of contract is to believe that behaviours inspired by motives other than self-interest are conducive to economic disaster. Trust, reciprocity and altruism contribute significantly to the civilization process of our economies. The *civil society*, which is based on the principle of subsidiarity and functions by the mechanism of reciprocity, could contribute to the development of capitalism, which is environmentally sustainable and socially just. The post-modern, global reality of our age requires a new model of social and economic governance that is a constructive symbiosis of the invisible hand of the market, the visible hand of the government, and the humanizing hand of civil society.

The *stakeholder relationship* is a key to understanding the functioning of business in today's globalized world. Edward Freeman (2002) emphasizes that identifying and analysing stakeholders is a way to acknowledge the existence of multiple constituencies in a company. The more the stakeholders participate in the decisions that affect them, the greater the likelihood that they will be committed to the future of the business enterprise.

The Principle of Stakeholder Co-operation says that value is created because stakeholders can jointly satisfy their needs and desires. The Principle of Complexity says that human beings are complex creatures capable of acting from different values. The Principle of Continuous Creation says that business, as an institution is a source of the creation of value. The Principle of Emergent Competition says that competition emerges from a relatively free and democratic society so that stakeholders have options (Freeman, 2002).

The Need for Responsible Economizing

The underlying idea of responsible economizing is that responsibility implies choice. The greater the adequacy of the decision-maker's conception of responsibility in the given situation, the greater the chance that he or she will make a decision which is an appropriate response to the situation (Zsolnai, 2008).

In the praxiological tradition, Wojciech Gasparski introduces the "triple E" criteria for judging human actions. The triple E refers to effectiveness, efficiency, and ethics (Gasparski, 2002).

Effectiveness, efficiency and ethics reflect three irreducible aspects of human choices. Stakeholders, goals, and ethical norms constitute the value-space within which decisions are made. Responsible decision-making means finding an optimal balance among the different and often conflicting requirements in human choice situations.

The responsible decision-making model (Zsolnai, 2008) deals with the category of 'ought' but assumes real persons, not ideal ones. Although real people may not make decisions as they ought to according to the responsible choice model advanced here, they are capable of using the model directly in real world situations if they want.

The most important choices are made in *complex choice situations*. In such situations the choice has wide-ranging consequences, and not only the decision-maker but also other parties are affected by the outcome of the choice.

Responsibility is unavoidably present in complex choice situations. This is the main reason the standard economic model of choice is not adequate in solving large, multi-agent problems of economics and public policy. A lot of work has been done in ethics on the topic of retrospective moral responsibility. However, we have only one comprehensible theory of prospective moral responsibility. It is presented by *Hans Jonas* in his opus magnum "The Imperative of Responsibility" (Jonas, 1979, 1984).

According to Jonas, responsibility means *caring* for the *beings* involved in our actions. This imperative presents a basic nonreciprocal duty toward other beings, including nonhuman beings and future human beings.

Jonas' theory of responsibility has important similarities with *Carol Gilligan*'s understanding of female morality. Gilligan interprets the moral experience of women as an *ethic* of *care*, which is contrasted with the *ethic* of *rights* represented by men. In mature morality these two disparate modes of moral experience are connected. A mature concept of responsibility should integrate the reverence for rights emphasized by men and the nonviolence of care represented by women (Gilligan, 1982).

The standard model of choice in economics and other social sciences is the well-known *rational choice model*. The model states that the agent should maximize her or his utility function in order to be considered rational. It requires that the agent's preferences are transitive and complete. (In circumstances of risk and uncertainty there are additional requirements, such as continuity and independence concerning the agent's preferences.)

The rational choice model represents a formal theory that says nothing about what human agents prefer or should prefer. Regardless of whether their preferences are self-interested, altruistic or even sadomasochistic, the agents may be equally rational in making their own choices. I refer to this model of choice as the weak form of rationality.

In economics and other social science literature, we often find a much stronger version of rationality. Assumptions of self-interest and perfect knowledge are added to the rational choice model. This is the famous *Homo Oeconomicus* model, according to which agents maximize their self-interest under perfect knowledge of the consequences. This model has a substantive claim about what people want or should want. I refer to the Homo Oeconomicus model as the strong form of rationality.

Both the weak and the strong forms of rationality have been heavily criticized by psychologists, sociologists, economists, political scientists, and philosophers on descriptive as well as on normative grounds.

Nobel laureate economist Herbert A. Simon (1982, 1987) states that the rational choice model has very strong claims concerning the cognitive capacity of human beings. Real world people have rather poor cognitive capacity and the information available to them is quite limited in most cases. Real world agents are not capable of maximizing their utility functions (if they have any). Instead of maximizing, they make "satisficing" decisions. According to Simon, human *rationality* is essentially *bounded*.

Princeton University psychologist Daniel Kahneman (1994) criticizes the rational choice model on the basis of experimental research. It has been found that people usually make *myopic choices*. They lack the skill to predict the utility of their chosen options. In addition, people have *fallible memories* that lead to incorrect evaluations of their past experiences.

Behavioural-decision researchers have discovered that people systematically violate the axioms of rationality, especially in circumstances involving risk and uncertainty. The most famous cases are the Allais' paradox, the Ellsberg's problem, the preference-reversal effect, and the framing effect. These violations of rationality are so fundamental that no hybrid, nearly rational model can possibly capture this type of behaviour.

Nobel laureate economist Amartya Sen (1987) criticizes both forms of rationality. He refers to the weak form as internal consistency of choice and to the strong form as maximization of self-interest. Sen shows that internal consistency cannot guarantee a person's rationality. A person can always choose exactly the opposite of what would enhance those things she or he wants or values. Some *correspondence* between the choice and the aims and values of the agent is certainly required.

Sen notices that selfishness as a universal pattern of human choice behaviour may be false, but *universal selfishness* as a requirement of rationality is patently *absurd*. The self-interest view of rationality does not reflect the complex motivations of agents in their economic affairs (duty, loyalty, and goodwill in addition to self-interest).

Cornell University economist Robert Frank (1988) emphasizes the strategic role of *emotions* in making choices. Frank shows that passions often serve our self-interest because we face important problems that are simply unsolvable by rational action. The modular brain theory seems to support Frank's arguments. According to this new theory, the brain is organized into a host of separate modules. Not all modules are equally well connected to the central language module of the brain that is viewed as the centre of our rational consciousness. The rational choice model reflects only the working of the language module of the left hemisphere of the human brain. However, a lot of information is simply not accessible to the language module of our brain.

Columbia University sociologist Jon Elster (1990) contrasts rational action with *norm-guided* behaviour. While rational action is outcome oriented, social norms are not. Social norms have a grip on the mind that is based on the strong emotions that their violations can arouse. According to Elster, human actions are determined jointly by self-interest and social norms. Social norms are only partly shaped by self-interest. They have an independent motivating power.

Communitarian philosophers such as Charles Taylor (1985), Michael Sandel (1982), and Alasdair MacIntyre (1981, 1988) forcefully criticize the liberal conception of the self, which is the underlying assumption of the rational choice model. They consider this conception of the self as being basically an atomistic one that denies the *relational, intersubjective* nature of human agency. It also neglects the constitutive role of communities and moral traditions in the deliberation of choices individuals ultimately make.

Sociologist Amitai Etzioni (1988) has developed the 'I & We' paradigm, which sees individuals in perpetual dialogue with their communities. Etzioni describes human choice behaviour as an attempt at finding a balance between pleasure and morality. He advances a *co-determination* model in which choice is affected by both pleasure and morality, which are in turn partly shaped by one another.

The rational choice model can also be criticized from an *environmental* point of view because the sustainability of natural systems cannot be assured on the basis of individual self-interested choices. Feminist criticism states that the rational choice model presupposes a *male-biased* conception of the human person known as the separative self.

Harvard University sociologist and political scientist Jane Mansbridge (1990) has developed a tripartite scheme of human motivation. She identifies *duty*, *self-interest*, and *love* as irreducible motives of human behaviour. This model goes back to David Hume, who acknowledges the rich variety of human behaviour when speaking about principle-driven, interest-driven, and affection-driven actions. Mansbridge favours the coincidence of duty and love with self-interest. She argues that in society, some 'ecological niche' should be arranged for non–self-interested behaviour to be protected from self-interested behaviour on the part of others.

Choice can best be seen as problem solving. The agent experiences some tension between the perceived state of affairs and the desired state of affairs. There is a gap between 'is' and 'ought' in the given situation.

Complex choice situations usually present ill-structured problems where the solution is far from clear or trivial. Russell L. Ackoff (1974) coined the term 'mess' to describe such decision situations. The decision-maker should use some heuristics for framing the decision he or she is facing. First, the decision-maker sets his or her aspirations concerning the solution of the problematic situation. However, other normative-affective factors are also at work, namely, ethical norms that apply in the given context and perceived other parties that can be affected by the outcome of the decision-maker's choice.

Ethical norms represent a subclass of social norms. They pose specific demands, which place *duties* on the decision-maker. A great variety of duties may apply in complex choice situations. The decision-maker may have perfect or imperfect duties that are either universal or special.

Stakeholders are those parties that can be affected by the choice of the decision-maker, and they are not limited to individuals, groups, and organizations. Natural entities such as biological creatures, ecosystems, and the Earth as a whole might also be included among the stakeholders of a decision. Similarly, future generations should be considered as stakeholders if their positions are affected by the choice of the decision-maker.

Goals and *alternatives* are not prearranged and given for the decision-maker. The applicable ethical norms, the aspirations of the decision-maker, and the perceived stakeholders together form the normative-affective basis that serves in the search for goals and alternatives. Goals and alternatives are not independent of each other but rather *co-evolve*. The generated alternatives influence the goals that are already in motion.

Business ethicist Kenneth E. Goodpaster (1983, 1991) has presented the most developed model of moral responsibility in an economic context. He proposes that moral responsibility should be understood as *rationality* and *respect* in making decisions.

Rationality is described by the following attributes: (i) lack of impulsiveness, (ii) care in mapping out alternatives and consequences, (iii) clarity about goals and purposes, and (iv) attention to details of implementation.

This concept of rationality does not imply that the decision-maker is preoccupied with maximizing her or his self-interest only.

Respect means having a special awareness of and concern for the effects of one's decisions and policies on others. It goes beyond seeing others as being merely instrumental to accomplishing one's own purposes and goals. Respect for the lives of others involves taking their needs and interests seriously.

Goodpaster's responsibility model is largely a *consequentialist* model of choice. It seems to favour an evaluation of the decision alternatives in terms of consequences from the perspectives of both the decision-maker and the stakeholders.

A consequentialist accounting can be criticized on different grounds. In complex choice situations there are phenomena whose consequentialist evaluation presents decision traps. We may think of marginal contributions as those described by American ecologist Garret Hardin (1968) in his famous 'tragedy of the commons' model, effects that are distant and/or dispersed in space and time, and consequences that are highly uncertain and partly unforeseeable.

The consequentialist accounting is also challenged from a deontological point of view. The essence of *deontology* is that the value of an act is determined not by its consequences but by its conformity to a relevant moral principle or duty. Philosopher Thomas Nagel (1988) generated crucial examples in which the agent has good deontological reason not to do something unless it would lead to good consequences.

I think it is better to deconstruct the ambiguous notion of 'respect'. I propose to define respect by referring exclusively to altruistic orientation toward the affected parties. Also, I propose to introduce deontological considerations as a separate component into the model of responsibility.

In this way we get a robust model of moral responsibility. Responsible decision-making is characterized as a synthesis of deontological considerations, rationality in goal achievement, and respect for the stakeholders. This model might be called the *3R model* since responsible decision-making equals reverence for the applying ethical norms plus rationality in goal achievement plus respect for the affected parties (Zsolnai, 2008).

Complex choice situations often present incommensurability for the decision-maker because of differing value dimensions. It is observed empirically that decision-makers seek to *avoid making tradeoffs* across incommensurable value dimensions. This regularity has been confirmed by the game experimental results of the Nobel laureate German economist Reinhard Selten (1994).

The natural heuristic of decision-makers facing incommensurability is depicted by Herbert A. Simon (1987). He states that decision-makers concentrate initially on *improving* the *most critical problem area* until it has achieved a satisfactory level of performance.

Complex choice situations have the following basic features: (i) more than one decision alternative is available to the decision-maker; (ii) at least one ethical norm applies to the decision-maker; (iii) the decision-maker has at least one goal to achieve; (iv) at least one stakeholder is present in the situation.

Responsible decision-making involves finding and implementing the decision alternative that best fits to the idea of responsibility in the given context of choice. I propose using the *maximin rule* for making responsible choices. It implies the maximization of the minimum payoff of decision alternatives. The rule is intuitively well known to chess players who select the branch that will provide the best response in the face of an aggressive opponent. However, it was formally described as early as 1912 by the Austrian logician Ernest Zermello. The rule was developed further in game theory by the Hungarian-American mathematical genius John von Neumann.

Responsible decision-making means selecting of the *least worst alternative* in the decision space of deontological, goal-achievement, and stakeholder values. The underlying principle is that the decision-maker should find an optimal balance across different value dimensions.

Responsible choice provides a Pareto optimal result in the sense that given the set of decision alternatives, it is not possible to increase the payoff in any decision alternative in one value dimension without decreasing its payoff in at least one other value dimension.

Rational choice can be considered a reduced form of responsible decision-making. If there are neither applying ethical norms nor affected parties in the choice situation, then the ethical-decision-making model falls into the rational choice model.

The procedural model of responsible decision-making can be summarized as follows (Zsolnai, 2008).

I Framing the choice situation by

  i Identifying the applying ethical norms.
  ii Mapping out the affected parties.
  iii Defining goals and generating alternatives.

II Multiple evaluation of each alternative regarding

  i The ethical norms.
  ii The goals to be achieved.
  iii The affected parties.

III Selecting the alternative whose minimum payoff is maximal in the decision space of deontological, goal-achievement, and stakeholder values.

Quality of Life

Complex real-world cases can be solved by using the responsible-choice framework. Multiple satisficing solutions are attainable if equal attention is paid to all of the relevant value dimensions; that is, if deontological, goal achievement, and stakeholder considerations are regarded simultaneously and the least worst options are consistently chosen.

The responsible-decision-making model can provide new insights into some basic problems of economics and public policy.

John Rawls's famous principle of justice (Rawls, 1971) can be defended on the basis of responsible choices made by people when they know perfectly well their own positions in a society. Responsible people in average, above-average, and below-average positions will accept the 'difference principle'.

The so-called Paretian Liberal Paradox (Sen, 1970) and other difficulties in aggregating individual preferences cannot be solved on the basis of information provided by the self-interested preferences of individuals. In the evaluation of states of affairs, deontological and stakeholder evaluations should also be used in order to broaden the information base for the evaluation of the state of affairs.

In prisoner's dilemma situations, if each agent pursues her/his self-interest, the result will be suboptimal solutions. In light of the responsible-choice model, the cooperative and non-cooperative strategies can be re-evaluated. Responsible agents who evaluate the strategies from multiple perspectives can arrive at optimal, that is, multiply satisficing, solutions.

Cost-benefit analysis can provide misleading results if environmental and social externalities are present and a high degree of uncertainty is involved. In such cases monetary evaluation of the state of affairs is not enough, no matter how sophisticated the applied procedure of assessing costs and benefits is in monetary terms. The state of affairs should also be evaluated from the ecological and social points of view. The maximin rule implies that a project is worthy of being undertaken if the worst aspect of the state of affairs with the project is better than the worst aspect of the state of affairs without the project.

The ethical performance of a business organization can be determined by evaluating its activities from the perspective of the applying ethical norms. The social performance of a business organization can be determined by evaluating its impacts on the stakeholders. Profit-generating activities of a business organization are acceptable if they do not violate the relevant ethical norms and cause no harm to the stakeholders. Hence, nonviolence emerges as a necessary and sufficient condition for the ethical and social acceptability of profit-making.

Any economic arrangement affects nature, society, and future generations. An economic arrangement is hardly legitimate if it produces negative payoffs for these primordial stakeholders. Justice among nature, society and future generations is established if the economic arrangement produces approximately *equal values* for nature, society and future generations. This may lead to an amendment of the biblical adage to the form, "Love nature and future generations as your own society".

Complex choice situations require *multiperspective* considerations. The crux of the matter is how the evaluative space of decision-making is defined. The *informational basis* of business and public decision-making should be extended to include ethical, social and ecological values.

The universal substitutability of values propagated by mainstream economics should be challenged. The *quality of life* can be preserved and enhanced if decision-makers pay equal attention to all the relevant value perspectives in the decision situation. The maximin rule permits only limited trade-offs among different values to keep life as diverse and complex as possible. Responsible decision-making is not a luxury; rather, it is a precondition of a life worthy to live.

References

Ackoff, R. L., 1974, *Redesigning the Future*, New York & London, John Wiley & Sons.

Elster, J., 1990, "When Rationality Fails" in Karen Schweers-Cook and Margaret Levi (eds.): *The Limits of Rationality*.University of Chicago Press. Chicago & London. pp. 19–51.

Etzioni, A., 1988, *The Moral Dimension*, New York, The Free Press.

Frank, R., 1988, *Passions Within Reason*, New York & London, W. W. Norton.

Freeman, R. E., 2002, "The Possibility of Stakeholder Capitalism" in Laszlo Zsolnai and Wojciech W. Gasparski (eds.): *Ethics and the Future of Capitalism*. Transaction Publishers. New Brunswick and London. pp. 111–116.
Gasparski, W. W., 2002, "Effectiveness, Efficiency, and Ethicality in Business and Management" in Laszlo Zsolnai and Wojciech W. Gasparski (eds.): *Ethics and the Future of Capitalism*. Transaction Publishers. New Brunswick and London. pp. 117–136.
Gilligan, C., 1982, *In a Different Voice: Psychological Theory and Women's Development*, Cambridge and London. Harvard University Press.
Goodpaster, K. E., 1983, "The Concept of Corporate Responsibility" *Journal of Business Ethics*, No 1. pp. 1–22.
Goodpaster, K. E., 1991, "Business Ethics and Stakeholder Analyses" *Business Ethics Quarterly*, No. 1.
Hardin, G., 1968, "The Tragedy of the Commons" *Science* 1968 December. No. 162. pp. 1243–1248.
Jonas, H., 1979, *Das Prinzip Verantwortung. Versuch einer Ethic fur die Technologische Zivilization*, Frankfurt am Main, Insel Verlag.
Jonas, H., 1984, *The Imperative of Responsibility: In Search of an Ethics for the Technological Age*, Chicago & London, The University of Chicago Press.
Kahneman, D., 1994, "New Challenges to the Rationality Assumption" *Journal of Institutional and Theoretical Economics*, No. 1. pp. 18–36.
Koslowski, P., 2002, "Ethics of Capitalism" in Laszlo Zsolnai and Wojciech W. Gasparski (eds.): *Ethics and the Future of Capitalism*. Transaction Publishers. New Brunswick and London. pp. 43–67.
MacIntyre, A., 1981, *After Virtue*, Notre Dame, University of Norte Dame Press.
MacIntyre, A., 1988, *Whose Justice? Which Rationality?* Notre Dame, University of Norte Dame Press.
Mansbridge, J. J., 1990, "On the Relation of Altruism and Self-Interest" in Jane Mansbridge (ed.): *Beyond Self-Interest*, Chicago & London, The University of Chicago Press. pp. 133–143.
Mlcoch, L., 2002, "Misunderstood and Abused Liberalism" in Laszlo Zsolnai and Wojciech W. Gasparski (Eds.): *Ethics and the Future of Capitalism*. Transaction Publishers. New Brunswick and London. pp. 69–87.
Nagel, T., 1988, "Autonomy and Deontology" in Samuel Scheffler (ed.): *Consequentialism and its Critics*, Oxford, Oxford University Press. pp. 142–172.
Rawls, J., 1971, *A Theory of Justice*, Cambridge, Harvard University Press.
Sandel, M., 1982, *Liberalism and the Limits of Justice*, Cambridge, Cambridge University Press.
Sandel, M., 2013, *What Money Can't Buy: The Moral Limits of Markets*, Farrar, Straus, and Giroux, New York.
Selten, R., 1994, "New Challenges to the Rationality Assumptions" *Journal of Institutional and Theoretical Economics*, No. 1. pp. 42–44.
Sen, A., 1970, "The Impossibility of a Paretean Liberal" *Journal of Political Economy*, No. 78. pp. 152–157.
Sen, A., 1987, *On Ethics and Economics*, Oxford, Blackwell.
Simon, H. A., 1982, *Models of Bounded Rationality*, Cambridge & London, The MIT Press.
Simon, H. A., 1987, "Satisficing" in Steven N. Durlauf and Lawrence E. Blume (Eds.): *The New Palgrave: A Dictionary of Economics*, London, Macmillan. pp. 243–245.

Soros, G., 1997, "The Capitalist Threat" *The Atlantic Monthly*, February.
Soros, G., 1998, *The Crisis of Global Capitalism*, Little, Brown and Company, London.
Taylor, C., 1985, *Philosophical Papers*, Cambridge, Cambridge University Press.
Zamagni, S., 2002, "Humanizing the Economy: On the Relationship of Ethics of Human Rights and Economic Discourse" in Laszlo Zsolnai and Wojciech W. Gasparski (eds.): *Ethics and the Future of Capitalism*. Transaction Publishers. New Brunswick and London. pp. 89–110.
Zsolnai, L., 2008, *Responsible Decision Making*. Transactions Publishers, New Brunswick and London.

Notes about the Authors and Editors

Timo Airaksinen (PhD Turku University, Finland, 1975) is professor emeritus (moral and social philosophy), University of Helsinki, Finland. He is a life member of Clare Hall, Cambridge, and honorary member of the Learned Society of Praxiology. He has written *The Philosophy of the Marquis de Sade* (Routledge, 1995), *The Philosophy of H.P. Lovecraft* (Lang, 1999), *The Ethics of Coercion and Authority* (University of Pittsburgh Press, 1988), and around 300 papers on various philosophical topics.

Victor Alexandre was a professor of social psychology at the University of Franche-Comté, Besançon, France. Specialized in attitudes, praxiology, structural analysis of acts, identification of acts, and environmental psychology. He published the following books: *Eléments de praxéologie,* L'Harmattan Paris, V. Alexandre et W. W. Gasparski (ed.) (2003); *The Roots of Praxiology*, The International Annual of Practical Philosophy and Methodology, Vol. 7, Transaction Publishers, V. Alexandre et W. W. Gasparski (ed.) (1999); *French and Other Perspectives in Praxiology,* Praxiology: The International Annual of Practical Philosophy and Methodology, Vol. 12, Transaction Publishers (2004); *Penser et agir, Actes de colloque*, Editions le manuscrit Paris, Alexandre V. (ed.) (2009).

Marek Arszułowicz is an academic and entrepreneur based in London, UK. His main interests focus on understanding the source of efficiency of an acting person, an entrepreneur in particular. His interdisciplinary research embraces decision-making, cultural background, language studies, mental conditioning, and innovation. He is currently working on his 'first line' theory, where he presents his understanding of a project's execution as an allegory of painting on a white canvas. He earned his PhD at Kozminsky University, Warsaw, under the supervision of Professor Wojciech Gasparski.

Jérôme Ballet is assistant professor in economics at Gretha-University of Bordeaux. He is also editor of the review *Ethics and Economics*. His main contribution concerns the integration of ethics in economics, and he has published on environmental ethics and development ethics.

David Botham began a long and varied career in further and higher education in 1968, working in material sciences and later in behavioural sciences. Alongside this, he worked as a session musician with various bands and recording companies. In 1994, he was invited to work closely with R. W. Revans in the role of first director in the newly created Revans Centre for Action Learning and Research, University of Salford. Shortly afterwards, he received a personal research chair during which time he continued to work as an academic until his 'retirement'. In 2009, he was invited to assist in the Business Systems Division within Manchester Business School in the Faculty of Humanities until he finally retired from academic responsibilities in 2012. Over the years he had the pleasure of working alongside some of the greatest academics and scholars and musicians in the world. To all of them he dedicates his work in this volume in humble appreciation.

Joanne B. Ciulla is professor of leadership ethics and academic director of the Institute for Ethical Leadership at Rutgers University. She has published extensively on leadership ethics and business ethics. Some of her books are *The Ethics of Leadership* (Sage), *Honest Work: A Business Ethics Reader* (Oxford), and *The Working Life: The Promise and Betrayal of Modern Work* (Times Books). She is the former president of both the International Society for Business, Economics, and Ethics, and the Society for Business Ethics.

Georges Enderle conducts research on the ethics of globalization, wealth creation, business and human rights, and corporate responsibilities of large and small companies, with a view on developments in China. Included among his new publications are his book *Ethical Innovation in Business and the Economy* (co-edited with P. E. Murphy, 2015), his chapter "Business and the Greater Good as a Combination of Private and Public Wealth" (in English and Chinese), and his articles "Exploring and Conceptualizing International Business Ethics" and "How Can Business Ethics Strengthen the Social Cohesion of a Society" in the *Journal of Business Ethics*. Enderle is co-founder of the European Business Ethics Network and a former president of the International Society of Business, Economics, and Ethics (ISBEE; 2001–2004). He teaches undergraduate courses on business ethics and corporate responsibilities and MBA courses on international business ethics and ethics in finance and banking. After gaining master's degrees in philosophy (Munich), theology (Lyon) and economics, he earned a PhD in economics from the University of Fribourg (Switzerland) and a PhD in business ethics from the University of St. Gallen (Switzerland).

Wojciech W. Gasparski is a professor of humanities, Dr. Sc. professor emeritus, former chair in business ethics and honorary director and founder of the Business Ethics Center, past vicerector for research of the Koźmiński University, and professor emeritus of the Institute of Philosophy and Sociology, Polish Academy of Sciences, where he chaired its academic board and headed the Department of Praxiology as well as the Research Group for Ethics of Business and the Economy. His publications on human action theory (praxiology), general and design methodologies, business ethics, management philosophy, science studies, and systems theory are numerous. He is a member of the Warsaw Learned Society; Learned Society of Praxiology (founder and life honorary president); Polish Philosophical Society; International Society of Business, Economics, and Ethics; and the Science Studies Committee of the Polish Academy of Sciences (life honorary member). He is also editor-in-chief of *Praxiology: The International Annual of Practical Philosophy and Methodology* and member of the editorial boards of the *International Journal of General Systems*, *African Journal of Business Ethics* and *Prakseologia*. He was awarded the *Commander Cross of Polonia Restituta Order*, the *Tadeusz Kotarbiński Medal* by the Polish Academy of Sciences, the *Medal of the Commission of National Education*, the CEEMAN *Champion Award in Responsible Management Education*, and the *Copernicus Medal* by the Polish Bank Association.

Krzysztof Klincewicz is professor at the Faculty of Management, University of Warsaw and rector's deputy for intellectual property management. He specializes in management of technology and innovation, with particular interest in strategies of technology firms and R&D management. Prior to joining the university, he had worked for high-tech industries in Poland, Finland, and in the UK (1997–2004), as well as at the Tokyo Institute of Technology, Japan (2004–2006). Expert in analysing innovation policies of EU member states in the "ERAWATCH", "Research and Innovation Observatory" and "Stairway-to-Excellence" projects of the European Commission and in a project of the Committee on Development and Intellectual Property, World Intellectual Property Organisation. He was a member of the UN Technology Executive Committee (2011–2015) and the lead EU expert, negotiating climate technology development and transfer at the UNFCCC (2011–2015). Between 1997 and 2000, he studied praxiology and business ethics in the Collegium Invisibile under supervision of Prof. Wojciech Gasparski.

Anna Lewicka-Strzałecka, PhD, is a professor at the Institute of Philosophy and Sociology, Polish Academy of Sciences (PAS). Her primary research interests include praxiology, practical philosophy, science of science and business ethics. She has published several books and almost a hundred articles and conference papers. She is an editor-in-chief of *Prakseologia*, a Polish journal on human action theory (PAS, Poland).

Olli Loukola (doctor of social sciences, University of Helsinki, 1999) is docent of practical philosophy and senior lecturer in social and moral philosophy, Department of Political and Economic Studies, University of Helsinki, Finland. He is also a member of the Teachers Academy of University of Helsinki. He has led a number of research projects in practical philosophy, among them Responsibility: A Philosophical Enquiry into Ethics and Politics of the Concept; The Anatomy of Environmental Responsibility, Redefining Concepts and Practices of Environmental Law and Decision-Making; and Sustainability in Forest Use. He has edited *Environmental Political Philosophy: Praxiological Considerations*, together with Wojciech Gasparski, published in 2011 by Transaction Publishers.

Piotr Tomasz Makowski (1982) is an assistant professor at the Institute of Philosophy, Adam Mickiewicz University, Poznan (Poland). He is specialized in metaethics and philosophy of action. The areas of his current research interests include (but are not exhausted by) theories of intention, philosophy of psychology, theories of rationality, praxiology, and management science. He authored two books, *Tadeusz Kotarbiński's Action Theory—Reinterpretive Studies* (2017) and *Po metaetyce* (*After Metaethics*, 2012), over a dozen papers issued in Polish and international publications, and edited two collections of papers: *Reasons for Action and Praxiology* (together with M. Bonecki and K. Nowak-Posadzy, Transaction Publishers 2015) and *Intersubiektywność* (*Intersubjectivity*, Universitas 2012). He was a visiting fellow at the University of California, Davis (USA), Roma Tre University (Italy), and University of Helsinki (Finland). He gave invited talks (inter alia) in Germany, Finland, India, Italy, Switzerland, Turkey, and the USA. He is an awardee of the Fulbright Foundation and the Polish Ministry of Science and Higher Education.

Piotr Masiukiewicz, PhD of economics, is a professor in Warsaw School of Economics, Institute of Value Management. Concerns of his research include the following areas: management of bank and banking crisis, financial enclaves on the market (include pyramid schemes), management of restructuration and recovery of enterprises, marketing, credibility of the enterprises and enterprise value management. He was president and vice-president of Polish banks (fourteen years) and advisor to the prime minister of Poland. Piotr Masiukiewicz is the author of more than 300 publications, including sixteen books, such as *Innovations in Customer Value Creation*, B. Dobiegała-Korona, P. Masiukiewicz (eds.), Warsaw School of Economics Press, 2011; *Customer Value Creation: Theory and Practice*, B. Dobiegała-Korona, P. Masiukiewicz (eds.), Warsaw School of Economics Press, Warszawa, 2012; "Dec P. Stress Test in Banking—Case of Europe and USA", in International Scientific and Practical Congress, *Economic Development of the EU and CIS Countries in Globalization*, ISAE Consilium, Bern, Switzerland, 2013; "Resistance of Islamic Banking to Crises", in *Considerations about the Eco*nomy, D. Niedziółka (ed.), Warsaw School of Economics Press, Warsaw, 2015, and articles in different journals around the world (seventeen countries). He is presently manager of postgraduate studies in WSoE (Management of Restructuration and Recovery Enterprises), editor-in-chief of the monthly scientific journal *Ekonomika i Organizacja*

Przedsiębiorstwa, vice-president of the Scientific Board of Institute Orgmasz in Warsaw, and president of The Learned Society of Praxiology in Poland.

Tufan Orel, PhD, is a consultant in design management. He formerly participated as a freelance consultant at the French National Computer Science Institute (INRIA, Sophia-Antipolis, Nice). In the 1990s, as co-editor-in-chief, he was in charge of the *Journal of Design Sciences and Technology*, published in France. He also worked as a researcher in sociology (CEAQ-Universite de Paris V, Rene Descartes) and lectured on the history of science at an engineering school for many years (Universite de Technologie de Compiegne-UTC). In sociology, his research was dedicated to the evolution of individualism since the 1980s. In 2016, he published in Paris a book that is mainly based on his research papers on design, entitled *Ecrits sur le design*.

Emmanuel Petit is professor of economics at Gretha-University of Bordeaux. His main topic concerns how emotions shape behaviours. Focusing on economic analyses, he is currently working on care economics.

Gunnar Skirbekk is professor emeritus at the Department of Philosophy and the Centre for the Study of the Sciences and Humanities, University of Bergen. He has written extensively on rationality and modernization, on political philosophy and the theory of the sciences, and on the history of western thought. Skirbekk is a member of the Norwegian Academy for the Sciences and the Arts and of the Royal Norwegian Society of Sciences and Letters.

Mirosław Sułek is a professor of social sciences. He got his M.A. in economics from Military Academy in Warsaw. Since 2012, he has been working at the International Relations Institute, University of Warsaw, Poland. His primary research interests include economics of national security, praxiology, strategic studies, geopolitics, and powermetrics. In 2001, he published *Podstawy potęgonomii i potęgometrii* (*Foundations of powernomics and powermetrics*). *Powernomics* means a science of national power and *powermetrics* means a science of measurement of national power. In this book, he introduced his own model of measurement of national power. There is a website (http://powermetrics.bplaced.net/) devoted to measuring national power formulas and authors. This website contains an article by Mirosław Sułek entitled "Synthetic Approach to Measurement of National Power". Other publications include *Potęga państw. Modele i zastosowania*, 2013 (*Power of Nations: Models and Applications*) and *Prognozowanie i symulacje międzynarodowe*, 2010 (*International Forecasting and Simulations*). He is an executive committee member of the Scientific Society of Praxiology (Poland).

Andrzej Sztylka, born in 1949 in Warsaw, is an alumnus of University of Warsaw's Higher Teachers School (1971) and University of Warsaw's Psychology and

Pedagogy Faculty (1973). In 1984, he gained a doctoral degree based on his thesis "Art and Humanistic Strategy of Life" (*Sztuka a humanistyczna strategia życia*), written under the supervision of Professor Irena Wojnar. He is a politically non-aligned humanist, teacher, educationalist, and philosopher. In the early 1990s, he was vice-president of the Committee of Education, Labour Market and Professional Ethics of the Polish Chamber of Commerce. He was an active participant in conferences organized by the Committee of Prognosis Poland 2000 Plus of the Presidium of the Polish Academy of Sciences; a member of the Scientific Society for Praxiology; and a member of Trentowski's Society of Philosophical Pedagogics. Between 1995 and 2015, he was a teacher in University of Natural Sciences and Humanities in Siedlce. He is the author of two books and a number of articles on pedagogy, ethics, philosophy, and art.

Laszlo Zsolnai is professor and director of the Business Ethics Center at the Corvinus University of Budapest, Hungary. He is president of the European SPES Institute in Leuven, Belgium. He is a fellow of the Royal Society of the Arts in London, UK. He serves as editor of the "Frontier of Business Ethics" book series at Peter Lang Publishers in Oxford. Laszlo Zsolnai's books include *Europe-Asia Dialogue on Business Spirituality* (2008, Antwerp and Apeldoorn), *Responsible Decision Making* (2008, New Brunswick and London), *The Future International Manager: A Vision of the Roles and Duties of Management* (2009, Palgrave Macmillan), *The Collaborative Enterprise: Creating Values for a Sustainable World* (2010, Peter Lang, Oxford) and *The Palgrave Handbook of Spirituality and Business* (2011, Palgrave-Macmillan). His website: http://laszlo-zsolnai.net.

For Product Safety Concerns and Information please contact our EU representative GPSR@taylorandfrancis.com
Taylor & Francis Verlag GmbH, Kaufingerstraße 24, 80331 München, Germany

www.ingramcontent.com/pod-product-compliance
Lightning Source LLC
Chambersburg PA
CBHW071110100726
47908CB00008B/2335

* 9 7 8 1 1 3 8 1 0 2 6 6 8 *